Six approaches
to the person

Also by Ralph Ruddock

Roles and Relationships
(reprinted 1972)

Six approaches to the person

Edited by
Ralph Ruddock

Department of Adult Education
University of Manchester

Routledge & Kegan Paul
London and Boston

First published 1972
by Routledge & Kegan Paul Ltd
Broadway House, 68–74 Carter Lane,
London EC4V 5EL and
9 Park Street,
Boston, Mass. 02108, U.S.A.
Printed in Great Britain by
Butler & Tanner Ltd
Frome and London
© Routledge & Kegan Paul 1972
No part of this book may be reproduced in
any form without permission from the
publisher, except for the quotation of brief
passages in criticism

ISBN 0 7100 7335 6 (c)
ISBN 0 7100 7382 8 (p)

Contents

presented and the final one, the person as an actor in a drama, is chosen for fuller treatment. Social behaviour can be classified under the headings of drama, ritual and routine. The individual is most fully a person when engaged in drama.

A review of some psycho-analytical and some sociological approaches identifies concepts for a model with six components: self, identity, personality, role, perspective and project. Self-realization is seen to depend on congruence between these components. The model is used for the analysis of congruence in selected examples.

The claims for the self-actualization thesis in the writings of Maslow, Rogers, Jung and several other authorities in clinical psychology are reviewed and compared. The case is argued for mystical and drug-induced experience in self-realization and therapeutic practice.

The person is seen to travel through many different mental states, average and unusual, happy and sad, dreaming and waking. A systematic classification based on descriptions drawn from mystical, psychiatric and other literature is elaborated into a three-dimensional model. The relevance of this model to the brain and to personality variables is developed.

Some areas of concern common to two or more of the contributors are identified, with concluding observations on the ontological problem.

Figures

Tables

Contributors

John H. Clark   Senior Lecturer in the Department of Psychology, University of Manchester. Formerly an M.R.C. Clinical Research Fellow following training in medicine and psychiatry. Interests include brain research, altered states of consciousness and behaviour therapy. Author of a chapter on medical cybernetics in *A Survey of Cybernetics*.

Dan Gowler   Senior Lecturer in Industrial Anthropology in the Manchester Business School. His work brings methods of analysis found useful for the understanding of pre-literate societies to bear upon the problems of contemporary work organizations, e.g. the socio-cultural influences on the operation of wage payment systems.

John F. Morris   Professor of Management Development in the Manchester Business School; formerly Senior Lecturer in Psychology. His interest has always been in the exploration of social behaviour in face-to-face settings in education, social work, family life and industry. Co-author and editor, with E. A. Lunzer, of *Development in Learning*.

Ralph Ruddock   Senior Lecturer in Adult Education, University of Manchester. Teaches social science to mature and post-graduate students in social work and education, exploring the relevance of the Freudian, Marxian and religious systems. Author of *Roles and Relationships*.

John W. Shaw   Staff Tutor in Psychology, University of Manchester Extra-Mural Department. Has taught psychology and philosophy in a long-term adult college and served as a research and training psychologist with the Northern Ireland Ministry of Agriculture. Has interests in personality measurement and in the theories of clinical psychology.

Ninian Smart Professor of Religious Studies in the University of Lancaster. His department is unique in respect of its uncommitted philosophical and comparative approach to religion. Author of several books in this area, including *The Religious Experience of Mankind*; *World Religions—a Dialogue*; *Reason and Faith*; *Secular Education and the Logic of Religion*.

Preface

There is an urgent need for systematic treatment of the whole person. The need is felt by specialists in many fields and in all the professions, wherever advice is to be offered to a client who has to be seen as a person in a situation. The need is also felt by academic specialists in the social sciences, who find themselves working with concepts for the behaviour of people, concepts for systems within or between people, but not with concepts *of* people. Beyond this, each person in everyday life experiences a need of this kind. Everyone who observes the changing social scene and reflects on his own experience asks himself how he is to think of himself and of other people. So far, psychology and the other social sciences have been careful to limit their fields of enquiry and to avoid such questions.

The present time sees a resurgence of interest in the whole person, and a greater readiness to examine the issues involved. This is becoming evident in medicine, in philosophy, in social work, in counselling, as well as in psycho-analysis and clinical psychology. To attempt to construct an all-purpose theoretical model has always seemed an absurd undertaking. Within the disciplines, however, systems have developed which call for exploration of ways in which the individual may be conceptualized for specific purposes. It therefore seemed appropriate to invite five scholars to join with the editor in describing their own approaches. The scholars concerned all had a lively sense of the qualities of the living being that could not be captured by any model. They were nevertheless prepared to write about *persons* and to set out the positions they had reached in according to the person the central place in their own academic work.

Contributors were encouraged to have in mind the interests of readers in many professions and disciplines, and not to address their essays solely to colleagues within their own specialism. Nor have they discussed the content of their essays with each other during preparation. Each stands as an individual presentation. The styles and approaches are widely different, but not, I think, divergent. Some attempt at drawing threads together is offered in the last chapter.

The order in which the essays have been arranged is as follows. After the editor's introductory chapter on the need for models of the person, four essays present views of the person as created by 'society' —other people. Ninian Smart is concerned with problems of autonomy, ethics and ontology; Dan Gowler with personification as determined by social and biological factors in inter-action; John Morris with metaphors for the person and his realization in dramatic involvement with others; and Ralph Ruddock with the choice of identity. The last two essays are psychological. John Shaw reviews the arguments for a basic drive towards self-realization. John Clark identifies and orders 'altered states of consciousness' which the person may be subject to, or may attain to. This sequence was not planned in advance. Later essays do not build upon earlier ones. The chapters of the book may therefore be read in any order. Some readers may choose to start with the essay by John Morris, who writes with an awareness of being a person writing about persons. He consults his immediate experience, as well as his observation, and has a minimum of academic reference.

I am most grateful to my colleagues for their willingness to contribute. All of them work under the pressure of unceasing demands, and I have warmly appreciated their undertaking to write and their production of scripts on time. My own writing has greatly benefited from discussions with them; and also from the textual criticisms of Miss Helen Hodgkinson.

1 The need for models

Ralph Ruddock

Concepts of the person and the use of models

This introductory chapter will be concerned with theoretical issues. The aim will be to present one perspective. It will be argued that there is a need to make explicit whatever assumptions about the individual person are implicit in the writings of social scientists and others; and that 'models', as small-scale conceptual systems, have certain advantages for this purpose. Their nature will be briefly examined. The argument will be set out in basic terms for the general reader rather than for the theoretician, but the issues are recognized to be difficult and to require discussion in somewhat abstract terms. Some readers may prefer to read first the six approaches in chapters 2 to 7, and to turn back to the present chapter for reading in conjunction with the concluding one.

The need for explicit formulations

A criterion for the assessment of the social sciences is their relevance to professional practice. All of the contributors to this book have experience of teaching adults and discussing their specialisms with professional workers. Such workers tend to demand teaching that is 'relevant'—meaningful in terms of their tasks. In general they do not appear to 'apply' much conceptual thinking to their problems, nor do they seek to add an area of knowledge to the areas they already command. Their effort is directed towards the integration of learning and practice. In favourable instances, they make a shift in position as a result of what they learn, and achieve a new understanding of their task by seeing it in a new perspective. In making this shift, sophisticated professional workers will usually discuss people with a disregard for academic demarcations. The attempt to construct a sociology without a psychology may be understood by these practitioners as an enterprise a sociologist is required to attempt only for academic purposes. Professional workers seek an account of man that will help them to understand their clients more fully. In their training they were offered a selection of disciplines drawn from sociology, psychology, history, economics, anthropology, physiology, philosophy and theology. To bring these disciplines into a focus upon the person, and to trace out their inter-relations, was a task their teachers did not in general attempt. It is a task that appears to be left to students and to professional workers. It is understandable if they sometimes shrink from the problem, and function on a basis of naïve common sense.

Humpty Dumpty, as R. D. Laing has pointed out, cannot be put together again by any number of hyphenated or compound words, such as psycho-somatic, psycho-pathological, psycho-social or socio-technical. No doubt there are immense problems. As long ago as the 1930s the major causal connections in psycho-somatic illness had been mapped out by Franz Alexander, Flanders Dunbar, Weiss and English and others. To an observer who has understood these interconnections, it is evident that psychic factors play a large part in most illnesses and a decisive part in many. Illness, and death itself, are frequently intelligible forms of *behaviour* in terms of the life situation of the person concerned; a fact which is often clear to relatives but not to the doctor. Yet these insights have influenced the practice of medicine very little. The splitting of the person into 'mind' and 'body' militates against it.

No doubt there would be wide agreement that a set of generally accepted concepts about the person would be of the greatest value in many fields of study and practice. It is a condition that appears to be at the same time necessary and impossible. Consider what has been said, and is being said, about man. His nature is said to be divine; God is in him, or he is in God; or he is a creature guided by rational self-interest; his nature is social; his nature is anti-social; he is an animal driven by instinctual forces. Alternatively he is a machine; a probability-programmed computer; a homeostatic cybernetic system; a hierarchically organized stimulus-response system; or he is *sui generis*; or an uncharacterized and unintelligible existent; or he is a social construct, a cultural and historical product; or man is a fallen or alienated caricature of Man; or man does not yet exist, man is his own project. H. J. Blackham has written: 'These different concepts of man are not of merely speculative interest, for they have practical consequences. They have governed different systems of ethics. Human nature is linked with human destiny, that is to say with goods to be chosen and pursued, evils to be recognized and avoided, heaven and hell.'

It is not always made clear whether these images of man are presented as matters of faith, as ideological constructs, hypotheses, working models or established findings of scientific enquiry. Yet each of them is seen as basic by one or other school.

While the psychologists cannot avoid taking a position on some of the issues involved, the sociologist usually prefers to avoid them altogether. He attempts to abstract for study the properties of social systems and relationships, disregarding whatever properties derive from the systems of individuals. This may involve him in teaching a course on inter-personal relations with no indication of what is to be understood as a person.

Dahrendorf is a sociologist who reacts to the assumption of a right to pre-empt the entire field of action. He claims that the model of *homo sociologicus*, like the economists' model of economic man, must be pushed as far as it will go for scientific ends, but be preserved as sharply distinct from the living person: 'the person has no place, yet he must never be forgotten.' In all his work the sociologist must be committed to the autonomy of the real person, as a counterweight to the 'moral insufficiency' of his discipline. We may agree that this is ethically admirable, while remaining uncomfortably aware, as Roland Robertson reminds us, that Dahrendorf fails to offer us a route from *homo sociologicus* to real man.

The sociologist views the individual as the product of the processes of socialization and role-training. He sees him as taking his identity from the roles he has to play and as perceiving the world from a position inside his roles. If this offers a way of understanding the members of societies studied by sociologists, it may help us to understand the problems of the sociologist also. What of *his* role-training? His aims, his self-image, his professional culture? If the role of the sociologist requires that he spends much of his working life studying, reading, teaching, thinking and writing sociology, then he runs the risk of excluding—of needing to exclude—views of the human condition peculiar to artists, theologians or psychiatrists.

Perhaps the sociologist, rather than his subject, is the prototype of Dahrendorf's *homo sociologicus*.

Marxism may be the one system which is equipped to gather the diverse problems touched on here into a dynamic unity. None of the contributors to this book has offered a Marxist approach to the person, although a respect for Marxian analysis reveals itself here and there. This is perhaps the appropriate point to recognize the tremendous scope of Marxian scholarship and thinking around issues very close to those discussed here. For Marxists, the absence of a fully human figure at the centre of the social sciences is a mark of alienation. They argue that only a society which has gone very far in dehumanizing itself could have generated so much arid theory. They call for a fully developed account of man in his historical, social, economic, political, ideological and cultural setting. They deplore the fragmentation and dissociation of the academic disciplines, which are seen as in a state of flight from their primary tasks. A very powerful review of the recent cultural history of Britain is presented by Perry Anderson (1969); the following is a brief extract:

> Simultaneously, the absence of a centre produced a series of structural distortions in the character and connexions of the inherited disciplines. Philosophy was restricted to a technical inventory of language. Political theory was thereby cut off from history. History was divorced from the exploration of political ideas. Psychology was counterposed to them. Economics was dissociated from both political theory and history. Aesthetics was reduced to psychology. The congruence of each sector with its neighbour is circular; together they form something like a closed system. The quarantine of psychoanalysis is an example: it was incompatible with this pattern. Suppressed in every obvious sector at home, the idea of the totality was painlessly exported abroad, producing the paradox of an anthropology where there was no sociology. In the general vacuum thus created, literary criticism usurps ethics and insinuates a philosophy of history.

The grand sweep of this perspective has much to commend it. It is, perhaps, necessary, and has a direct bearing on our main theme. For the moment however we must return to the problems of the contemporary academic sociologist.

Social scientists have untiringly explored the perceptions, attitudes and value systems of others. It is now becoming necessary to know a social scientist's own position if we are to read him with understanding. He will usually be ready to agree that although he prefers not to formulate his assumptions about the individual, they could be discovered by an examination of his writing. They would be revealed in the accounts of events in which a causal sequence is implied and expected to be understood by the reader. The assumptions are implicit, and they have significant consequences. 'All study of human behaviour is explicitly or implicitly based on what may be called a general image or model of the nature of man, which determines problems, methods, vocabulary, frame of reference' (Lindesmith & Strauss, 1968).

In a discipline so sophisticated as sociology, it seems naïve to call attention to this matter. A naïve viewpoint will often discover a simple truth, however. Questions that the sociologist might put to himself are of this kind. Does he agree that he is in fact already working with an image or model of the nature of man? Does he feel a need for concepts in this area? As his discipline seeks to elucidate the action of individuals, can he satisfy himself that he can rightly exclude consideration of the nature of individuals? Does he see his academic field as a total system offering an account of all social action? What legitimacy does he concede to other disciplines focusing on aspects of the individual? How are the disciplines, or 'universes of discourse' to be brought into relation with each other?

A social scientist willing to make the attempt to formulate his concept of the person will face formidable difficulties. He may wish to disengage himself from a traditional doctrine that sees man as composed of body and soul, without coming to be hailed as an ally by 'rationalists'. He will need to be clear about the metaphysical status he wishes to claim for his concepts. His main embarrassment however will arise from the complexity of the processes he wishes to encompass (although it is fair to comment that the sociologist has not been unduly inhibited by the complexity of 'society'—where individual process is further complicated).

A sociologist might well feel inclined to accept the advice of Gluckman (1964) and make do with abridged formulations taken over from psychology. If he attempts this however he discovers that the psychologists can present no agreed account of mental function. Psycho-analysts, psychiatrists and psychologists commonly discredit each other's basic postulates. The cleavage is most acute between those adopting a behaviourist positivist approach modelled on the physical sciences and those preferring such terms as phenomeno-logical, psycho-dynamic, existential, to describe their approach. To some extent the opposition may reflect differences in roles—research versus clinical practice. The possibility that the choice of roles and the choice of approach are both expressions of innate tempera-mental dispositions—tough or tender—needs to be considered. Polarities of this kind, and their associated modes of perception, thought and feeling, have had much attention from psychologists during the last generation. The contrasts were recognized and sharply expressed long before psychology emerged as a discipline. David Roberts summarizes and quotes Pascal as follows:

If this creature sets himself to get at the truth by 'pure reason', he discovers that reason is surrounded by countless self-deceptions and limitations. There are, of course, truths which can be grasped by mathematical minds 'provided all things are explained to them by means of definitions and axioms; otherwise they are inaccurate and insufferable, for they are only right when the principles are quite clear'. But there are other truths which can be grasped only by the penetrative mind. 'On les voit à peine, on les sent plutôt qu'on ne les voit, on a des peines infinies à les faire sentir à ceux qui ne les sentent pas d'eux-mêmes . . . Il faut tout d'un coup voir la chose, d'un seul regard et non pas par progrès de raisonnement, au moins jusqu'à un certain degré.' 'They are scarcely seen; they are felt rather than seen; there is the greatest difficulty in making them felt by those who do not of themselves perceive them . . . We must see the matter at once, at one glance, and not by a process of reasoning', and since the two aptitudes, mathematical and intuitive, are rarely combined in the same person, most men are able to see one kind of truth only at the cost of being blind to the other . . . Reason is also frequently at the mercy of imagination, custom and will. Imagination is 'cette partie dominante de l'homme, cette maîtresse d'erreur et de fausseté, et d'autant plus fourbe qu'elle ne l'est pas toujours, car elle serait règle infaillible de vérité . . . Je ne parle pas des fous, je parle des plus sages, et c'est parmi eux que l'imagination a le grand droit de persuader les hommes. La raison a beau crier, elle ne peut metter le prix aux choses.' 'That deceitful part in man, that mistress of error and falsity, the more deceptive that she is not always so . . . I do not speak of fools, I speak of the wisest of men: and it is among them that the imagination has the great gift of persuasion. Reason protests in vain; it cannot set a true value on things . . .'

Nowhere in the literature of psychology is the difference so sharply and so relevantly stated as by Robert Graves:*

He is quick, thinking in clear images;
I am slow, thinking in broken images.

He becomes dull, trusting to his clear images;
I become sharp, mistrusting my broken images.

Trusting his images, he assumes their relevance;
Mistrusting my images, I question their relevance.

Assuming their relevance, he assumes the fact;
Questioning their relevance, I question the fact.

When the fact fails him, he questions his senses;
When the fact fails me, I approve my senses.

He continues quick and dull in his clear images;
I continue slow and sharp in my broken images.

He in a new confusion of his understanding;
I in a new understanding of my confusion.

This leads towards the possibility that the theoretical systems of social science are functions of personality. Instead of a systemized body of knowledge 'out there', each school becomes a sophisticated way of perceiving the world *proper to the individual*, who could only hope to teach it to others of similar constitutional type and cognitive habit. Perhaps this is not so far from experience, in fact. Aaron Cicourel has argued that sociology can do little but offer highly selective accounts of social events, usually arbitrary and naïve in their assumptions. He reports that his exposition is depressing for his students, at least temporarily; but impossible for his colleagues.

If one's account of persons, or of social action, is a derivation from one's personal cognitive system, one cannot claim generality for it. Scholarship in the social sciences has been based on an assumption

* From 'In Broken Images', *Collected Poems 1965*, by kind permission of Robert Graves.

that general statements can be made, although such statements have always come under attack almost as soon as they were formulated. There is a suspicion of general system-building at the present time, and much sympathy with Nietzsche's pronouncement that a systematic theory is an act of bad faith. The global systems of Comte and Spencer are now seen as mistaken endeavours. Marx has done better because he offered the dialectic, and analytical and synthetic method, which has survived the failure of his system in some other respects. William Blake is reported to have said, 'To generalize is to be an idiot.' (Even Blake however was not free of the need to construct a system out of arcane components. For him the need was defensive. 'I must create a system or be enslaved by another man's.') He directed our attention to the 'minute particulars' and the last decade has seen a concentration of interest in the minutiae of social interaction—eye-contact, gesture, proximity; the nuances of role-behaviour and of the 'presentation of self'; self-perception, the perception of other's perception of oneself. Significant detail is finely observed in the studies of Goffman, Laing, Argyle, Sommer, Garfinkel and many others. We should also recognize that the psycho-analysts have erected their interpretative systems on the basis of 'nameless unremembered acts'. Whereas eye-contact, gesture, proximity, appear to be dependent on common culture, the interpretations of the psycho-analysts are dependent on the unique life experience of the patient.

The term 'nomothetic' is used for reference to the establishment of laws, and 'idiographic' to individual instance. Thinking in terms of such apparently polar opposites does not take us far, even when we are prepared to recognize their inter-dependence. A middle position is possible. Kluckhohn and Murray in their compendium on personality, published in 1949, write:

Every man is in certain respects
(a) like all other men,
(b) like some other men,
(c) like no other man.

What could be more obvious? Yet much effort has been employed in seeking to reconcile (a) with (c) without recourse to the helpful middle term. The probabilistic nature of general propositions is now better understood. Modern mathematics also invites us to consider sets of individuals with common characteristics.

The social scientist need no longer think of himself as either constraining the belief of his readers by making empirically validated general statements on the one hand, or as developing an idiosyncratic perspective that few can be expected to share on the other. There is an acceptable middle position. To paraphrase Kluckhohn and Murray, every social scientist is in certain respects like some other social scientists, and may hope that a *part* of what he has to say will be understood by *some* of his readers.

Models

The tendency to think of the idiographic and the nomothetic as polar opposites is a matter of convenience. Suppose we see them as lying at the extremities of a continuum; then we can ask, what positions can we identify at the intermediate points? The answer is likely to be a position defined by a model.

Models have been much in favour during the last decade, following the retreat from general theory. The use of the term is various. Models may be specific or general, metaphoric, analogic, mathematical or verbal. They may be used to organize thinking in natural science, and equally helpfully in the field of total subjectivity, of which Dr Clark's essay in this volume is an example. Geographers, amongst others, have experienced difficulties in setting up a general theory, and the recent development of economic, demographic, urban and sociological models in that field has proved so promising as to merit the title, the New Geography. Several of the quotations and points made in the following paragraphs are taken from the first chapter of Chorley and Haggett's useful book, *Socio-Economic Models in Geography*.

Events around us and within us are far too complex for us to hope to accommodate all available data about them in our thinking. Thought requires simplified concepts. Apostel writes that in this way we can achieve 'an overview of the essential characteristics of a domain' and goes on to say:

the mind needs to see the system in opposition and distinction to all others; therefore the separation of the system from others is made more complete than it is in reality. The system is viewed from a certain scale; details that are too microscopical or too global are of no interest to us. Therefore they are left out. The system is known or controlled within certain limits of approximation. Therefore effects that do not reach this level of approximation are neglected. The system is studied with a certain purpose in mind; everything that does not affect this purpose is eliminated. The various features of the system need to be known as aspects of one identical whole; therefore their unity is exaggerated.

Reality has to be explored by the use of simplified patterns of symbols, rules and processes (Meadows). Chorley and Haggett describe models very much in these terms as 'highly subjective approximations . . . valuable in obscuring incidental detail and in allowing fundamental aspects of reality to appear', and quote Bambrough, 'each of these pictures gives undue prominence to some features of our knowledge and obscures and distorts the other features that rival pictures emphasize. Each of them directs such a bright light on one part of the scene that it obscures other parts in a dark shadow'; Black writes on scale models: 'only by being unfaithful in some respect can a model represent its original'.

Models are aids to thinking, and in respect of some problems may be a necessary condition for thought. New thinking is likely to arise from an insight, a new understanding. Chorley and Haggett quote Bridgman: 'Explanation consists in analysing our complicated systems into simpler systems in such a way that we recognise in the complicated systems the interplay of elements already so familiar to us that we accept them as not needing explanation.'

Whereas general theory is required to approximate to the condition of truth, to bring all concepts in a field into a single system, to demand high levels of validity or statistical probability, the criteria for models are different. An efficient model must be simplified, explanatory, suggestive and heuristic. It must, like a Marxian dialectic, expect to be transcended, discarded, or conserved in a new unity. In writing about human individuals as whole persons, this approach will relieve us of any absurd attempt to do justice to our subject in all its complexity.

The contributors to this book have not set out to devise models; but in each essay the argument has led in this direction. These arguments have used concepts derived from the social sciences, and behind these concepts lie philosophic questions. It is not enough to say that models are useful—we have to say for what purpose. Nor can we be content to say that models have heuristic value; that might mean that basic concepts lead to a proliferation of secondary concepts. We need to know what can be claimed for the model as representing some aspect of reality. We are at once involved in problems relating to the nature of scientific explanation and discussion about the reference theory of meaning. The attempt to make statements about the world around us may involve us in metaphysics. The relativity of our perception of it leads us into phenomenology. None of these philosophic fields however offers us a language adequate to the description of individual experience. For that purpose we have to speak of ontology, the science of being, a branch of philosophy revitalized by the philosophers who have been grouped together as 'existentialists'.

Psychology painfully separated itself from philosophy at the turn of the nineteenth century. Sociology was similarly implicated in social philosophy in the writings of Comte, Spencer, Hobhouse and others. The separation became destructive, and exposed the social sciences to the pull of the natural sciences, with some unfortunate results. The current trend is to repair the damage, and to bring philosophy and the social sciences together again. It is one distinction of Marxist thought always to have insisted on this unity, brilliantly developed by Sartre and others. From a quite different position the phenomenology of Alfred Schutz has influenced such sociologists as Garfinkel and Cicourel. Ninian Smart is a philosopher who has cogently argued the case for an increased traffic between his discipline and the social sciences, as has Alasdair MacIntyre. It will be apparent that Ninian Smart's essay in this book touches on many themes treated by other contributors, especially by Dan Gowler.

As indicated in the preface, no attempt was made to constrain the contributors of the following chapters to adhere to a pre-planned sequence. It was thought that the essays might prove to be more significant if each was written in ignorance of the context of the others, and to accept the risks involved. The reader must expect a very different experience as he moves from one to another. The editor has included a brief terminal chapter which identifies some themes of common interest.

Bibliography

Alexander, F. (1932), *The Medical Value of Psycho-analysis*, New York, Norton.

Anderson, P. (1969), 'Components of the national culture', in *Student Power*, ed. A. Cockburn and R. Blackburn, Penguin.

Apostel, L. (1961), 'Towards the formal study of models in the non-formal sciences', in *The Concept and the Role of the Model in Mathematics and the Natural and Social Sciences*, ed. H. Freudenthal, Doordrecht, Holland.

Argyle, M. (1967), *The psychology of Interpersonal Behaviour*, Penguin.

Bambrough, R., *see* Chorley & Haggett.

Blackham, H. J. (1970), 'The concept of human nature', in *Question Three*, Rationalist Press Association annual publication, Pemberton.

Bridgman, P. W., *see* Chorley & Haggett.

Chorley, R. J. & Haggett, P. (1967), *Socio-Economic Models in Geography*, Methuen.

Cicourel, A. V. (1964), *Method and Measurement in Sociology*, New York, Free Press; London, Collier-Macmillan.

Dahrendorf, R. (1968), *Essays in the Theory of Society*, Routledge & Kegan Paul.

Dunbar, F. (1943), *Psychosomatic Diagnosis*, Paul B. Hoeber.

Garfinkel, H. (1967), *Studies in Ethnomethodology*, Englewood Cliffs, Prentice-Hall.

Gluckman, M. (ed.) (1964). *Closed Systems and Open Minds*, Oliver & Boyd.

Goffman, E. (1968), *Stigma*, Penguin.

Goffman, E. (1968), *Asylums*, Penguin.

Goffman, E. (1969), *Where the Action Is*, Allen Lane.

Graves, R. (1957), *Poems Selected by Himself*, Penguin.

Hobhouse, L. T. (1957), *Morals in Evolution*, Chapman & Hall (first published 1906).

Kluckhohn, C. & Murray, H. A. (1949), *Personality in Nature, Society and Culture*, Cape.

Laing, R. D. (1959), *The Divided Self*, Tavistock.

Lindesmith, A. R. & Strauss, A. L. (1968), *Social Psychology*, New York, Holt, Rinehart & Winston.

Meadows, P., *see* Chorley & Haggett.

Pascal, B. (1958), *Pensées*, ed. L. Lafuma, Paris, Le Club du Meilleur Livre.

Roberts, D. (1959), *Existentialism and Religious Belief*, New York, Oxford University Press.

Schutz, A. (1967), *The Phenomenology of the Social World*, Evanston, Illinois, Northwestern University Press.

Sommer, R. (1970), *Personal Space*, Englewood Cliffs, Prentice-Hall.

Weiss, E. & English, O. (1943), *Psychosomatic Medicine*, Philadelphia, W. B. Saunders.

2 Creation, persons and the meaning of life

Ninian Smart

Introduction

In approaching the concept of the person I owe something to recent philosophical debate and something to the study of religion. I hope that what I have to say will also have some relevance to sociology and psychology. Since knowledge and insight often advance through discussion, I would not worry if a lot of what I have to say can be shown to be misguided and false: but it would be upsetting if it turned out to be so unclear and confused that it would not be capable of being argued about. I only hope that I have at least avoided that misery.

In the first main section I consider the old question of freedom, but from a 'social' point of view. I wish to argue that freedom is a power precipitated in the individual by society. This leads on to the second main section where I wish to argue that in an important sense the concept of the person is culturally determined, and has (so to say) an ethical component. That is, it is wrong to think of personhood as something simply given, like bipedhood. This leads on to a third section which considers whether an 'ontological basis' of personhood exists. That is, I consider what realities underlie the ascription of personhood, and in doing so consider the place of myth and *Weltanschauungen* in explaining and expressing what a person is. Some concluding remarks deal with the present apparent predicament of many Westerners in coming to terms with an alteration in world views and with their proliferation. Is the person as well as nature to be disenchanted?

Freedom, creativity and society

Since the war one fashionable philosophical view about freedom of the will has been summed up in what has been called 'the Compatibility Thesis'. It is the view that freedom of the will and causal determinism are compatible, given what we ordinarily mean by terms such as 'free'. The argument, briefly and too simply, is as follows. First, on the one hand, the notion of causality can be analysed as being equivalent to, or replaceable by, that of predictability in principle. Thus to say that event C causes event E is to say that given C, together with the other relevant conditions and a knowledge of the relevant laws, one could predict E with certainty. Of course, we cannot always predict well; knowledge is incomplete and patchy—hence predictability has to be qualified by the words 'in principle'. On this analysis, then, to say that an action of a human is determined is to say that it could be in principle predicted, given a knowledge of the prior relevant conditions, etc. The thesis that *all* human acts are causally determined (the thesis of determinism) is simply that they are all in principle predictable. The next and second stage in the argument is to consider what 'free' and its cognates mean. To say that I am free to choose eggs rather than sausages for breakfast means (apart from the fact that these choices are *available*) that no one is forcing me, by a gun or otherwise by imposing unreasonable restraint, to choose one rather than the other. Of course, there are kleptomaniacs—that is, not all constraints upon freedom come from outside. The compulsive shoplifter, alas, cannot help herself. In that way she is not free—some hidden internal constraints operate in her. In brief, freedom consists in the absence of serious external or internal constraints. This part of the argument derives simply from an examination of the concepts as they are used ordinarily. The third part of the argument consists in the observation that freedom is not constrained by prediction. If you (knowing my character) correctly predict that I will choose eggs rather than sausages, you are in no wise forcing me. It is a very different matter from holding a gun at me.

Of course, it makes a difference if you tell me your prediction (I may be cussed and react against it, and so falsify it). Of course, there are many queries and holes in the argument as here presented also. In many respects it is simplistic and doubtful. But it serves as a useful starting point, for it raises the question of the limitations which may in principle lie upon our knowledge of persons and of the future. I hope to bring this out in a way relevant to the thesis that freedom is, so to say, a power precipitated in the individual by society.

The problem of freedom has tended to be seen by Western philosophers as being much bound up with the possibility of moral
action. It is interesting that the problem is called the problem of the
freedom of the *will*, and the will has typically been conceived as a
shadow organ (so to speak) which is brought into operation in the
making of moral decisions. But I think that it is useful to extend
the problem beyond morality, and this for a number of reasons.
First, what counts as a moral choice and what is not remains
unclear. Is choosing a cream puff a moral choice? (What if I am
overweight; what if I am not?) Is deciding the colour of wallpaper?
Second, even if it were possible to carve off a range of decisions
which are not moral, it does not appear that the processes involved
in coming to a decision materially differ, even if the considerations
do. Choosing between going to a film and a brothel and choosing
between going to a film and a Chinese meal involve differing considerations; but it seems unrealistic to suppose that there is an ontological difference between the one set of events and the other.
Third, moral choices may have quite as much to do with imaginative
attitudes as with strength of will. Two hundred years ago there
wasn't much thought given to animal rights; but now there is,
partly because of an existential realization on the part of many folk
that animals actually suffer. There has been a shift in imagination.
In many instances, men's moral choices are affected by, and up to
a point effected by, the way men look at the world. Thus even from
the point of view of moral action, will power is not all (or even
much). But imaginative changes, and connectedly changes in the
state of knowledge, are not necessarily directly moral. Hence it is
reasonable to treat freedom in the wider context of attitudes and
knowledge, not just in the context of moral decisions.

In any event, the person is a complex whole where it is simplistic
to match conceptual decisions to psychological powers. Because I
can do sums, it does not follow that there is a sum-making faculty
embedded in the psychophysical organism, like an inner eye. Because
I can make choices, it does not follow that there is an entity called
'the will', with which I make them. In brief, we must be sceptical of
faculty psychology. Once we have rid ourselves of this illusion, there
no longer seems to be much sense in treating freedom in the narrow
context of moral choices. If it exists, it does so as a property of a
decision-making, exploratory, imaginative animal.

In this case it becomes useful to look at the person as being capable of change. Can people take imaginative decisions, and change creatively? Well, the answer is at one level quite obvious, since we have a use for the expressions 'imaginative' and 'creative'. But I want to suggest something about the nature of these possibilities in human beings. I want to argue that there are necessary limits upon predictability. This is an argument that is clearer in regard to the history of ideas than it is in relation to moral choices of the ordinary kind. Indeed, there are contexts where choices are quite predictable (or if it is preferred, causally determined).

Given a certain social framework and milieu of ideas, moral choices made by individuals may be highly predictable. But, nevertheless, any given system—even if it be closed—may be invaded, so to speak, by new influences, whether these be the creative ideas of a member of the group or forces acting from without. Looking at matters sociologically, for a moment, my argument is relevant to the concepts of prophecy and charisma in the writings of Max Weber: however, the range that needs to be taken into account is wider—the inventor of radio or the discoverer of penicillin has a role similar to that of the prophet, in 'breaking through' existing patterns of thought, behaviour, technology, etc. Also, though I have written above of a 'member' of a group, there is no reason why a breakthrough of ideas should not be a joint effort. Though committees are not often creative, there is no reason in principle why they should not be. Group discoveries are not discoveries by individuals or by a sum of individuals.

Now to the main argument. Let us use as examples the history of science and the history of art. Consider the state of physics towards the end of the nineteenth century. To a great extent it looked as though classical physics had reached a final form. True there had arisen one or two nagging discoveries, notably radioactivity. Still, it was possible for Kelvin to discourage a young man from taking up work in physics on the ground that all the major problems had been solved. Yet it was a relatively short time later that physics underwent a tremendous revolution—through relativity and then through quantum physics. Some of the central assumptions of classical physics had been challenged, and Newton survived as a special case, not as king.

There are two main reasons why the details of the revolution could not be predicted, and why only the vaguest premonition of a revolution could be had in Kelvin's time. First, looking at matters from the side of the facts which a theory has to take account of: these as collected represent a finite group—but the theory of course goes further in proclaiming its validity over facts which could in the future be collected. The theory in this respect has predictive value. It contains universalizations, to the effect that all X's are Y-ish (e.g. that all atoms have certain properties in common, or that all events of a certain sort are followed by other events of a certain sort). But in the nature of the case the present collection of facts cannot *guarantee* the nature of the facts which can be collected in the future. It is not that one should be, in Humean mood, uncertain that the sun will rise tomorrow; no such scepticism is justified by the lack of guarantee. But at the same time one should acknowledge that nothing can absolutely *exclude* the possibility of awkward facts being encountered, which will necessitate the scrapping or at least modification of the previously held theory. Thus from the side of the brute world which theories set out to describe and explain, there is liable to be an army of factual guerrillas lying in ambush for the most secure theories.

Second, from the side of any present development of science, there is no guarantee of the unchangeability of the *concepts* which we use. Scientific revolutions may be precipitated by factual ambushes as described above; but they can also be precipitated by the change of concepts. In any event the factual ambush may require conceptual changes of a radical kind. But the present state of science cannot predict the conceptual changes which precipitate its demise. Let us put this point in a different way. To predict, one needs some kind of theory. But the present state of theory cannot be used to predict the emergence of concepts which overthrow it. (It is true that we may discover some contradiction or disquieting disharmony which leads us to suppose that a new theory is called for—but the contradiction or disharmony will not supply the details of the concepts crucial to the new theory.)

For these two reasons there is an ineluctable openness in principle in the ongoing progress of science. There is a theoretical limit upon predictability. Thus one aspect of human existence is unpredictable in principle. But we may note that science, though a matter for the specialist, is liable to wide dissemination. It can be disseminated by its applications, such as atom-bombs; and it can be disseminated conceptually through the difference it makes to our vision of the world, i.e. through its philosophical importance. Thus, although I am no scientist, I am affected by the scientific revolutions—for example, I remember sitting in a truck after an army exercise in a wet wood and hearing about the dropping of the first atom bomb. We had been using sten guns. We all felt like throwing these nasty toys away, for they would not be needed at the fag-end of the war. This is rather a banal and obvious point. It is mentioned here to remind us that we cannot ensure any kind of ultimate insulation from what other men may achieve. Thus every scientific advance is like a stone thrown in a pond: the ripples spread outwards.

This is part of what is meant by saying that freedom is a power precipitated in the individual by society. For rational action and decision depend upon a certain degree of sophistication in dealing with the world, and a prime condition of this sophistication is the use of language. It is by communication that we participate in traditions of know-how, and it is by the use of language that we can envisage alternative future courses of action on a scale quite outside the reach of other animals. Thus the emergence of personhood in an individual as he progresses onwards from the foetus depends heavily upon his becoming a linguistic animal. But once this capacity of communication and thought is achieved, the individual is necessarily liable to influences from outside. Admittedly, through brain damage or through senility and so on it may come about that a linguistic animal no longer functions as thus open to visionary and conceptual influence. Or it may be in fact that his community is very static and cut off from the wider world. Nevertheless, there can be no guarantee that those who have, as linguistic animals, attained personhood will not be affected by unpredictable creativities arising elsewhere. At a humbler level, new imaginative ways of dealing with people and problems may arise from the example of others, through conversation and so on. Thus because the social group precipitates its language in the individual, and so the individual becomes in part a cultural creation, any creative unpredictability accruing to a member of the group or to part of the group will be liable to be transmitted to the rest and in particular to the individual we have in mind. The plasticity of his behaviour and thinking is thus a product of the group.

Or to put things in another, and more provocative, manner: freedom is essentially a property of the group, and only secondarily of the individual. Yet this provocative remark is liable to misinterpretation. For obviously the group is made up of individuals and does not have an abstract, separate existence of its own.

I have been making much of unpredictability in principle. It is, of course, only one condition (if it is at all a condition) of creative freedom. For mere unpredictability is a sort of randomness. And randomness is not enough. Consider: it is alleged that the behaviour of electrons is not totally determinate, i.e. that it cannot be fully predicted, so that within a certain range of possibilities the outcome is random. As we may recall, Einstein was rather dissatisfied with the state of quantum mechanics and claimed that God does not play dice. Nevertheless, there are good theoretical reasons why there is randomness in sub-atomic events. Now suppose for the sake of argument an action of mine was (so to speak) triggered off by a sub-atomic event occurring somewhere in my brain, so that I do A rather than B simply because of a random and unpredictable cause. This would hardly be accounted free. Mere randomness does not, then, give freedom. It is the difference between the case of electrons and the case of the creative human that is important.

This difference can be represented as in part consisting in the following fact: that the inventive scientist (for example) finds his problems in an ongoing tradition of doing science. It may be that in important respects he overthrows the tradition, by his creativity. But, nevertheless, the problems which are posed are scientific problems and, for example, more narrowly physical problems. His very capacity to envisage a new bit of theory arises from his already having been initiated into existing theories and more fundamentally from his having learned the language of science. Thus the situation is in a sense dialectical: he needs the thesis before he can pose his antithesis. All this implies that there is a logical or *conceptual* connection between his new bit of theory and the old theory. The one follows the other in an 'internal', not merely an external way. Thus the work of the Copenhagen school might be followed by the blowing up of Copenhagen by an H-bomb. This would be an external, merely temporal, following. But the work of the Copenhagen school may be followed up by the postulation of quarks. This is an 'internal' connection. It is this main fact that distinguishes the case of human creativity from the randomness of the behaviour of a particle. If you like: the scientist has a project, but electrons do not have projects. (For which reason the attempt to read free will into electrons has always seemed rather laughable.)

The situation echoes something in classical Christian thinking, the idea, namely, of grace—which implies that the good I do comes, so to say, from outside me, though in another important respect it comes from within. This is why the occurrence of a bright idea is likened to inspiration.

The argument that has here been put forward in relation to the example of the progress of the sciences could also use the example of the arts. The sculptor working in the modern tradition may, if he is truly distinctive, create a new style. But the theoretician of sculpture, who might wish to foresee trends, needs to have imagined in detail, i.e. in effect to have created, the very style which he hopes to foresee.

All this is not to deny that futurology (as it is now fashionably called) is in some degree possible, though its achievements are bound to be rather severely constrained by the sorts of consideration that I have been advancing. And, of course, there is nothing in the arguments to deny that hypothetical predictions are quite feasible, even in the areas like scientific discovery which have been used as examples. Thus we can predict that unless some unforeseen discovery takes place, more evanescent examples of elementary particles will be turned up by the use of cyclotrons.

The general argument might, however, be attacked at a fundamental level by denying the equation of determinism and predictability. Maybe there are causal transactions at work which are in themselves perfectly determinate even though *we* are in principle precluded from getting at them. For instance, it might be argued that an advanced computer, one which is more advanced than anything which exists at the present time, might turn out to be creative in the manner, roughly, in which men are—by discovering, say, new theorems in mathematics or by experimenting successfully with new ways of classifying objects—and so coming up with a sort of conceptual revolution. Anyway, let us suppose such a creative computer, and one which is in some sense in communication with other computers. Then the argument I have used would apply equally to the computers. But do we want to claim that there is not as much causal determinacy as could be expected (namely every event in the computer being caused by another event)? It might be that the computers would be precluded from prediction, in principle. But we would not. This objection is a confused one, however, though it expresses a strong feeling which we need to take into account. It is confused because *ex hypothesi* the computers are being creative, and even from our point of view they are producing novel ideas. The fact that we *built* the computers does not as such give us any superiority (any more than the fact that my wife and I produced a son makes us cleverer). Or we can put the point differently by saying that the computers are in communication with us as well—they are mechanical individuals, but for the purposes of the argument individuals none the less.

What then is the strong feeling which has to be taken into account? I think it can be brought out in the following way. The general argument which I have pursued assumes that we must look upon man as an historical being. The history of science (for example) remains open always at its cutting edge. It is replete with instances in the past of how certainties can come to be transformed into dubieties and special cases. Of course, it would no longer be open if the planet was destroyed with all its inhabitants. But it is essentially open so long as the enterprise of investigation goes on. But perhaps we do not need to look at man from an historical perspective. The strong feeling to which I referred is what may be called the sentiment of timeless Godhood—the sentiment, namely, that it is right and proper also to look upon the world *sub specie aeternitatis*, perhaps in the manner of Minkowski. We are encouraged in this sentiment by the example of the computers for we are their creators: we can take, so to say, a timeless God-like view of them.

The strong sentiment, then, suggests a manner of seeing men ahistorically. But the timeless vision cannot have real content: it is rather a reminder that there may be a way of describing the world in which we step out of our historical nature, which we cannot (however) do. In other words, it is possible that there is a secret determinism which must in principle remain opaque and unavailable to us. I do not mind if this be so—it hardly affects the correctness of the conclusion I have been offering, about the unpredictable creativity which remains a possibility for human groups and individuals.

To recapitulate, then: I have argued that freedom has a wider range of application than moral choice, and can be applied to thinking and imagination. I have tried to indicate the way in which scientific and artistic history is open-ended and unpredictable. This is enough, given the linguistic, communicative nature of persons, to show that individual action etc., is unpredictable, in the required sense—since it cannot be guaranteed to be insulated from the creativity of others. Thus we live in an indeterministic, historical mode. I have also tried strongly to emphasize that personhood is not simply something given, but something acquired, through the learning of language and through being inducted into a social mode of existence. From this point of view, freedom is not naturally given, but is a power precipitated, so to say, by society in the individual. (This however is not to deny that some basic physiological and psychological equipment is necessary if the individual is to be capable of attaining personhood. For this reason, cats cannot properly speaking become persons.)

The way in which I have attempted to deal with the problem of freedom is a shift away from 'will-centred' moral psychology. With the moralizing of the notion of sin, and with the doctrine of man's fall, Western men have tended to concentrate upon the notion of will-power—as though what is wrong in men's condition has to do with failures in making the correct choices. Perhaps we have not paid sufficient attention to the importance of knowledge and vision —for many of our ills stem from failures in imagination and insight. There is something to be said, therefore, for the Indian idea of what I may call 'original ignorance' as lying at the root of our dissatis-factions and sufferings. Neither model is complete, nor are they jointly complete—for very often our miseries come from outside, from earthquakes and from failures in the psychological and physio-logical equipment that keeps us going. But if anything, my account of freedom veers more towards the Eastern conception than to the dominating concern with will-power.

Personhood as an ethical concept

As I have argued, personhood is not something given biologically like being a biped. An individual has to *become* a person. There is another way also in which personhood might appear to be a cultural and social creation. It is, however, a very different, though not unconnected, way. We can approach the matter from the standpoint of the moral status of the person.

Let us begin with a macabre example. Suppose I am tending an enormous bonfire in the garden, and keep throwing heavy objects on to it, soaked in petrol. Suppose I am asked what these are, and reply, 'Oh, just some spare persons I wanted to get rid of.' That the idea is immediately disgusting perhaps relates to the way in which we almost instinctively treat persons in certain situations—say a number of people are lying on the ground watching a cricket match and I come walking over them: I do not tread on them as though they are logs or stones, but gingerly step between them. It would require considerable training to rid oneself of this almost instinctive tenderness towards persons.

Thus already at quite a primitive level recognizing an individual as a person involves being prepared to act towards him in certain ways. For this reason, as well as for a number of other well-canvassed ones, the model used by some philosophers to account for belief in other minds, namely that we perform a sort of inference in ascribing mental attributes to others, is unrealistic. A similar remark applies to a range of the animal kingdom. A Catholic philosopher and theologian once remarked that we know too little about animal psychology to be certain that animals feel pain. But if one sees a cat writhing on the road with its back broken by a passing car one is already (not calculating whether it feels any pain) getting ready to *do* something about it. It does not mean, incidentally, that one actually *does* do anything: for all sorts of wicked reasons one might repress the incipient actions, but the incipience is there. I leave out of account here complications arising from sadism and so on—but note that delight in others' pain does presuppose ascription of pain; in this kind of way, hate too is a kind of compliment, for at least it treats its object as human. Perhaps this is why some S.S. men were trained by the Nazis to handle human skulls until they could treat a human with complete indifference and detachment. This is the higher cruelty, which in a sense is not cruelty at all.

The fact that already at the primitive level we do not just step on cats when walking across rooms, the way we might step on rugs, indicates that some animals have an analogy to persons. More sophisticatedly they may be regarded as having an analogy to human rights. But they are not fully persons, because of the lack of language and social initiation. (I guess however if we could really get super-dolphins bred, which could converse squeakily about Aristotle, we would think of them as persons.)

Moving now beyond what I have called the primitive level: the person is seen as being the bearer, in principle, of certain rights, and also as the locus of certain values and disvalues. Thus a person appears not only with rights but also with human attributes which we may cherish or otherwise. Thus the concept of a person is not simply descriptive, but imperatival and expressive. Crudely, the ascription of personhood in these latter two respects incorporates imperatives about not infringing certain rights etc., and expressive utterances about the value of humanity.

But this raises questions immediately about the extent to which the concept of the person is culturally determined and historically rather particular. In brief, is it a way of looking on people which is essentially latter-day Western? The question is posed as soon as we begin to speak of rights, since the notion that a human being has certain rights, irrespective of his group, does not seem to be universally shared. There are many different ways of classifying people, and to classify people as essentially persons is only one of them. A lot must depend on the weight also which is attached to different ways of differentiating between classes of people.

Consider for instance the ancient Indian classification of people in terms of the *varṇas*—the four classes, Brahmins, Kṣatriyas and so on together with those outside (and typically socially below) the system. It is clear from ancient Hindu law that in terms of rights, the lowest in the hierarchy had less protection than some animals. From the point of view of a sacred hierarchy of beings, the distinction 'human' (non-human' was less important than distinctions of sacred value. Indeed the realm of living beings (and gods and spirits, demons and so forth) represents in the ancient Indian tradition a continuum, across which lines are drawn in a disconcertingly different way from the modern Western tradition (it is of course only disconcerting from *our* cultural viewpoint). This difference in the way the world is looked at is brought out by the doctrine of souls. Except in Advaita Vedanta, Buddhism and Indian materialism, one can say that every system of belief involved the assertion of innumerable souls or life-monads. The soul or life-monad is of great importance, for it is this element that is to be liberated. The 'essential' being existing in the state of salvation or release is this soul. Now universally among these Indian systems of belief the souls are possessed equally by non-human beings, for example animals. Hence the most important distinction now becomes 'living)(non-living', or 'animate)(non-animate', not the distinction between humans and non-humans.

Again it is a feature of some tribal languages that the word for man coincides with the word for a member of the tribe. It is as though all men are people, but only some count as persons. This feature of tribal languages is reproduced in modern societies, e.g. when they are at war. It is not uncharacteristic that a word like 'gook' should be invented to refer to Vietnamese, by American soldiers. It begins to create a licence to treat Vietnamese as less than persons. Similar phenomena can be observed in colonial situations, where the ruled are natives and wogs (but here the rulers can come into conflict with missionaries, for instance—whose 'all men are equal in the sight of God' is a different mode of classifying).

These and other examples might lead us to suppose that the concept of the person is culturally particular, and thus in a sense open to challenge. We shall in due course have to examine the problem of whether there is an ontological basis to justify the concept in a way which would free it from the charge of mere cultural particularity. But in the meantime let us notice that in having imperatival and expressive elements built into it, it is not unlike a number of other concepts. Examples which can be cited are 'worker', 'the reverend', 'wife'. Thus a man of the Left, in classing someone as a worker, is not merely drawing attention to certain economic facts and to the mode of the person's occupation. He is also by implication placing him in a context of action and value. One has to have a special attitude, of course, if the appropriate imperatives and expressive utterances are to follow—that is, the man of the Left is appealing to the solidarity, if one may put it this way, of the hearer. It is a feature of imperatives and expressives that they can generate resistance as well as acceptance, for they in effect pose a choice and a challenge to the hearer. In a highly integrated and non-pluralistic society there is little in the way of problems about this. All members of a tribe may accept, consciously or unconsciously, the value judgments incorporated in their modes of classification. But in a more pluralistic milieu it often happens that the commendation of X by A leads to the rejection of X by B. Correspondingly, the expressive side of the term used to categorize may be (so to say) counter-productive. This is a topic ill researched by demonstrators, who often have the effect of bringing about the opposite attitudes to those being inculcated by the demonstration. However, it is hard for this to happen over the expressive aspect of the concept of a person, since it is not easy to sign out of the category. But to return to the concept of the worker, I hope that the point is enough made that it has its imperatival and expressive aspects, having a certain communicative (mainly evocative) effect for those who share the values of the utterer, or (if he is clever) for those who in due course *come* to share those values.

But as has been hinted at, the case of the person may be different. How can we *reject* the moral and valuational aspects of the concept if we recognize, as we must, that we are all persons? How indeed? But then it must be seen that the question has been posed in a certain way, namely in terms of the concept of universal human person-hood. The question can well be transcended by the use of differing ways of classifying living beings or of another way of carving up the human territory. For the very appeal of the concept of the person is universalistic; while it may well be that the world is not viewed in this manner. Thus the contingency of the idea of the person, as expressing a universalistic and cosmopolitan ethic, means that the employment of it represents a moral stance.

Let us illustrate this by the following analogy. A few years ago the notion of 'squares' became current. Young folk often accused their elders of being square. Those who rejected squareness did so in part by employing the concept: that is, by using the category they were able to discriminate with a certain subtlety between square and other behaviour, and thus they were enabled to avoid squareness in a subtle way. By endorsing the notion of squareness (by endorsing the disvalue of the square) the antisquare individual was taking a kind of moral and customary stance. Now it will be readily conceded that there is no 'transcendental deduction' of squareness: it is not a concept inextricably embedded in any coherent view of the world. It is not necessary to any and every language. It is, in brief, a con-tingent concept, which means that it is always open to a group or an individual to repudiate the distinction which it makes. In this way the concept is not endorsed, but rather repudiated, replaced or ignored. Thus the moral attitude encapsulated in it is not a neces-sary, ineluctable one. This being so, it represents a certain choice, and this is what is meant by saying that the use of the concept expresses a particular moral stance. By analogy, therefore, we may say that the employment of the concept of the person represents such a stance. It is not, in other words, an ineluctable concept. This reinforces the earlier suggestion that it is culturally and historically particular. Though it enshrines a universalistic ethic (as far as humans are concerned) it is not itself universal.

I have hinted earlier at the differing ways in which individuals may be looked at in differing social systems and conceptual schemes. If the conclusion of the argument just given is a sound one, the concept of the person is definitely a moral option. It is a way of looking at humans given a certain ethic. But though I have tended to stress the contingency of the idea, it should not be thought that the idea is, therefore, merely arbitrary. In the next section we shall be considering the 'ontological' basis for the idea of the person.

If I may now draw together the two strands that have been spun out in the first two sections. In the first it was argued that freedom as a power or property of the individual was precipitated in him by his social group. In the second section it has been argued that on the ethical front the concept of the person represents a particular (though universalistic) moral stance. The attempt therefore to derive morality from the assumption of respect for persons is perfectly fair, except that it does not amount to a necessary demonstration of moral rules, since respect for persons represents a particular moral stance. Hence the rest of morality would share in this 'contingency'. It is true that some moral rules are such that their general observance is a necessary condition of the existence of a society—to this extent they are not contingent. But even then they can vary in form. Thus the Buddhist prohibition of killing extends to animals, while the Ten Commandments' version does not. And in any event the two codes allow of differing exceptions (thus killing in war is not an infringement of 'Thou shalt not kill' as usually interpreted). The case of war is perhaps of very deep significance. The existence of society is not necessarily the existence of planetary society—the very idea has been only patchily expressed in human history. Rather the observance of bans on stealing and so forth have been a necessary condition of the existence of particular societies. Thus if British people go around killing Britons too much, British society will collapse. But of course Italian society will not. Thus the ban on killing as being a rule whose general observance is a necessary condition of the existence of a society need not be taken to mean that one cannot kill members of an external group. Thus typically in human history, 'Thou shalt not kill' and its equivalents in other religions and cultures has been *primarily* applied to kith and kin. The notion that members of other societies—of *all* other societies—are persons with the same rights of protection as members of one's own society has not been all that widespread.

The two strands are intertwined because freedom as a power precipitated in the individual does not flourish greatly in a closed society. It does not do so, for the closed society does not encourage speculation and new uses of imagination—those 'conversions' which direct men away from dull stereotypes. The 'open' society is one which is bound to be critical of traditionalist barriers between men. To this extent it will drift towards the universalistic ethic which operates with the idea of the person as the primary bearer of rights and as the locus of human values. However, though the two strands may be intertwined they remain separate, and I am far from arguing that they entail one another or that one entails the other. Much, of course, depends on whether any strong ontological basis of the idea of the person can be discovered, and on the nature of that basis. To this topic I now turn.

Souls, persons and meaning

Religions have sometimes expressed the ontological basis of universal personhood. Thus, for example, the Christian tradition has spoken of men as being made in the image of God, or as having souls, and these models have been meant to apply to everyone, across tribal, national, social and other barriers. Again, many Indian systems of belief have claimed, as we have seen, that all living beings have souls, which contain, so to say, the potentiality of release. Buddhism has given an analysis of persons, via the five *skandhas* or constituent factors, which is meant to apply universally to all humans. In such religious beliefs we can see a variety of models of the person. We find other models in modern existentialism, Marxism and materialism.

These models have to explain somehow the 'worth' of persons. They are models which both attempt to describe or analyse on the one hand and attempt to express the value and meaning of persons on the other. They thus have a kind of mythological function. But this remark needs a little explaining.

First, of course, I use the word 'myth' in a high not a low sense. By 'myth' I do not mean false story or false idea (which it means so often in popular usage). By it I mean what historians of religion mean by it, namely a story or account of things human and divine, like the myth of Adam or the myth of Christ's birth, death and resurrection. Now a myth is more than a mere story or account. It has a certain kind of function. To put the matter over-simply, a myth is co-ordinated to ritual. It is a story repeated in ritual contexts, like the story of the Last Supper as used daily and weekly in communion services. The story both validates and expresses the meaning of the rite. It thus is a celebratory story, and it vindicates the celebration. To say that the models of humanity which one finds in religions and metaphysical schemes have a mythological function can be explained as follows.

As we have seen in the second section, the concept of the person expresses a certain moral option. We have seen too how at a very basic, almost instinctive level, we behave towards other persons in a manner different from the way in which we behave towards rocks and flowers. And at the more sophisticated level our behaviour becomes in a sense ritualized, in love and hate, concern and cruelty. Persons are to be responded to in action, and as it happens our mutual relationships employ not only the conventions of language but also a whole host of meaningful gestures. Thus in so far as the concept of the person represents a certain moral option, it must involve an expression of the way in which one should respond to persons. It both describes and lays down the right ritual. It is to this extent a validating and celebratory idea, like a myth. This, crudely, is the justification for seeing the concept of the person as having a mythological character.

But myths do not stand isolated. They mutually support and illuminate. They show forth further reasons for the rite. The question about the moral option incorporated in the concept of the person is: Why adopt this option? The model we have will help to justify the option and to add a further layer to the meaning of persons.

Let us begin by considering some religious models. The belief that men are all children of God, for instance, provides a model which (typically for a religious one) links people to the transcendent realm. God as eternal creative spirit is, of course, not just a timeless entity of a special kind, but the being of supreme value. God is worshipped, and in so far as the worship is successfully integrated into life, God becomes the apex of human values—the sincerity and magnificence of the worship testifying to this, it being men's most intense expression of their relationship to reality. Thus in relating humans to the timeless apex and source of values, expression is given to the value of persons. The timelessness and unchangeability of God may have come in for criticism in recent times from the 'process theologians', and one can understand the metaphysical and other reasons for their adopting the idea of a changing and suffering God. What needs, however, to be understood is the old attraction of the timeless. Not only in the Christian tradition but in others as well the idea of transcendent stability and changelessness is very evident. Why?

More generally, why is there so often expressed the contrast between the changeable world of human existence and the pure realm of the changeless? Life, it might be thought gains such attractions as it possesses from the novelties and happy surprises and repetitions of existence, and such a broken rhythm obviously implies change. Part of the reason for the model of the timeless lies in the nature of mystical and contemplative experience, and this aspect of the matter need not detain us here. But there is at least one other, and from the point of view of our interests here, vital reason for the model. It can be summed up as the result of the quest for the unchallengeable, the secure. Let us expand this more intelligibly.

There is security in what is timelessly valuable since it is the prime instance of what is to be prized for its own sake. Crudely, we may divide goods into two classes—those things, actions, events and so on which are instrumentally good, and those which are good in themselves. Thus a radio set is not good in itself (typically) but because it is a means to an end, such as my listening to Mozart or pop. On the other hand, playing cricket is typically not a means to some further end, but a thing to be enjoyed, if indeed it is enjoyed, for its own sake. The usual relationship between means and end is temporal (the story can become quite complicated, as over a radio; but there is little need to demonstrate this point in detail). This temporal relation does not obtain in the case of things prized in and for themselves. I do not of course deny that intrinsic goods of this sort can be temporal—can last a while, like a cricket match, and so forth. Nevertheless, the means–end relation is, so to say, aimed at the future in the way in which the other is not. Not for nothing did Horace commend the slogan *carpe diem*. Or, in more exalted terms, 'Sufficient unto the day is the evil (or good) thereof.' Thus, to conclude this first reason, the figuring of the state of release or being with God as somehow timeless is intelligible as a means of expressing the absolute security of that which is good for its own sake and not as a means to an end.

Second, things which are 'intrinsically' good, chosen for their own sake, may have a short life and need to be renewed. Thus making love to a wife is an activity which is good for its own sake (and hopefully is from her point of view as well), but it is not a once for all operation. It of its nature requires repetition. This is a charm;

but yet the idea of a completely timeless and sublime joy appears to go one better. In the timeless state there is no repetition, but that charm is replaced by the immeasurably greater satisfaction of a joy which looks neither forward or backward, utterly complete in itself. This is the second reason for the fascination of the timeless.

Third, as has been hinted at in the foregoing discussion, there is the question of security. What exists now can fall away and crumble. Any joys that you may attain can cease to be available. Any loved one may die. Any project can go sour. All this can be represented as follows: that what is now may not be soon. The insecurity of this suggestion is naturally countered by the idea of the transcendentally timeless. For if the transcendent cannot change, then there can be no falling away from the present supreme state. This, then, is a third reason for the prizing of the timeless.

Let us then concede that the supremely excellent timelessly transcendent is a figure of the apex of value. The connection of man to that timeless being, through the myth of the creation of the world and its inhabitants by the Creator and through the myth of the special relationship between God and man (the latter being made in the former's image and being also in special communication with him), confers an ontological benefit on man. For as is typical in mythic thought man participates in what makes him, deriving, so to say, some of the substance of the Creator. This is typical of mythic thought for, to put the matter with great but necessary crudity, just as the repetition of the myth in the ritual context confers on the ritual event the substance of the original event (consider the Lord's Supper), so *within* the myth there is the transfer of substance from the Originator to its or his 'descendants'. Consider in this connection how in the Christian tradition men have been conceived as sharing in the Fall of Adam, the Original Man. So, in brief, the myth of the Creation of man (in the image of God) succeeds in conferring upon persons something of the timeless and unassailable substance of the transcendent. The myth gives an account of why it is that persons have their own solid value, in themselves. Rationalized, the myth becomes, in the Enlightenment, Kant's dictum that one should treat another never merely as a means but also always as an end.

However, the myths of Creation and the Fall seem to land persons in a stereotype. It is a common humanity, via Adam, which they share; and no doubt the image of God is similar in each person. The same style pertains to the idea of the eternal soul in the Indian tradition. Normally there is nothing to distinguish one soul from another. It is as though everyone carries within himself a standardized electric light bulb. This is surely one way in which we try to cope with the idea of the person, for in so far as it is by sharing similar characteristics that different entities warrant the tender and humanized behaviour which we reserve for one another, the person must be seen in a sense as 'standardized'. Yet there is a paradox in this, for when it comes to individual love and concern (or for that matter hatred) the particularities of the person, not his standardization, become of the utmost importance. This aspect of the matter is offered by the model supplied by the existentialists, dangerous as it may be to generalize about such an individualistic breed of philosophers and mythmakers. Let us turn briefly to the myth supplied by them—a myth which can in a certain respect be connected to that of the idea of non-self in Buddhism, to which we shall come later.

One element in existentialism, put with great force by Jean-Paul Sartre, has been the idea that man is not to be defined, that the individual is perpetually liable to escape from preconceived blueprints, that any role which is laid down for him can be left behind. In this lies the individual's essential freedom, that he can transcend by a kind of 'irrational' choice the roles and routines that even reason may prescribe to him. In brief, a man makes up his character as he goes along. He is only a standardized entity when he is being inauthentic. Genuine life consists in transcending externally derived roles.

However, there is some tension between this model of man and the picture painted earlier in this essay, in which the social, cultural aspect of an individual's existence has been stressed. (There is, incidentally a like tension between Sartre's existentialism and his Marxism.) Before attempting a resolution of the tension, let us note where there is a congruence between the two approaches. In both of them there is a repudiation of a standard essential humanity.

The earlier doctrine of the 'precipitation' of personhood in the individual by society does not of itself entail that individuals become stereotyped. Both from the point of view of the genetic material out of which the individual is constructed, and from the point of view of the particular circumstances of the individual's childhood and growing up, there is bound to occur a vast, indeed infinite, range of variations in individual properties. Further, it was emphasized, in the discussion of creativity and freedom, that the elements in a social group or enterprise, namely individuals (for of what else is a group built) can display unpredictable new properties. Thus the doctrine of the 'social precipitation' of personhood does not conflict with the existentialist notion of the possibility of role-transcendence.

Further, if the existentialist model stresses individuality, the other doctrine must emphasize cultural differences. For though we may abstractly talk about 'society', what we have in fact is societies and, more narrowly, institutions and groups within societies. My linguistic apparatus, for example, is English, and this gives a different style of thinking from Chinese. More narrowly, because of being brought up in a middle-class Scottish environment, I begin from a certain base of acquired values (even if some or all be repudiated, the result is different from the repudiation of some other set—the ex-Catholic is different, as they say, from the ex-Presbyterian). Again my thought is in part acquired from the intellectual initiations I have undergone and maintain, through belonging to such groups as historians of religion and so on. Thus both the individualistic emphasis and the social precipitation theory indicate a pluralism about human nature which is glossed over by ideas of a standardized soul. There is, therefore, a congruence between these ideas and the Buddhist model of 'non-soul' or 'non-self' (*anatta*).

Yet the Buddhist doctrine reminds us of a problem if we dissolve away the eternal substance within the individual. If he consists in a congeries of powers and events—conscious and other states in a complex flow—what is the ontological basis of treating him as 'sacred', as worthy of the most profound reverence and love? Is it just that human beings feel pain and pleasure, and so should attract, perhaps on a higher plane, the concern which we sensitively show towards animals?

Clearly the deeper attitudes of religion and morality go beyond this idea of the sacredness of the individual. The notion of the eternal soul or the ultimate, unchallengeable worth of the human as being made in the image of the Eternal is a 'myth', as we have seen, which seeks to symbolize and express something about the 'meaningfulness' of human life. It must be noted, however, that this idea of meaningfulness is not to be equated with the idea that life has a purpose. The picture of a purposive universe is certainly a religious option; but meaningfulness pertains to human life even beyond any purposes or projects which we may fulfil. We may perhaps reinforce the earlier account of the Eternal as representing the apex of value by considering what the meaningless is.

When some activity becomes meaningless it may be because it can no longer serve a useful purpose—like keeping a donkey in the age of the motor-car. But a deeper sense of meaninglessness arises when what has been prized and valued somehow loses its savour. Old men, for example, in rapidly changing societies see the old rituals and customs which conferred meaning on their social life wither away. Again, a person may be very much bound up in sharing his interests and pursuits with his wife. Her death would then render them meaningless, in an important sense of this term. Indeed in the non-linguistic context, this is the dominant sense. 'X doesn't mean anything to me any more' refers, that is, to x loss of value by X, which has to be explicated in terms of changes in my loves and concerns. All this, then, throws some light upon the doctrine of the eternal in man, or of the reflection at least of the Eternal in men. It is a doctrine which indicates that we should not get into the mood of thinking life and human beings savourless—and that if we do perchance get into this mood we should be reminded that the attitude is 'not true' to the realities of existence. There are of course real questions about how we know the truth in this context: there are for instance different mythic pictures of the way in which men participate in the Eternal, and so there are problems about which are incompatible and how to choose between them—there must also be the question as to whether *any* of them are true. Into these questions it is not possible to enter here, partly because I am primarily concerned with the concepts applied to persons, rather than with the direct question of which are correctly applied. Be that as it may, it is worth briefly pointing out that the establishment of non-linguistic meaning, i.e. value, is something like the establishment of an aesthetic judgment. For this reason, those with an eroded sense of other people's humanity are rightly dubbed 'insensitive'.

It is now possible to give some account of the relation between the role of the myth of the Eternal as giving sense and meaning to human life and the pictures supplied respectively by individualistic existentialism and by the doctrine of the social precipitation of personhood in individuals. Both the latter doctrines open the way to the exploration of the ideas of freedom and creativity. They also form a mutually illuminating way of regarding human pluralism, both social and individualistic. But though freedom and variety may be grounds for coming to some sort of semi-aesthetic judgment about the meaning and worth of human life, the doctrines do not strongly express the worth of uncreative and inauthentic people. More generally they do not strongly bring out the indelible worth of persons— the ultimate basis, one may come to see, of the morality of love. (Incidentally, those myths which also relate animal life to the Eternal provide a wider scope for this morality, and non-human life is seen as partaking in the sacred quality the Western tradition has usually reserved for human beings.)

In brief, then, the myth of man's being made in the image of the Eternal by itself is inadequate. It gives the impression of standardization, which runs contrary to the anthropological and social facts and which can also stifle the sense of individuality so sharply brought out in the existentialist tradition. But it is an important adjunct to the other doctrines, which could err in another direction, by being élitist and by failing to establish the indelible worth of each person.

Though I have by implication been speaking about relatively traditional religious pictures of men and their Creator or of men and their transcendental goal, the myth of the Eternal can be expressed in humanist form; or rather, the problem of humanism is to provide an adequate alternative myth which would with equal power bring out the worth of persons.

Problems about the disenchantment of the world

This last remark brings us all too briefly to look at the predicament of contemporary Western man. It is clear that the traditional myths have, for many people, faded. Mastery over our outer environment has in part disenchanted nature, and we see ourselves whizzing round on a fragile planet. It is not surprising that the trend has been to mythicize the inner life, and even to try out technological means, by drugs, to enchant the mind. But the very fact that we can change mental states somewhat is the harbinger of a new psychotechnology (electrodes buried in the brain, memory-molecule injections and so on) which will allow us to make ourselves thoroughly artificial. When this happens, our temptation will be to look upon humans as machines in a sense, i.e. as entities to be manipulated in the furtherance of projects. Or else the temptation will be to look upon ourselves and others as playthings, toys. In all this we shall be exaggerating tendencies which have long existed in human societies (the prostitute being an old example of the human toy).

The sense of our fragility is a major source of the attractions of new eschatologies—the evolutionary consummation promised by Teilhard de Chardin and the various futures offered by varieties of Marxism and anarcho-syndicalism. For the future becomes a kind of Eternal place in which our present strivings and sufferings and joys can be tied to a supreme consummation. The problem, though, is to make these new humanist myths consonant with realities, scientific and otherwise.

Thus we can conclude that at the present time the concept of the person is beset with question marks. What I have attempted to do in this essay is to bring out fresh ways of looking at persons—fresh, though, only because what we already know about persons needs bringing to the surface of our consciousness.

Bibliography

Kuhn, Thomas (1962), *The Structure of Scientific Revolutions*, University of Chicago Press.

Pike, Nelson (ed.) (1964), *God and Evil*, Prentice-Hall.

Popper, Karl R. (1960), *The Poverty of Historicism*, Routledge & Kegan Paul (2nd edn).

Popper, Karl R. (1963), *Conjectures and Refutations*, Routledge & Kegan Paul (3rd edn).

Roberts, David E. (1957), *Existentialism and Religious Belief*, Oxford University Press.

Smart, Ninian (1969), *Philosophers and Religious Truth*, SCM Press (2nd edn).

3 On the concept of the person: a biosocial view*

Dan Gowler

A man begins as a biological entity, is given status and
becomes a social entity, then dies and again becomes a
biological entity, although some of his experiences as a social
entity may adhere to him. Only the group has continuity. It
accepts a man provisionally at birth and rejects him at death.

Paul Radin: *The World of Primitive Man* (N.Y., 1953)

Introduction

This chapter discusses what might be described as the 'biosocial'
view of the person. In this perspective, a person is defined as a biological entity, which has been endowed, or has achieved certain social
rights and duties. Further, the following discusses the proposition
that these two categories, which combine to provide this idea of a
person, are in a dynamic relationship, where each defines the other,
and where, in consequence, the result of their combination also
undergoes redefinition.

To restrict the discussion to this proposition would obviously
limit it to the rather narrow view that a 'person' must be a biological
entity with social status, in other words, the human biological entity.
This would, however, neglect the whole question of personification
and animism, where non-human organisms, e.g. animals and in-
organic phenomena, e.g. rocks, are attributed with life and/or the
status of a person. Furthermore, an extension of the discussion to
encompass non-human organisms and inanimate objects would
still be inadequate, since it would restrict the analysis to the sole

* I am grateful to Karen Legge and Professor John Morris for their generous
help and encouragement, which both lightened my labours and improved
their outcome.

SAP—D

consideration of concrete categories, omitting the whole sphere of abstract categories, e.g. gods, ghosts and other such 'artificial' persons as companies and corporations. Therefore it is necessary to discuss a second proposition; that is, that a 'person' may also be defined as any concrete or abstract category which has been endowed with or has achieved certain social rights and duties, and where the categories concerned are in the same mutually defining relationship as commented upon above.

The first proposition—persons and individuals

In his celebrated paper on social structure, Radcliffe-Brown makes the point that every human being living in society is two things: he is an individual and a person. Further, he defines an 'individual' as a biological organism and 'a person' as 'a complex of social relationships'. He also observes:[1]

> If you tell me that an individual and a person are after all
> really the same thing, I would remind you of the Christian
> creed. God is three persons, but to say that He is three individuals
> is to be guilty of a heresy for which men have been put to death.
> Yet the failure to distinguish individual and person is not
> merely a heresy in religion; it is worse than that; it is a source
> of confusion in science.

This raises several interesting issues, the most important of which is the value of separating the biological and social categories. Of course, one cannot contest the validity of this separation for certain purposes. For example, to be able to arrive at a concept like social structure, which distinguishes the abstract notion of a network of rights and duties from the concrete individuals who perform them. However, this rigid separation of the social and biological categories ceases to be useful when one wishes to consider a human being as an entity which undergoes both physical and social transformations, and *between which transformations there is a continuous process of inter-action*. In the paper referred to above, Radcliffe-Brown comments upon the changes which occur in the biological 'individual' and the social 'person', but does not relate the one to the other.

This relationship, which defines the nature and type of person, is illustrated in diagrammatic form in figure 3.1.

In figure 3.1, arrow b represents the fact that all societies allocate a number of social rights and duties (box B) on the basis of certain physiologically determined differences in the human biological entity (box A). It is an anthropological commonplace that societies use classifications of age and sex to distribute certain rights and duties in social life. Beattie, for example, observes,[2] 'in all societies known to us (but perhaps least in modern Western societies) the physiologically determined differences of role which distinguish men from women are associated with important social and cultural differences' (p. 132). He also adds: 'The division of tasks on the basis of age is also physiologically determined in some degree' (p. 189).

Arrow a represents the fact that the human biological entity (box

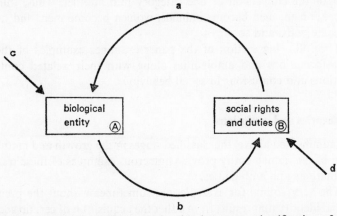

Figure 3.1 Mutually defining relationship between a classification of biological entities and a classification of social rights and duties

A) is likely to undergo a change in categorization when a change occurs in its social rights and duties (box B). This relationship is often expressed in a dramatic fashion. For example, when a change in social rights and duties alters the moral and/or jural status of the person, it has often been accompanied by symbolic mutilations of the body. Thus, Goffman, when commenting upon the subject of social stigma, observes:[3]

> The Greeks, who were apparently strong on visual aids,
> originated the term *stigma* to refer to bodily signs designed to
> expose something unusual and bad about the moral status of
> the signifier. The signs were cut or burnt into the body and adver-
> tised that their bearer was a slave, a criminal, or a traitor—a

blemished person, ritually polluted, to be avoided, especially in public places.

Arrows c and d represent the fact that changes in the categorizations of both the biological entity and social rights and duties may be generated independently of one another. Therefore, changes in social rights and duties may occur without a change in the biological entity and vice versa.

The combinations of the internal inter-actions between boxes A and B, as indicated by arrows a and b, coupled with independent, externally induced changes in either one or both of them, as indicated by arrows c and d results in the creation of ambiguous categories and/or the conversion of one category into another. Thus, things become men, men become animals, women become men, and men become gods, and so on.

The following section of the paper examines examples of these transformations and ambiguities along with their related contradictions and confusions in social behaviour.

Categories and confusions

As commented above, the classified stages in the growth and maturation of the human entity provide numerous examples of these transformations and ambiguities.

The very young, for example, are sometimes without the precise social identity that results from either the acquisition of certain social rights and duties or a clear definition of what kind of entity they are. In consequence, they may be regarded as an ambiguous category, part object, part animal, part spirit and part human.

A not uncommon example is reported among the Lugbara of Uganda, where 'Babies are not social beings, and have no souls; they have neither authority nor responsibility.'[4] In this case, one assumes that when these Lugbara babies are eventually regarded as social beings, that is, 'persons', they are transformed from one biological category to another.

Another clear example of this type of transformation has been reported among the Ashanti:[5]

It is by the father's ritual act of naming his children and so distinguishing them from other children of the same lineage that patrifiliation is formally validated. It is significant that this personal name is not given until the eighth day after the child's birth. *Until that day it is not regarded as fully human.* If it dies unnamed, the body is not given proper burial, no funeral is held, and the parents dress and behave as if rejoicing. *It is said to have been a ghost child, not a being of flesh and blood* [my italics].

It is interesting to note in this respect that in contemporary British culture it is not uncommon to hear a very young child referred to as 'it'.

Further, this throws some light on a number of important contemporary issues. For example, the debate about the legality and morality of abortion. It seems to me that a major aspect of this controversy is concerned with the topic under consideration here, that is, at what stage in its development does the biological entity become a person. Is it at the moment of conception, or at some later stage in the development of the foetus, or perhaps at the time of birth? This is an important question, since, by definition, a person possesses social rights and duties, the most fundamental of which is the right to life. However, this raises a rather complex difficulty. This is that one cannot have rights without duties, and therefore the biological entity which 'claims' rights without being able to perform duties, as is the case with unborn and very young children, cannot be a complete person. In this event, the biological entity concerned is an ambiguous category, and as such, I think, tends to confuse our thinking about these issues.

The same problem appears at the other end of the individual's life span. For when does the living person become a dead 'non-person'? This contentious issue has been emphasized in recent debates about the legality and morality of 'spare parts' surgery, where the rights of the donor of some vital organ are subject to much controversy. Here again we have the question, is the donor a person? And again, if the biological entity cannot perform social duties, its social rights must obviously be queried. These points are discussed in detail later in the chapter, but suffice it to say at this point that the unequivocal right to life rests upon the biological entity's ability to perform certain social duties. Looked at this way, it becomes apparent that the definition of death does not rest entirely with the physical state of the biological entity, for death is also a social event and, as such, requires a given degree of 'decomposition' of social rights and duties.

The treatment of twins provides another illustration of the relationships and processes described in figure 3.1. Twins present an anomalous biological form. They are, in a sense, both one and two, and as such do not, in some cultures, qualify for social status. They are ambiguous, confused, mysterious and possibly dangerous.

Turner, when discussing the view of twins among the Ndembu comments:[6]

> Professor Schapera (and other scholars) have drawn attention to the fact that wherever kinship is structurally significant, and provides a frame for corporate relationships and social status, the birth of twins is a source of classificatory embarrassment. For it is widely held, in Africa and elsewhere, that children born during a single parturition are mystically identical. Yet, under the ascriptive rules associated with kinship systems, there is only one position in the structure of the family or corporate kin group for them to occupy. There is a classificatory assumption that human beings bear only one child at a time and that there is only one slot for them to occupy in the various groups articulated by kinship which that one child enters by birth. Sibling order is another important factor; older siblings exert certain rights over junior siblings and may in some sense succeed to political office before them. Yet twinship presents the paradoxes that what is physically double is structurally single and what is mystically one is empirically two.

All cultures have to deal with similar classificatory embarrassments. For example, malformed, illegitimate and adopted children all present problems of classification and, depending upon the society concerned, rules and procedures have to be developed to 'fit' these embarrassments into the simple model outlined in figure 3.1.

The type of solution used in such circumstances depends upon the values, beliefs and institutions of the people concerned. For example, in the case of twins, at least in those societies organized mainly through kinship, there are only two solutions.

> Either you can say, like the little boy on first seeing a giraffe, 'I don't believe it' and deny the social existence of the biological fact; or else having accepted the fact, you can try to cope with it. If you try to cope, you must make it, if you can, appear to be consistent with the rest of your culture (ibid., p. 49).

In some societies, either one or both of the twins is put to death, as among the Bushmen of the Kalahari, or accorded special status, as among the Ashanti.

It is now possible to relate these examples to the 'model' illustrated by figure 3.1. In the case of the Ashanti, for instance, the acquisition of social rights and duties, initially conferred by the father's ritual act of naming his children, defines them as human, and is, therefore, a clear example of the processes represented by arrow a. Further, the fact that the Ashanti ascribe a special status to twins illustrates the processes represented by arrow b. That is, where an anomalous biological 'entity' is accommodated by a special set of social rights and duties.

The child, once having been accepted into the moral and legal community of its parents, qualifies for recruitment to a series of social statuses, some of which are, as commented above, allocated on the basis of certain physiological characteristics and/or the stages of development in the human biological entity. For example, in contemporary British society, eighteen years' physical maturation confers full adult status upon the individual concerned. Furthermore, those classified in this society as either mad or mentally sub-normal do not qualify for a number of these adult rights and duties, even though they may have attained the age of majority. Also, to illustrate the feedback aspects of the same example, that is, the process represented by arrow a in figure 3.1, it is not uncommon to hear someone addressed or referred to as 'grown up' (a physiological metaphor) when they are either possessed of adult rights and duties or perceived to be behaving as if they had.

In all societies, a major transformation occurs when the individual dies and his social rights and duties are reallocated among other members of his group. The dissolution of the biological entity being reflected in the dissolution of its related social rights and duties. Further, and to look at the reverse of this process, it might be said that it is only after the deceased person's rights and duties are completely reallocated to the living that he is finally classified as dead, which fact is eloquently expressed in every culture's mortuary rites and observances. (This draws attention to the well-attested fact that changes in social rights and duties do not always lag behind changes in the biological entity. Thus, in some societies, physical puberty might lag behind social puberty, and physical maturity might lag behind social maturity.[7]) However, the dead are inevitably ambiguous because the redistribution of their social rights and duties takes time and, in many cases, some are retained beyond the grave, with the consequence that the living and the dead still interact with one another as members of the same everlasting community.

Crimes, sins and the afterlife

In preceding sections of the chapter I have attempted to indicate some of the instrumental and expressive aspects of the relationships between the two elements distinguished in figure 3.1. Also this discussion has been accompanied by some examples of and observations about the confusions and difficulties which inevitably stem from the practical application of any system of classification. There is, however, another important facet of the relationship between the biological entity and social rights and duties, which, while interesting in itself, also provides a link between the first and second propositions stated in the introduction.

The point here is that changes in one or other of the elements under consideration may alter the moral status of the individual concerned. In certain circumstances, the process triggered by a change in either the biological entity or social rights and duties, may become self-perpetuating, and the continuous inter-action between these two elements may go so far as to redefine 'the person' as either a beast or a god. A neat example of this feedback process is provided by Hoebel, who when commenting upon the traditional society of the Cheyenne of the Great Plains, observes:[8]

A Cheyenne who kills a fellow Cheyenne rots internally. His body gives off a fetid odor, a symbolic stigma of personal disintegration, which contrition may stay, but for which there is no cure. The smell is offensive to other Cheyennes, who will never again take food from a bowl used by the killer. Nor will they smoke a pipe that has touched his lips. They fear personal contamination with his 'leprous' affliction. This means that the person who has become so un-Cheyenne as to fly in the face of the greatest of Cheyenne injunctions is cut off from participation in the symbolic acts of mutuality—eating from a common bowl and smoking the ritual pipe. With this alienation goes the loss of many civil privileges and the cooperative assistance of one's fellows outside of one's own family. The basic penalty for murder is therefore a lifetime of partial social ostracism.

Thus, in terms of figure 3.1, the abuse of social rights and duties (arrow d) produces (arrow a) a disintegration of the biological entity (box A) and then feeds back (arrow b) to emphasize and reinforce the original crime or sin.

In the last example, the complete feedback process was triggered by an abuse of social rights and duties by the Cheyenne killing another member of his tribe, but a similar process may be generated by the abuse of his social rights and duties occasioned by the killing of himself. Again Hoebel observes,

> For the Cheyenne there is no Hell or punishment of any sort in afterlife; no Judgement or Damnation. Although Cheyennes sin when they commit murder and they often do wrong, murder is expiated in the here and now, and wrongdoing builds up no burden of guilt to be borne beyond the grave. For the Cheyenne there is no problem of salvation; goodness is to be sought as rightness for its own sake and for the appreciative approval of one's fellow man. When at last it shakes free of its corporal abode, the Cheyenne soul wafts free and light up the Hanging Road to dwell thereafter in benign proximity to the Great Wise One and the long-lost loved ones. *Only the souls of those who have committed suicide are barred from this peace* (ibid., p. 87, my italics).

Though one must obviously be chary of making facile cross-cultural comparisons, one cannot but be impressed by the similarity between these examples from the Cheyenne and the situation in contemporary British society. In the latter, for instance, the murderer is also ostracized, either permanently or temporarily, and may even be said to carry 'the mark of Cain', despite the fact that, in this society, the crime of murder is no longer permanently physically imprinted on the body of the criminal. The 'punishment' meted out to the suicide is also very similar, for nowadays in British society his rights to certain forms of burial and so on are likely to be denied or reduced, and, possibly, like the Cheyenne, his soul may be believed to suffer eternal deprivation in the afterlife.

In both the societies discussed here, the crimes (or sins) of murder and suicide provide examples of acts which so abuse social rights and duties that they transform the moral status of the criminal (or sinner) and which situation is either permanently or temporarily expressed on the body of the transgressor. This then transforms 'the person' into a social being of a lower order or even some kind of non-human creature. For example, in Britain, it is not uncommon to hear someone, who has so abused his social rights and duties as to suffer this change in moral status, referred to as 'an animal', 'a beast', or 'a rat'. Moreover, this does not only apply to contemporary British culture, many examples have been recorded from all over the world, and where the animal status of the sinner or criminal is reflected on their bodies either living or dead.

Roscoe, when commenting upon the treatment of the corpse of a suicide in traditional Baganda society, observes:[9]

> The Baganda were very superstitious about suicides. They took innumerable precautions to remove the body and destroy the ghost, to prevent the latter from causing further trouble. Shame for crime committed led to suicide, but this occurred rarely in any section of the community, and most rarely among women. When a man committed suicide, he hanged himself on a tree in his garden or in his house. In the former case the body was cut down, and the tree felled also; then both the tree and the corpse, *the latter tied to a pole like the carcase of an animal*, were taken to a distant place where cross-roads met, and the body was burned, the tree being used for the firewood [my italics].

It is not suggested that all suicides are treated this way, but the argument is simply that certain abuses of social rights and duties, *which, of course, vary from society to society*, redefine the biological entity, and this is expressed in the treatment of and towards the body both before and after death. This is the type of process represented by arrow a in figure 3.1.

Those sins and crimes which are classified as attacks on the whole community often result in treatment similar to that meted out to murderers and suicides. It might be argued that the last mentioned crimes are often also regarded as offences against the whole community. However, it is interesting to consider the case of witchcraft.

Witches are 'the enemy within',[10] they attack members of their own community and are 'tremendously disruptive in terms of group integration', particularly in those kinship-based societies, where people have to depend upon one another in every area of their lives. Witches when detected are, therefore, burnt, poisoned, speared or drowned, and death has been the universal punishment for the crime. Further, like many murderers and suicides, their burials reflect their moral status and their corpses are not treated as those of normal members of society.[11]

Among the LoDagaba, but not among the LoWiili, a witch is buried in a similar manner. In Lawra, for example, such a person is carried to a marsh on the edge of the parish and buried there, together with his personal possessions. For witchcraft is an offence against the Earth, and formerly the shrine was used in order to test the validity of accusations of witchcraft. Among the LoWiili there is no special piece of ground put aside for the burial of witches, and I have only known this one case, not one involving witchcraft, when the body was interred in the bed of a stream. But there is no mourning and no playing of xylophones at the death of a witch. The body is simply disposed of as quickly as possible in an old grave, which is never again reopened.

In modern nation states treason is dealt with in much the same way. The individual guilty of treason is likely to be disposed of as if he were a beast, in fact, 'shot like a dog', or as formerly in Britain 'hung drawn and quartered' like an animal.

Another example of this relationship between the abuse of social rights and duties, moral status, and the condition or definition of the biological entity, is provided by those who are guilty of incest. This crime strikes at the whole fabric of society since, among other things, it confuses social relationships, and as Lévi-Strauss observes:[12] 'The violent reaction of the community towards incest is the reaction of a community outraged.'

As so often with this type of crime, the change in moral status of the criminal is not only expressed and reinforced by the punishments meted out by his society, which may or may not depersonalize him, but mystical retributions in the form of bodily afflictions, e.g. leprosy, are also likely to follow.

These dire consequences are also likely to be visited upon the children of an incestuous union. A very striking example of this has been reported by Warner in his study of the Murngin. Among these

Australian Aborigines the dead are disinterred at a stage in the mortuary rites, and Warner comments:[13]

> If the body has not started to rot it is often believed that the father and mother are the cause: they belonged to the same moiety and were incestuous. A man on the border line between two cultures, where the culture pattern was slightly confused, married a woman whom the natives of his tribe considered to be in his own moiety. They used to point to his children and say their bodies would never rot.

This raises two points. Firstly, it illustrates a neat reversal of the normal relationship between the elements, i.e. in the normal course

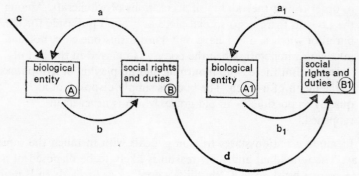

Figure 3.2   The transfer

of events the body corrupts, therefore, if the body has not corrupted, the normal course of events cannot have taken place. In the case of the Murngin, the parents of the individual concerned committed abnormal acts, that is, the sin of incest, but in other cultures the incorruptible corpse may be seen as the sign of a pure and blameless life, e.g. the claimed incorruptibility of Christian saints and the Virgin Mary. However, even in the latter case, the course of events was not perceived as normal, for people are not really expected to lead a completely blameless life.

The second point is that arrow c and d in figure 3.1 may also represent what might be called *transfers*. For example, people commit offences but the punishments are visited upon others, like the child of incestuous Murngin parents. Also bodily afflictions may be transferred directly in the form of illness from one individual to another. The result of such a transfer may be the transformation of the person involved into an entirely different and/or ambiguous category.

An interesting, though somewhat extreme example of such a transfer is the institution of 'ghost marriage'. Gluckman, when reporting on this institution among the Zulu, comments:[14] 'If a man dies leaving only daughters and no son, *the oldest daughter should take his cattle and marry wives for her father to produce sons for him*' (my italics).

This process may be illustrated in an elaborated version of figure 3.1, which is represented by figure 3.2.

The transfer process represented by figure 3.2 has four stages, and using Gluckman's Zulu example, they are:

Stage 1   redefinition (arrow c) of the biological entity (box A), that is, a father without sons dies.

Stage 2   redefinition (arrow b) of social rights and duties (box B) transforming the rights and duties of the living into the rights and duties of the dead.

Stage 3   certain of dead father's rights and duties are transferred (arrow d) to eldest daughter, which redefines her rights and duties (box B1).

Stage 4   the eldest daughter is redefined (arrow a_1) as a 'male' biological entity (box A1), or alternatively as a social and/or biological ambiguity. (It must be appreciated that Stage 4 of the process, the final conversion of the eldest daughter into a 'male father' is somewhat speculative, since the published ethnographic evidence is not really adequate enough to completely establish this point.)

It is now possible, having dealt with the question of transfers, to return to the issue of changes in moral status and the redefinition of the person. However, the last example, the institution of 'ghost marriage' introduces another aspect to this section of the analysis. For this example illustrates the fact that changes generated in, or introduced to the biological entity may alter the moral status of the individual to such an extent that changes are also wrought in its (and others) social rights and duties, and so on. These processes are, of course, represented by arrow b (figure 3.1), whereas the examples discussed so far in this section have been concerned with arrow a (figure 3.1), where changes in the biological entity 'result' from changes in social rights and duties and/or a related change in moral status. The following considers some examples of the former (arrow b) which when combined with those discussed above, are used to provide the evidence for further analytical distinctions.

Possibly the most dramatic examples of the relation between changes in the biological entity and moral status are provided by 'divine kings'. Here the physical, ritual, and moral condition of the monarch is reflected in the well-being of his people and their possessions. For example, Beattie writes that among the Nyoro of Western Uganda, the Mukama, or king is obliged to keep himself in good ritual, spiritual, and physical condition 'for the good of the country', since this is symbolically identified with the prosperity of the whole society.[15]

> In pre-European times, if the Mukama himself fell sick the
> matter was kept strictly secret. It is said that if his illness were
> serious, if he suffered any physical incapacity or mutilation,
> or if he grew too old and feeble to carry out his duties properly,
> he would either kill himself by taking poison or be killed by
> one of his wives. This was, of course, because any imperfection
> or weakness in the king was thought to involve a corresponding
> danger to the kingdom.

Many cultures, but particularly African ones, provide examples of these powerful ritual figures, who clearly demonstrate the principle that a degeneration of the biological entity is likely to be followed by a degeneration of social rights and duties. In those circumstances, where this sequence of events results in a dangerous change in moral status, the individual concerned is probably subject to social and mystical sanctions.

This process is not only reserved for the powerful and sacred members of society, but it is also observable in ordinary people who have been classified as ill. There are, however, two quite different aspects to the 'sick role.' First, as Loudon observes of contemporary Western society,[16]

> Someone who is ill is not expected to fulfil all the obligations
> of his social roles, though the degree to which he is exempted
> from them depends to some extent on the nature and severity
> of his symptoms. At the same time the absolution from social
> obligations in itself imposes certain duties on the patient. It is

taken for granted that if the state of being ill is acknowledged by him as something unpleasant and undesirable, it necessarily involves the duty of wanting to get well and taking of appropriate steps to that end. Failure to come up to these expectations may arouse suspicions that he is malingering and thus tend to abolish exemption from usual role responsibilities.

This example clearly illustrates the type of process represented by arrow b in figure 3.1. Very simply, social rights and duties are adjusted to conform with certain conditions of the biological entity, since the performance of these obligations are difficult or even impossible when an individual is very ill. However, this may be accompanied by a change in moral status, and this is the second of the two aspects referred to above.

Some illnesses so actually reduce the individual, both physically and socially, that they do not qualify as a 'person'. In Britain it is not unusual to hear people who are suffering from illnesses that inhibit or prevent speech, movement and other normal forms of social inter-action referred to as 'vegetables'.

The loss of physical and social identity may be accompanied by a concomitant change in moral status, e.g. vegetables (at least the British variety) do not have souls.

This situation is represented in diagrammatic form in figure 3.3.

Figure 3.3 makes the very simple point that a given state or change in either the biological entity or social rights and duties may be accompanied by a given state or change in moral status. What is meant here is that 'normal' physical states and social statuses are considered worthy, and the individuals who possess them are in what might be called a state of biosocial grace.

Examples of this process are relatively easy to find. For instance, what is the moral status of, say, children born with severe physical and mental handicaps, or people suffering crippling injury or disease? Very often one finds that individuals in these circumstances are perceived to be morally reprehensible. Of course, there are certain categories of people, e.g. negroes, whose physical characteristics are such that they are automatically attributed with low moral status, which in turn influence their claim to full citizen rights and duties, and so on.

Sickness and 'bad luck' which may influence the individual's physical state and/or social status, may well lead to such a change in moral standing. This last comment does, in fact, raise the general question of misfortune and its relationship with moral status.

Misfortunes and illnesses are often believed to have been sent by either (i) a malign agency, e.g. witches or evil spirits, or (ii) a mystical

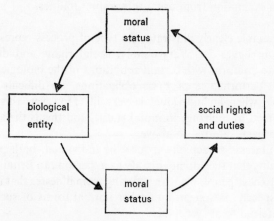

Figure 3.3 Change in moral status

or divine power who is exacting some kind of retribution for crimes and sins.

An example of (i) is provided by Leach who comments:[17]

Kachins make use of concepts concerning the supernatural for practical (technical) as well as ritual ends. The illnesses of men and the diseases of crops and animals are alike attributed to the malicious attack of supernatural beings. There are many different categories of such supernatural beings, each thought to be responsible for different classes of symptoms. Treatment consists of a preliminary diagnosis to discover the type responsible, followed by a sacrificial offering to the spirit concerned. This is an essentially practical procedure no different in principle from our routine of taking one kind of pill for a headache and another for a stomach ache. With us, if one course of treatment fails, we try another, Kachins do likewise.

An example of (ii), that is where illness and misfortune are seen to be sent as a punishment for sins and crimes, is provided by Hilda

Kuper, who, when commenting upon the Swazi of South Africa, observes:[18]

> Illness and other misfortunes are frequently attributed to the ancestors, but Swazi believe that the *emadloti* [the world of spirits] do not inflict sufferings through malice or wanton cruelty. The mean husband, the adulterous wife, the over-ambitious younger brother, the disobedient son may be dealt with directly or vicariously by the spirits, acting as custodian of correct behavior and tribal ethics.

The reason for presenting these two examples is simply to help make the point that a change in moral status is more likely to accompany situation (ii) than situation (i). For in situation (ii), where mystical powers are believed to be punishing the transgressor, the individual concerned has, by definition, already 'committed' some morally reprehensible act. Whereas, in situation (i), misfortune and illness are not seen to be the result of the 'victim's' moral shortcomings. However, even in modern Western societies, where illness and misfortune are seen to be visited on people by chance or by some malign agency, i.e. situation (i), the idea still lingers that these calamities may well be the result of some sin or crime, and where the 'victim' is getting his 'just deserts'.

This section has shown how the biological entity and social rights and duties combine to define and rank the person in his society's social, ritual and moral hierarchies. Further, it has been illustrated how a change in either the biological entity and/or its related social rights and duties may result in the person being redefined as something else, e.g. an animal or a vegetable. To develop this, the next section takes up the question of position in the social, ritual and moral hierarchies and shows how this is linked with the relationship between the two elements distinguished in figure 3.1.

Countervailing power

So far the analysis has suggested and indeed demonstrated that certain processes developed in and between the elements in figure 3.1 may become self-perpetuating and result in the redefinition of one or either of the components which comprise the person. This self-perpetuating process may lead either to the destruction of the individual's social rights and/or the redefinition of his biological form as non-human, e.g. an animal or a vegetable. Of course, this may all go the other way; the process may result in the accumulation of more social rights and duties and the redefinition of the related biological entity as some superior being, e.g. a saint or a god.

This, however, raises an interesting question, that is, what independently generated process tempers the self-generating reaction described above? Furthermore, is there anything in either of the elements which may be said to prevent the complete disintegration of the person brought about by this self-perpetuating process. This is a most important issue, since unless there is some 'brake' or 'resistance' to this type of inter-action, certain individuals and groups cease to have a foothold in society at all. The following suggests that such a brake on this self-generating process exists, i.e. the growth of *countervailing power* in one or other of the elements.

The concept of countervailing power was developed by the American economist, Galbraith, when describing and analysing the forces which had developed to counteract the private power which itself had replaced the power of market competition in capitalist economics. He writes:[19]

> In fact, new restraints on private power did appear to replace competition. They were nurtured by the same process of concentration which impaired or destroyed competition. But they appeared not on the same side of the market but on the opposite side, not with competitors but with customers or suppliers. It will be convenient to have a name for this counterpart of competition and I shall call it *countervailing power*. . . . The long trend towards concentration of industrial enterprise in the hands of a relatively few firms has brought into existence not only strong sellers, as economists have supposed, but also strong buyers as they have failed to see. *The two develop together, not in precise step but in such a manner that there can be no doubt that the one is in response to the other* [my italics].

How does this concept from the spheres of politics and economics apply here? The answer to this question lies in the last sentence of the last quotation, since this situation may also be said to apply to the two elements under consideration here. In other words, when 'powers' vested in social rights and duties diminish or increase, powers vested in the biological entity do so also, but in an inverse manner, and vice versa. These points are illustrated in the following examples.

Firstly, it has often been observed that there 'is some degree of negative correlation between administrative capacity or political powers and ritual authority'.[20] Further, it also appears that this 'inverse correlation' assists in the maintenance of social cohesion, and as Gluckman comments,[21] 'The distribution of ritual power helps achieve a balance against competing secular interests . . . This general hypothesis can be applied to domestic relations well as political relations.' It is contended here that this general hypothesis may be applied to the person, or more precisely to those two elements which comprise the person. In other words, there is a negative correlation between the 'powers' vested in the biological entity and its related social rights and duties. This relationship maintains the balance between these elements, thus preventing the growth of the self-perpetuating processes which result in the redefinition or even destruction of the person.

An example of this countervailing power in the biological entity is provided by those individuals who are in a weak or inferior social position. The case of illegitimate children in traditional British culture is relevant here. It was formerly held that an illegitimate child, though deprived of certain social rights and duties, particularly the inheritance of property and status, may possess exceptional personal qualities and talents, and so Gloucester's bastard, Edmund cries,

> Why brand they us
> With base? with baseness? bastardy? base, base?
> Who, in the lusty stealth of nature, take
> More composition and fierce quality
> Than doth, within a dull, stale, tired bed
> Go to the creating a whole tribe of fops
> Got 'tween asleep and wake?
>
> > (*King Lear*, Act 1, Scene ii, lines 9–15)

Thus the social inferiority of the illegitimate child is compensated for in some measure by the physical qualities provided by nature.

Another example of this inverse relationship between low social status and exceptional powers and talents is provided in Southall's study of political structures and processes among the Alur of the Congo and Uganda.[22]

Rain power also contributes to the important function of ritual which is to afford consolation prizes to groups which are not powerful. Just as within the status system of a chiefdom, groups of low status find positive consolation in some speciality of function or uniqueness of position, so between chiefdoms of varying political power special ritual claims console for lack of effective authority or importance.

Finally, the lowly and the weak may be attributed with a special relationship with the divine powers of the universe, and this is well put by Mary Renault in her novel, *The Bull from the Sea*, where she writes: 'Don't we say all helpless folk—the orphan, the stranger, the suppliant, who have nothing to bargain with and can only pray —are sacred to Zeus the Saviour? The king must answer for them; he is next the god. For the serfs, the landless hirelings, the captives of the spear; even the slaves.'

The reverse process, that is where countervailing power develops on the social rights and duties side of the equation, is perhaps best exemplified by the special treatment of the aged, crippled and infirm, and where weakness in the biological entity is compensated for by a particular social status. However, this situation is not quite so clear cut. Certainly people categorized as infirm in some way may be allowed many privileges, but these are often only *temporary* concessions and cannot in any way be said to improve the social status of the individual concerned or add any 'real' power to that he already holds.

This distinction suggests a number of hypotheses that are specifically concerned with the problems of social cohesion and social change.

First, it may be hypothesized that the countervailing power which develops in social rights and duties helps to counteract perceived weaknesses and ambiguities in the biological entity. This serves the function of maintaining certain individuals in a viable position in their group. This is particularly the case with illness and injury, where the victim is either permanently or temporarily prevented from performing his full social rights and duties, and, as such, is in danger of becoming redefined as a non-person. This process also has the function of maintaining *intra-group cohesion* in the face of 'disturbing' events, such as the birth of twins, providing a means by which the group may deal with the problems posed by such occurrences.

The simple point here is that, since the biological entity is often the source of classificatory confusions and ambiguities, the social group must develop some mechanisms whereby these events do not destroy its continuity and cohesion. The provision of special social status (a form of countervailing power) for anomalous biological forms and conditions is one example of such a mechanism.

Second, the countervailing power that develops in the biological entity provides not only individual security and group cohesion in a manner similar to that described above, but also functions as a means of *inter-group cohesion*, by allocating some protection for low status groups who have limited economic and/or political power. Briefly, this means that those groups in society who have a relatively weak claim to power and resources are often attributed with either mystical powers and/or extraordinary physical abilities and talents (see p. 55). And it is contended here that this mechanism, by providing these low status groups with this protection, contributes to inter-group cohesion, where the balance of power between the 'haves' and 'have nots' does not widen to intolerable and destructive limits. This particular mechanism has not escaped the notice of certain political theorists who argue that here we have the example of the way in which 'superstition' and traditional value systems contribute towards exploitation and tyranny and the maintenance of control of the many by the few.

These hypotheses suggest that the two elements which comprise the person, the biological and the social, combine and inter-act in such a way as to assist in the maintenance of intra and inter-group cohesion, while at the same time providing the individual with some economic, social and psychological security.

The equilibrium provided by these processes is, as suggested earlier, of a very precarious nature. Certain actions and events may so disturb it that the person may disintegrate and subsequently be biologically and/or socially defined as something else, producing a number of adverse effects on social cohesion in and between groups. Furthermore, while countervailing power may develop in either of the elements, the form that evolves around the biological entity is fundamentally unstable and, as such, contributes towards the possible breakdown of this delicate equilibrium. The point here is that, while it 'costs' nothing to attribute certain classes of individuals with rather diffuse talents and ritual capabilities, it is a rather different matter where real economic and political powers are involved. It

costs very little to credit the gipsy with his curse and psychic powers
or the negro with his sexual potency, sense of rhythm and musical
abilities, but job opportunities, income, political and legal equality
are too scarce and expensive to be dealt with in this way. (It is perhaps interesting to note that it is only when classes of individuals
cease to be attributed with these special abilities that they might
claim to have improved their social status. A fact which any feminist
in our society will no doubt attest.) Obviously such a state of affairs
is not likely to continue indefinitely, and low status individuals and
groups will eventually disturb this equilibrium by a rejection of such
social arrangements.

The latter introduces the fact that the relationship between the
elements influences and is influenced by social change. And where
the rate of social change is accelerating, as it is in contemporary
Western society, the balance between these elements is very likely
to be disturbed, with consequences similar to those described above.

Social change is a very large and extremely complex topic. Nevertheless, it is generally agreed that it is faster and more far reaching
in modern Western societies than in the technologically under-
developed kinship-based ones. Therefore the following comments
are to be taken to refer mainly to modern Western societies, and as
Alvin Toffler comments,[23]

Western society for the past 300 years has been caught up in
a fire storm of change. This storm, far from abating, now
appears to be gathering force. Change sweeps through the
highly industrialized countries with waves of ever accelerating
speed and unprecedented impact. It spawns in its wake all sorts
of curious social flora—from psychedelic churches and 'free
universities' to science cities in the Arctic and wife-swop clubs
in California. It breeds odd personalities, too: children who at
twelve are no longer childlike, adults who at fifty are children
of twelve.

There are rich men who play act poverty, computer program-
mers who turn on with LSD. There are anarchists who, beneath
their dirty denim shirts, are outrageous conformists, and
conformists, who beneath their button-down collars, are
outrageous anarchists. There are married priests and atheist
ministers and Jewish Zen Buddhists. We have pop . . . and op
. . . and art *cinétique* . . . There are Play boy Clubs and

homosexual movie theatres . . . amphetamines, and tranquillizers
. . . anger, affluence, and oblivion. Much oblivion.

How does all this relate to the issues under consideration here?

First of all, as a result of the victories of scientific rationalism and
brilliant technical achievements, the human biological entity has
been redefined. We now perceive our bodies not as a sacred temple
of the soul but as something profane; we have secularized our physical form. For example, our bodies are often referred to as 'machines',
which may be redesigned and parts of which may also be replaced.
In terms of figure 3.1, this redefinition (arrow c) of the biological
entity (box A) influences (arrow b) the allocation of social rights and
duties (box B) and then, of course, the feedback relationship via
arrow a. At the same time the changes (arrow d) brought about in
social rights and duties (box B) by the increasingly 'temporary' nature
of all the social structures in which we are involved influences the
categorization of the biological entity (box A). This last point is
evidenced by the fact that permanent expression of social differentiation on the biological entity, e.g. mutilations of the body, have
been replaced by more temporary expressions, e.g. changes of
clothing, length of hair, body painting and decoration. The increasingly rapid change of fashion, therefore, expresses the equally rapid
change in the nature of social relationships. Obviously this analysis
might be extended to the arts, where there is evidence to support
the general proposition that Man's representation of himself is
certainly influenced by changing rights and duties (arrow a, figure
3.1) and vice versa (arrow b, figure 3.1).

Given the increasingly temporary nature of social rights and duties
and the related fragmentation of social life, and the fact that various
roles are played out in different ways in different places at different
times, behaviour has become more and more contingent. This has
led inevitably to the rise of moral relativism, what is 'right' or 'wrong'
becomes less absolute and social deviance, in so far as it can be
defined at all, might even be said to have become, like many other
forms of social behaviour, contractual.

Crimes and sins are no longer believed to be reflected in and on
the biological entity, while at the same time, illness and misfortune
are no longer believed by many to represent signs of divine punishment and disfavour.

To generalize and summarize all this: *in modern Western societies the relationship between boxes A and B in figure 3.1 is as valid as in any other society, but as a result of rapid social changes it is more varied and spasmodic.* Further, this variety has resulted in more choice for the individual, in that he now may choose (in fact *must* now choose) between a bewildering number of biosocial identities and so, in a sense, determine what type of 'person' he is. However, it must be added that this makes the psychological integration of the individual as difficult as the integration of society itself, and as Toffler again observes about the consequences of such social change:

> The individual searching for some sense of belonging, looking for the kind of social connection that confers some sense of identity, moves through a blurry environment in which the possible targets of affiliation are all in high-speed motion.
> He must choose from among a growing number of moving targets. The problems of choice thus escalate not arithmetically, but geometrically . . . The level of personality disorder, neurosis and just plain psychological distress in our society suggests that it is already difficult for many individuals to create a sensible integrated, and reasonably stable personal style. Yet there is every evidence that the thrust toward social diversity, paralleling that at the level of goods and culture, is just beginning. We face a tempting and terrifying extension of freedom (ibid., p. 264).

In these circumstances, it seems that countervailing power is unlikely to develop on either side of the model (figure 3.1). In which case inter- and intra-group cohesion and stability will become even more brittle, and this in turn will contribute to increased social differentiation and fragmentation, and so on.

The second proposition—gods and devils

Earlier in the chapter (p. 38), it was suggested that a person may also be defined as 'any concrete or abstract category which has been endowed or achieved certain social rights and duties', and this may be represented in a diagrammatic form in a manner similar to that of figure 3.1.

As can be seen, figures 3.1 and 3.4 are similar except box C and arrows e, f and g have been substituted for box A and arrows a, b and c. The difference here is that box C is all-embracing and therefore includes those categories, i.e. biological entities, represented by box A in figure 3.1.

Figure 3.4, therefore, represents the proposition that any category may be attributed with a number of social rights and duties, and, as such, may be perceived and treated as a person. Furthermore, and to extend the argument, *such an attribution tends also to credit the category concerned with the characteristic of the human biological*

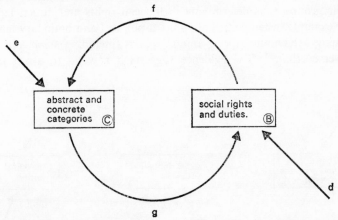

Figure 3.4 Mutually defining relationship between a classification of abstract and concrete categories and a classification of social rights and duties

entity. In this event, plants, natural physical formations and phenomena, animals, etc. are attributed with human sensibilities and, in some cases, human form.

There are many reasons that might be advanced to explain this universally observed fact. The following diagram, figure 3.5, presents an explanation which follows along the lines of the analysis already discussed in the paper.

In figure 3.5 the 'basic model' is represented by the relationship between boxes A and B which has already been illustrated in figure 3.1 and discussed in detail in the first four sections of the chapter. This relationship has been termed the basic model, since it seems reasonable to suggest that easily distinguishable physical characteristics of the human biological entity may well have provided the classification upon which the 'first' allocation of social rights and duties were based. Of course, this is all very hypothetical and certainly leaves the last statement open to the charge that it is just another *Just-So* story. (Freud suggested that Kroeber's criticisms may well have conferred this title upon his imaginative and highly controversial account of the origin of the incest taboo.[24]) Nevertheless, and speculations about origins apart, the ethological evidence appears to support the view that the characteristics of sex, age and physical strength determine social status in many animal species, particularly primates. In many instances they rank animals in the dominance hierarchies in their groups, thus determining their social rights and duties. Tiger, for example, when commenting upon political and boundary maintaining behaviours among animal species (including *homo sapiens*) observes that,[25] 'The evidence suggests it is valid to assert that

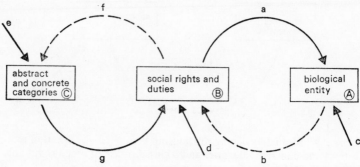

Figure 3.5   General application of the basic model

political groups occupying territory are centred and dominated by hierarchies of adult—usually senior—males. (Age limits for office-holders, e.g. U.S. Presidents must be at least thirty-five, reflect general concern with the broad biological characteristics of age and the experience it may represent.)

This basic model, which obviously forms such an important and deeply rooted aspect of individual and social life, may be said to have been used as a paradigm for the relationships between social rights and duties and *all* the phenomena, both concrete and abstract, which are perceived as meaningful to men. This occurs, I believe, for two reasons—one psychological and the other social.

The psychological reason why this paradigm is used to organize other relationships is the existence of the process of association, whereby one cognitive system is linked with another. This linkage occurs when objects and/or events are perceived to have some characteristic in common or are in close spatial and temporal proximity.

There is a direct connection between these psychological and sociological reasons for the general use of the basic model. First, men do not only interact with other men, they also interact with and through other 'things', e.g. property, and thereby these things acquire social rights and duties. (Perhaps the best example of this is provided by the 'corporate person', e.g. a business concern, where a legal entity possessing certain social rights and duties is often attributed with the characteristics of a living, sometimes human being.) And, second, since the basic model relates social rights and duties to a biological entity, these 'things' acquire through cognitive association the characteristics of the human physical form. Here is really nothing more than the use of a *metaphor*, which as other writers have observed, is often used in a reverse fashion. For perceived relationships among non-human phenomena, e.g. animals and plants, are, in a number of societies, used to regulate relationships in and between social groups. Claude Lévi-Strauss, who has been the chief exponent of this type of analysis in the fields of myth and totemism, observes:[26] 'In certain societies a very general tendency to postulate intimate connections between man and natural beings or objects is put into effect in order to qualify concretely classes of relatives, either true or classificatory.'

Figure 3.5 shows, in what I would certainly agree is an oversimplified manner, the relationships and cognitive processes discussed here. Very simply, when any category (box C) is attributed with (arrow g) social rights and duties (box B), it is cognitively associated with (arrow a) the human biological entity, or entities (box A). The reverse of this 'structural/perceptual' process, where men are 'converted' into something else, e.g. animals and inanimate objects, may be traced via box A, dotted arrow b, box B and dotted arrow f to box C.

Figure 3.5 is actually no more than an elaborate way of restating the ideas discussed earlier in the chapter, especially the various transformations of the person in the second and third sections. Nevertheless, it does raise several interesting questions concerning the pivotal position of social status, i.e. social rights and duties, in the model.

The first point to be made here is that it is impossible to have social rights without corresponding social duties and vice versa. The second is, as argued earlier, that social rights and duties are allocated and attached to a number of non-human categories. However, and this is a major issue, certain of these non-human agencies cannot exercise their rights and perform their duties, or can only do so in an indirect, often mystical manner, working through human agents. Moreover, there appears to be a certain ambivalence about attributing non-human categories with a full complement of social rights and duties. Complete adult social rights and duties mean control over substantial areas of scarce political, economic and ritual resources, and therefore can only be allocated to a full member of the community concerned. Gods and ancestors may have their due, but the practical men who make decisions about community affairs can treat the deities in a very cavalier fashion when the distribution of scarce resources is involved.

One consequence of this is for certain non-human categories to be perceived and treated as if they were in the possession of either social rights *or* social duties, *but not both*.

On the basis of this premise it is possible to construct a continuum including all the logical possibilities. This is illustrated by table 3.1.

Table 3.1 Continuum of social rights and duties

1 *Social rights and duties*	*2* *Persons/non-persons*	*3* *Abstract and concrete categories*
1 rights but no duties	1 non-persons, e.g. devils and malignant spirits	1 non-human, e.g. part animal, part human
2 rights and duties	2 persons	2 human biological entity
3 duties but no rights	3 non-persons, e.g. the benevolent and higher deities	3 non-human, e.g. part human, part abstract entity

The first column in table 3.1 represents three points on a continuum which ranges from rights but no duties through to duties but no rights. The second and third represent two parallel continua. The second column represents three points on a continuum ranging from non-persons of possibly evil disposition, through normal persons, to non-persons of possibly benevolent disposition. The third column represents three points on the continuum ranging from non-human, possibly part animal, part human, through normal human beings, to non-humans, possibly a part human, part abstract entity.

Only in the second rank, where appropriate social rights and duties (column 1) are coupled with the human physical characteristics (column 3) acceptable in the culture concerned, does one have the necessary conditions for the existence of that category we know as 'the person'. As much of this has been discussed already, I shall confine my comments to the question of the divorce of social rights from social duties.

Where some entity is attributed with social rights without corresponding social duties, it is credited with a position of power without responsibility and, therefore it is likely to be perceived as actually or potentially malignant. Further, it must be, by definition, a non-person, and as such is also likely to be attributed with only animal-like or malformed physical characteristics. The point, I think, is supported by the reverse situation, e.g. people who are unfortunate enough to be regarded by their fellows as physically malformed are also likely to be treated as if they are non-persons and possibly of evil and malignant disposition.

At the other end of the continuum, where some entity is attributed with social duties but not with corresponding social rights, the effect is to credit that entity with responsibility without power. This appears such an impossible situation that only divine beings of benevolent disposition fill the bill. Again, such beings must, by definition, be non-persons, but in this case their physical form is likely to be perfect (which itself is non-human) or in some way elemental and/or abstract.

The continuum represented by column 1 represents a number of ways in which men might think about the allocation of social rights and duties in society and must *not* be taken to illustrate some form of evolutionary development. I might, however, be prepared to accept the proposition that a move along these continua might be taken to represent the social, physical and moral development of the 'person' in any society, from irresponsible infancy, through full and responsible social membership, to death and incorporation into the community of saints or ancestors.

This is all very well, but to return to an earlier point, social rights cannot exist without social duties and vice versa. This logical and practical point must surely mean that the situation described above creates a number of ambiguous categories, the social rights and duties of which are at best unclear. And, to follow Leach on this issue, one consequence is that these ambiguous categories do not fit into the natural order of things and are therefore in some way dangerous and taboo to ordinary mortals.[27] As Mary Douglas observes,[28]

> Animal and vegetable life cannot help but play their role in the order of the universe. They have little choice but to live as it is their nature to behave. Occasionally the odd species or individual gets out of line and humans react by avoidance of one kind or another. *The very reaction to ambiguous behaviour expresses the expectation that all things shall normally conform to the principles which govern the world* [my italics].

Finally, these ambiguities, like those commented upon earlier in the chapter (see p. 59) may be brought about by changes of language and knowledge, in other words, changes of classification, indicated in figure 3.5 by arrows c, d and e. Variations, accelerations and lags brought about by the constantly changing nature of social rights and duties (see arrow d, figure 3.5) also contribute to this state of affairs, and all is compounded by the total inter-action of the elements concerned (see arrows a, b, g and f, figure 3.5).

I do not wish to suggest that all is ambiguity and confusion; it obviously is not. I have attempted through the consideration of the concept of the person, to show how ideas and social structures interpenetrate each other; and have offered some indication of the complicated dynamics of social change.

Conclusion

The last statement might be said to sum up my approach to the topic considered in this chapter. I appreciate that there is the strong probability that, in tackling the problem in this fashion, I may well be accused of having begged the question. That question being, of course, what do I understand by the concept of the person? For my answer has been that the person is what we define as the person; it is a matter of classification. But, and in my own defence, I have suggested that the person is defined and redefined where at least two 'planes of classification'[29] intersect, and where one of them is concerned with social rights and duties.

In this treatment of the question I have been very concerned to emphasize that it is 'in' the 'person' that society and the individual meet and combine, while at the same time maintaining the importance and relevance of biological factors.

Emphasis has also been laid upon the nature of the relationship between the biological and the social, particularly how the one defines and redefines the other. I have also suggested that this relationship may generate ambiguous biological and social categories, and this is, of course, exacerbated by social change, where social rights and duties and systems of classification undergo alteration.

Social change may also disturb the balance between the biological and social elements (what I have called countervailing power), which influences inter- and intra-group cohesion. This process appears to be accelerating in modern technologically advanced societies.

Finally, it has been suggested that the relationship between social rights and duties and biological entities provides a paradigm for other relationships, which, I think, throws some light on the question of personification and relations with and conceptions of spiritual entities.

Obviously the theoretical model discussed here is a gross over-simplification. For example, I have not adequately differentiated the categories I have used or the types of change that they may undergo. Also, I have taken a rather simple-minded approach to the cross-cultural data, and I am fully aware that there are dangers in using and comparing examples of apparently similar behaviour from various societies without due regard for the different and complex circumstances with which they are embedded.

It is perhaps necessary to explain my dual use of the concept of status, where I have used it to refer to bundles of rights and duties and also to refer to a position relative to another position, i.e. in its hierarchical sense. For I contend that social rights and duties entitle people to a differential command over scarce resources and as such they, i.e. statuses, *must* be hierarchically organized.

Theoretically speaking this chapter has presented considerable difficulties, since I have attempted to combine both cognitive systems and social structure in the one analysis. I am aware that these two theoretical perspectives may be incompatible because several of the assumptions which underly them differ in many ways. However, I am convinced that the attempt should be made, and would add that this approach is by no means original, having already received brilliant expression in the work of the 'structuralists' and 'new' anthropologists.

It seemed when first contemplating my approach to a definition of 'the person' that this structural/perceptual orientation was very suitable for the task. It was only during my development of these ideas that I realized that they might also throw some light on the vexed questions of 'personification' and 'animism', and I believe that the arguments I have presented here may well be followed up with advantage.

Critics will no doubt point out that my exposition of the concept of the person may be reduced to the simpler proposition that what man says he is influences what he does, and what he does influences what man says he is. Nevertheless, I believe that this relationship between biological classification and social status is of considerable importance. For, as argued above, it is not only one of the mechanisms which contribute to the maintenance of social cohesion but it is also extremely vulnerable. Moreover, it is both the weapon and target of prejudice, particularly racial prejudice. In Hitler's Germany millions of Jews found that, as far as they were concerned, the balance in this relationship had broken down, and they were reclassified both socially and biologically. The result of this was that they were perceived and treated as non-human, anti-social 'parasites', and went in their legions to unnatural and untimely deaths.

Notes

1 A. R. Radcliffe-Brown, 'On social structure', in *Structure and Function in Primitive Society*, Cohen & West, 1952, p. 194.
2 J. Beattie, *Other Cultures*, Cohen & West, 1964.
3 E. Goffman, *Stigma*, Penguin, 1970, p. 11.
4 J. Middleton, *Lugbara Religion*, Oxford University Press, 1960, p. 31.
5 M. Fortes, *Kinship and the Social Order*, Routledge & Kegan Paul, 1970, p. 199.
6 V. W. Turner, *The Ritual Process*, Routledge & Kegan Paul, 1969, p. 45.
7 A. van Gennep, *The Rites of Passage*, Routledge & Kegan Paul, 1960, p. 66.
8 E. A. Hoebel, *The Cheyennes*, New York, Holt, Rinehart & Winston, 1960, pp. 50–1.
9 John Roscoe, *The Baganda*, Frank Cass, 1965 (2nd edn), pp. 20–1.
10 E. H. Winter, 'The enemy within: Amba witchcraft and sociological theory', in *Witchcraft and Sorcery in East Africa*, ed. J. Middleton & E. H. Winter, Routledge & Kegan Paul, 1963.

11 J. Goody, *Death Property and the Ancestors*, Tavistock, 1962, pp. 152–3. It is interesting to note that Goody also records:

> 'An unweaned child is only a potential human being; he has not yet achieved a social personality. For the emergence of a new personality is not necessarily tied to the moment of birth . . . a child is not entitled to human burial until it has been weaned, a process that does not normally take place until the third year of its existence. . . . Thus the Lo Dagaa display no public grief at the death of an unweaned child, for it is not yet accorded human status. Indeed, if the child dies before being ritually taken out of the house three (or four) months after birth, not even the parents always mourn. For an older but still unweaned child the parents may weep, but the xylophones are silent; the funeral is almost entirely a domestic affair' (p. 149).

12 C. Lévi-Strauss, *The Elementary Structures of Kinship*, Eyre & Spottiswood, 1969, p. 62.
13 L. W. Warner, *A Black Civilization*, Harper Torchbook, 1964, p. 426.
14 M. Gluckman, 'Kinship and marriage among the Lozi of Northern Rhodesia and the Zulu of Natal', in *African Systems of Kinship and Marriage*, ed. A. R. Radcliffe-Brown and D. Forde, 1964, p. 184.
15 J. Beattie, *Bunyoro*, New York, Holt, Rinehart & Winston, 1960, p. 26.
16 J. Loudon, 'Religious order and mental disorder: a study in a South Wales rural community', in *The Social Anthropology of Complex Societies*, ed. M. Banton, ASA Monograph no. 4, Tavistock, 1966, p. 73.
17 E. R. Leach, *Political Systems of Highland Burma*, Bell, 1964, p. 172.
18 H. Kuper, *The Swazi*, New York, Holt, Rinehart & Winston, 1964, p. 59.
19 J. K. Galbraith, *American Capitalism*, Penguin, 1967, p. 125.
20 M. Young, 'The Divine Kingship of the Jukun', *Africa*, April 1966.
21 M. Gluckman, *Politics, Law and Ritual in Tribal Society*, Blackwell, 1965, p. 246.
22 A. Southall, *Alur Society*, W. Heffer, 1953, p. 95.
23 A. Toffler, *Future Shock*, Bodley Head, 1970, pp. 10–11.
24 R. Fox, '*Totem* and *Taboo* reconsidered', in *The Structural Study of Myth and Totemism*, ed. E. Leach, ASA Monograph no. 5, Tavistock, 1967, p. 161.
25 L. Tiger, *Men in Groups*, Nelson, 1969, p. 62.
26 C. Lévi-Strauss, *Totemism*, Merlin Press, 1964, p. 11.
27 E. Leach, 'Anthropological aspects of language: animal categories and verbal abuse', in *New Directions in the Study of Language*, ed. E. H. Lenneberg, MIT Press, 1964.
28 M. Douglas, *Purity and Danger*, Penguin, 1970, p. 210.
29 V. W. Turner, op. cit., p. 41.

4 Three aspects of the person in social life

John Morris

This chapter is a personal statement, expressing views developed through some years of teaching psychology, particularly social and developmental psychology, to a varied set of people—university undergraduates, some of them fresh from school, managers, doctors, social workers, architects, economists and policemen—to name most but not all of the audiences who quickly became participants, critics, and occasionally supporters.

Everyone, however varied in other ways, seems to expect psychology to be a sophisticated attempt to understand the individual person in all his diversity. But the most widely used research approaches in psychology, as in the other 'behavioural sciences', have been based on analysis rather than synthesis, and scientific experiment rather than sympathetic observation and understanding. On analysis, the person as we know him in everyday life disappears and is replaced by a welter of part-systems—thinking, remembering, feeling, deciding, behaving. One of the most difficult but rewarding activities for a psychologist in these closing decades of one of the most destructive yet creative centuries in history is to gain a clear understanding of the living person, as a whole rather than a set of parts, in adulthood as well as childhood and adolescence, in health as well as in sickness, and in his leisure as well as his work.

This is all by way of being a kind of throat-clearing before starting work. One more rumble and I shall get down to business. Innumerable writers have shaped the ideas presented here. But to avoid a tedious review, I shall mention only a few, and those will be placed at the end of the chapter.

Metaphors for looking at people

Suppose we start with some metaphors. One of the most natural ways of thinking about people is to use metaphors—'Lazy pig!' 'As usual, she steam-rollered her way through the discussion.' 'They are building quite an impressive firm there.' In listening to people using such metaphors over a number of years, I have noted six of them as particularly important. They are the metaphors drawn from building, engineering, agriculture, zoology, medicine and the theatre.

The building metaphor is often used about people at work, but we also talk of building a family, or even a friendship in one's leisure time. At the Manchester Business School, where I work, we have a splendid phrase in our postgraduate course brochure boasting of 'laying the foundations for a lifelong career in management'. The metaphor, in its strength and stability, conjures up a picture of reasoned, weighty and sober action, far from the colour and excitement of the activities evoked by some of the other metaphors. Clearly a person who is part of a building is solid and trustworthy, even if the load on his shoulders makes him pretty static and therefore boring, like those Greek ladies supporting great weights in the temples; the only interesting thing about whom is their name, Caryatides, which sounds like a sad pun.

The engineering metaphor, especially that which is drawn from mechanical engineering, adds movement to the building metaphor. Once again the metaphor is happiest when applied to people at work. Business organizations are full of examples: the activities a man engages in at work are abstracted from him and called 'the specification' of his job. It is quite a come-down from having a specification to being told bluntly that one is a 'weak link in the chain'. Better, perhaps, be dispensed with on the more grandiose grounds that one is a 'tractor' and the organization wants a 'sports car' (to use the language of a well-received recent report on management education and development).

Both the building and engineering metaphors reduce people to things. The third metaphor—agriculture—allows people to live, but only as plants. I have noticed that eager young technocrats at the Business School quite unselfconsciously slip into the first two metaphors, while older, more experienced practical managers rather relish seeing themselves as gardeners, farmers, or foresters. One such man said to me about the development of senior management,

'I want to grow my own timber!'; after cutting out the dead wood, no doubt. Others have spoken of the need to wait for people to mature at the 'natural' rate, as if they were plants with their own seasonal requirements, and like to speak of the need for a favourable 'climate' or the provision of appropriate nourishment. In some organizations there is a bitter little joke about the 'mushroom theory' of treating managers, namely, 'Keep them in the dark and cover them in excrement from time to time!'

The agricultural metaphor assumes that the plant stays where you put it. It may flourish or wither, but it does not move. But people do occasionally move from one place to another. Where this becomes evident, the agricultural metaphor gives place to the zoological. A verbatim extract, etched on my memory, from the conversation of a sardonic friend returning from an international encounter of managers and academics, provides an example: 'The managers are like tigers prowling in the jungle. What a contrast to the academics! They are like rabbits nibbling lettuce, safe in their hutches!' And when I objected to tigers and rabbits, he said, 'All right then— elephants and hyenas!' Rather sharp perhaps; but have not the major defence strategists of our time been characterized in terms of hawks and doves?

There are areas of commercial life so chaotic, so unregulated, that people say 'It's a jungle.' Others, more regulated, where competition may well be fair but fatal, are described as the rat race. A man with a heroic record in the underground resistance movement in Europe during the war was heard frequently to say to himself in moments of decision during his business life, 'Am I a man or a mouse?' Others had no doubt that he was a man, but his own uncertainty on the question seemed to be an important factor in the conduct of his life.

Animals represent for us our instinctual drives and dispositions— aggression, devotion, fear, mating, gregariousness. The animal metaphor serves to personify for us, with the dramatic simplification of the caricature, whichever of our characteristics we choose to think of as dominant. Think for a moment of the difference between seeing people in pet-shop terms when very young, jungle terms when they are in a lynching mob, and zoo terms when they are working in open-plan offices, sharply gossiping at the typewriters, clacking among the rubber plants.

And now, after moving slowly towards people, we actually arrive at the human condition itself. But it seems that we are not easily able to look directly at healthy people. So we now come to people in need of medical diagnosis, prescription and treatment. It is astonishing to see how often the fact that people have problems lead us to see these problems as some kind of sickness. We do this particularly often in psychology, perhaps because psychologists aspire after some of the prestige and confidence of medicine. I think it was Freud who said 'The whole world is my patient.' The widespread growth of psychiatric analogizing has continued unabated since his day. The question nowadays in some circles seems to be 'What kind of sickness is the current fashion?' This is brought out clearly in the enormous vogue of studies such as Eric Berne's *Games People Play* or the speed with which macabre studies of psychopathology such as *Who's Afraid of Virginia Woolf?* become internationally known in films, plays and television productions. The ills of the sick society are spelled out for us. A business firm persistently failing to show a profit is said to be sick, and therapists for this condition, basing their thinking on the medical model, are not slow to diagnose and prescribe. Managers must 'take their medicine'. Accountants also are often described as company doctors.

It is perhaps understandable that the medical metaphor is so often resorted to. What we know about health is largely derived from the study of sickness. The significance of Freud lay precisely in this, that he was able to use his remarkable discoveries about the origins oɪ neurosis as the basis for a uniquely insightful account of the total personality. Psycho-analysts however, have been ready to recognize that they understand mental disorder much better than they understand normal function. Indeed they have rather little to say about many aspects of normality. Perhaps we have to conclude that it is never possible to describe health in the language of sickness. We must look to other metaphors.

For me, the metaphors really come close to reaching their goal— the genuine illumination of the human condition, when they reach the theatrical metaphor. This is the first of the six that we have looked at that enables human beings to be seen in their full humanity, at least to the extent to which that humanity can be socially expressed.

The theatrical metaphor: love and war

The theatrical metaphor is especially good at showing people in action—that is, people committing themselves to lines of behaviour that they believe could have been otherwise. The theatre may not see its function as being that of holding a mirror up to nature. It might see itself as a scourge, an emetic, an amusing trifle, or a source of edification. And why not? Whatever can be represented, and responded to, is a possibility for the theatre. This is why the theatrical metaphor seems so wonderfully rich after the wretchedly unsatisfactory business of seeing real people as building blocks or machines, plants or animals.

There seem to be two great themes touched by the theatrical metaphor—love and war. Love is a deep concern for some person or thing (often we have to extend 'things' to ideas, such as pride, honour, or glory). The theme of love enables many of the more positive aspects of people to be depicted—their ability to sacrifice themselves for others, or for a 'cause', their ability to suffer with, or for others. War takes the other side of human nature, its belligerence, arrogance, assertiveness, its passion for expansion at all costs.

The theatre, though diverse, is usually afraid of being a bore, and sometimes love can be boring if it is solely concerned with sweetness and light. Most plays, then, at least in the Western tradition, manage to keep some element of contrast or conflict even in plays of love. This is the element of 'war', which appears to be the most certain source of interest in plays and all other situations having a dramatic form. The theatrical metaphor, however, does not make clear whether it is dealing with the element of the dramatic in real life, or the element of the theatrical. The difference is essentially this— drama is real-life at its most engrossing and significant, while theatre is an imitation or representation of life. From this point on, I want to use the concept of 'drama' in distinction from theatrical activities.

Drama and the individual person

I believe that any action is dramatic, for the person engaging in it, if it has three characteristics. First, the situation must be novel, within the person's experience. This does not mean that every aspect of it must be quite unfamiliar, but that important aspects of it are new. Second, the activity, or its outcome (or both), must be important to him, for whatever reason.

Third, the outcome must be in doubt, and he must feel that his actions may influence it.

I am confining the attributes of novelty and importance to the person himself, though society also expresses ideas about the kinds of situation that are generally dramatic. This is because experience becomes accumulated within social life, and becomes part of what social anthropologists call a 'culture'. The importance of this for the individual is incalculable, in providing cues for response and recognition. But society cannot enable a person to avoid feelings of drama, however possessive and pervasive it may be.

Let me give a homely example of drama in everyday life. Suppose I am on my way home from work. Eager to get back to my wife's excellent cooking, I cross the road without sufficient care, and am knocked down by a passing vehicle. The crowds part for a moment, though only those in my immediate vicinity (others are only dimly aware of a distant bustle and go on uncomprehending).

In a few minutes, along comes the ambulance and with great speed and care the ambulance men decide that my injuries are minor, but need hospital treatment (my leg is broken). For them, my accident is a routine. They know that there will be a number of accidents like mine in the course of the working day, together with some that are very serious. Even the serious accidents are taken in the men's stride. We could look at this event through the eyes of all those who have anything to do with it. For me, as the 'victim', the event is a drama, and a distinctly disagreeable one. For the ambulance men (assuming that they are experienced in their work) it is a routine. But part of their training, as well as (one hopes) their human sympathies, will enable them to realize that they are dealing with someone who is disturbed and shocked, and whose immediate family are also likely to feel concerned. The by-standers are more likely to see it as an incident of passing interest, perhaps worth mentioning to their friends and acquaintances (this of course depends on how many accidents they see during the week).

So what, then, about the person for whom an experience *is* a drama? It is worth asking some questions, such as how often in his life the person experiences drama, what forms the dramas take, and what happens when situations that have been dramatic recur. The first question takes us back to childhood.

For the child, almost everything that happens is new. There seems to be a survival instinct among animals, vestiges of which remain among human beings, to assume that things which are new are also important. The young child is also notoriously inclined to believe that he can change things by getting involved. So our three requirements of drama are all met in childhood. The link between childhood and the dramatic is well recognized in the symbolism of the Christian religion. Birth, death and re-birth are the key themes. 'Except you become as a little child.' But in everyday life, the spiritual implications of the child's freshness and ever present sense of wonder give place to a feeling of oppression. By general agreement among parents, their children's endless dramatism is exhausting . . .

Although it is from the theatre that the idea of drama usually derives, drama is unusually *real*, rather than entertaining or unreal. I mean 'real' in the sense of significant, memorable. I would remind the reader that our lives are focused on our personal dramas. These punctuate the banalities of every day, and enable us to recall events in terms of before and after the particular dramas we have in mind. This is delightfully expressed by James Thurber in 'The Day the Dam Broke' and 'The Night the Bed Fell'.

Breakdown dramas and development dramas

Two concepts that I have found useful in throwing light on the dramas of individual life are *breakdown dramas* and *development dramas*. As its name suggests, a breakdown is a sequence of activities that is set off by an unexpected event. 'Breakdown' indicates that what we have expected to happen has not—a train has not turned up to take us to London, we have had an accident (my 'homely example' of a page or so back would be a breakdown drama), or we find our country has declared war and is determined to involve us in it, whether we like it or not.

The usual reaction to a breakdown is to make attempts to get back to the expected state of affairs. Even if we had doubts about the desirability of a particular state of affairs, it has only to break down for most of us to work enormously hard to get things 'back to normal'. The general manager of a chemical plant observed that his operatives only worked hard when there had been a serious breakdown—a fire or an explosion; he wondered (not too seriously) how far morale and long-term productivity would be improved by some skilfully timed breakdowns. In the life of the child, a break-down often occurs, partly because of the fact that the child has too little experience to make accurate predictions as to what is likely to happen (we are speaking of breakdowns *of expectations*, of course, when we talk of breakdowns); partly because the child has little control over situations and therefore cannot steer things along the lines of his desires.

When most of us think in a common-sense way about 'dramas', we think about breakdowns. This is because we have experienced so many in our individual careers. Growing-up is a hazardous business at the best of times, and one of its most typical experiences is to expose people to their own ignorance of things, others and them-selves. In this connection, 'society' provides a lot of help, and it is no accident that as social life has become more complicated, the time, energy, skill and money spent on full-time and part-time education has increased.

Development dramas have three inter-linked aspects. All of them centre on an improvement of state, in relation to the person's goals. The most commonplace (though still welcome) is a growth in size. The growth of a firm frequently involves all its personnel in a development drama, casting employed persons in more specialized roles and senior managers in more general ones. The person as he grows up not only gets physically larger, but knows more, has to develop greater skills, and more sophisticated attitudes and values. The second aspect is the growth of specialized skill, rather more difficult than just adding, but still perhaps less difficult than the third aspect—the growth of integration, in the ability to live and work as a unity, without sacrificing one's achievements in size or specialism. This ability, let us call it 'wisdom', is not readily found in education designs, whether at the primary, secondary or higher levels of education. Perhaps it cannot be taught, but only deve-loped. But we clearly stand in great need of it in this troubled century.

Taking a role

The idea of a person playing 'roles' fits very well with the metaphor of drama. But the essential point about dramatic roles, in the sense in which we are discussing them here, is that they are deeply felt—

the individual is not so much 'playing' a role (with the implications of 'not really taking it seriously' which the idea of playing carries along with it) but is *taking* a role. The person is committing himself to a situation, working within certain guidelines which he believes to be appropriate for him in that kind of situation. A person in a particular situation is not showing the whole range of his attitudes, values, skills, and knowledge. But this does not mean that he is putting on a façade, or deliberately deceiving the observer as to his 'real' qualities. He may be, but then it is always possible, since man is a creature possessed of some measure of self-consciousness and self-control, that he is trying to mislead. I merely want to distinguish between selection and simulation. Role-taking is an example of the former rather than the latter, in most situations.

The social psychologist Herbert Kelman makes a useful distinction between three levels at which an attitude or a form of social behaviour can be maintained and developed. The first, and most shallow, he calls 'compliance'. Here the person is doing or believing something because of rewards and punishments in his social environment. When these disappear, or change, his behaviour or his attitude changes. At a somewhat deeper level we find 'identification'. This refers to behaviour supported by some respected or loved person in the immediate environment. If the relationship with the person changes, then the behaviour is no longer supported and therefore itself changes.

Third, there is an 'internalization' of behaviour, meaning that the person finds intrinsic satisfaction in behaving in this way. We must not assume that role behaviour is always a matter of compliance or identification. It may often be the result of having 'internalized' (though I shudder at the word, the concept that it refers to is perfectly legitimate). The role expectations have become a part of one's self. Even professional actors may do this, though they know that they are not taking a role in real-life, but playing a theatrical role in depth.

At this point in describing the individual in relation to drama, I am beginning to feel quite uneasy. So many concepts and so little in the way of situations to apply them to! I realize that I am engaging in a form of behaviour that *I* have deeply internalized—the academic inclination to start with the concepts as intellectual instruments, rather than the problems which made the concepts seem useful in the first place. I shall hurry to repair the omission.

A person in the role of an author

A good way of starting is to look more closely at my own behaviour and attitudes as I sit here at the typewriter trying to write an account of these three aspects of the person. First, what I am doing now is dramatic for me, in the sense of being novel, important and (I sincerely hope) capable of being influenced by my own activity. But it is not all that novel, and, if I am honest with myself, not all that important. It would be more dramatic, in a disagreeable sense, if the editor, Ralph Ruddock, were to burst into the room where I am typing, and say, 'I've had enough of this! If you don't give me your completed chapter by tomorrow, I'll get another contributor. Come to think of it, I will anyway!' Even this would be mild compared with other possibilities that fantasy can conjure up. It is when we let our ideas run on this way that the feeling of excitement grows, and, in my case, the chapter starts moving ahead at an unprecedented rate.

But this, you might quite rightly say, is a form of cheating. I am engaged in the quite serious business of writing a chapter in a book on different ways of looking at the person. If I fool around by blithely imagining quite unlikely ways in which the editor, the publisher, or any possible reader might behave, I am being theatrical rather than dramatic. That is, I am playing a kind of game. But whereas the actor is not cheating, because he knows that members of his audience understand that his job requires him to simulate a person other than himself, I am not in the role of actor but expositor. And if I am not careful my exposition, by using myself as a subject, will become so complex and inward-looking as to defy understanding, even by the most intelligent and careful reader.

Yet as I type these words I feel a certain quickening of the blood, a feeling that I am not putting down on paper the words that I have often used in talks and lectures to a variety of audiences, but am exploring, in the context of readers who have to be imagined rather than seen and conversed with, a kind of social relationship that I find unfamiliar and quite exciting. It is a deferred relationship with people in a role, the well established but not very well defined or well understood role of 'reader'. Reader, that is, not of a novel or a poem, but of a piece of exposition about people in social relationships.

How do *you* feel as you read? Where are you reading this? I wish I could see you, hear you. Are you reading so quickly that you cannot hear my voice? If you have been through a quicker reading course and possess the proud reading speed of 800 words a minute with full comprehension I imagine that you cannot afford to hear my voice. Presumably it would be like one of those comic voices on a speeded-up tape-recorder.

I suddenly notice that attention to my own activity has introduced a ritual note. I want to talk about ritual later (why, I wonder, am I trying to be so orderly and sequential; after all, I am not expounding symbolic logic but conveying a sense of the self in drama . . .) Still I will talk about ritual later. Although I have read Marshall McLuhan and been duly impressed, irritated, overwhelmed, confounded, and impressed again, I cannot manage to write for you without some sense of the order in which I am going to say things to you.

Back to drama. It is much easier to get a sense of drama in personal encounter. Yet there is something strangely personal about writing, here and now. The overhanging light glows hypnotically bright upon the page, the clack of the typewriter badly used, is awkwardly honest, and the solid feel of the great oak dining-table gives me a sense of immediacy.

We create each other

I remember reading that D. H. Lawrence had no sense of an audience as he wrote, in his beautiful longhand, smoothly and gracefully across the page; no feeling of the reader reading his words. Only a sense of what it was necessary to say. Yet have you noticed that when we know people really well, we talk to them as if we were talking to our better selves? And when you come to reflect on the matter, how could you talk to anyone, except through your own understanding of them? In one sense you are talking to yourself, but possibly in a rather trivial sense. Because it is more true to say that our selves *are* a kind of social anthology of people encountered, represented or imagined. Yet not a passive anthology. Surely the people that we have, in some sense, experienced, are our own responsibility. The people we know, whether real or imaginary, are in a sense our creations. *But in a more important sense, because there are more of them than there is of us, we are theirs.*

This is being dramatic with a vengeance. And yet not theatrical.

It is real, a part of our actual experience, and not knowingly simulated.

I have come to the conviction that the apparently objective concept of 'observable behaviour' is rather a will o' the wisp, except in a fairly trivial sense. Once we get away from reflex behaviour on the level of sneezing and kneejerks, all behaviour is whatever we define it as *meaning*, with the agreement of others whom we accept as reasonable and informed observers. This can take us a long way into the person, through the medium of what a person tells us about himself through posture, gesture, words, silences, inflexions of speech and so on, if we can guess what they mean for him.

I feel that a very odd thing is happening now. I am a little uncomfortable about my ruminations. They seem self-indulgent. I have often shared this kind of experience with a group of people that I feel I can trust, and will take the self-revelation in the spirit in which it is meant: as an exploration of experience as one experiences it, rather than a formal statement of standardized categories and 'behaviour-measurements'. But now I am seeing you, the reader, as a demanding collection of readers, far more critical, impatient, and demanding, than any of the groups I meet in everyday life. Are you in fact feeling irritated, critical, bored? If you were feeling like this in a group, I could sense your feeling of tedium and irrelevance, and change tack . . .

There is a kind of silence. The reader within me withholds assent, letting me go on. Are you more *un*critical than the real reader? If I cannot create you, how can I create for you?

Courage, I feel. The writer is more courageous, or more insensitive, than the speaker. Taking courage, I break off, to take the dog for a walk which I would not give him if my commitment to what I really want to express to you about development dramas had not been so shaken. Yet as I leave for the walk, I know that when I return, it will be in the knowledge that you will understand that development dramas, if they are really dramatic, must risk being breakdown dramas.

Now I have returned, having thought the matter through a little more clearly, even more convinced that only the more trivial kinds of development can be simply added to the previous acquisitions of knowledge and skill. Development dramas, then, to be worthy of the name, must be rather powerful experiences and are not likely to come about out of a blue sky. The study of child development suggests that some of the crucial development dramas—the Oedipal conflict of early childhood and the 'identity crisis' of adolescence—are fraught with deep inner turmoil, and accompanied by breakdowns or threats of breakdown. Again, to move to a later epoch in personal development, the self-questioning and major reorientations of the middle years of life, in the late forties and early fifties, are experiences of breakdown followed by a change rather than by mere restoration of the *status quo*.

I think it was Jung who first drew attention to the positive aspects of 'nervous breakdowns' as indications of a person's unconscious wish to move to a 'higher' and more satisfactory level of functioning, often a new level of spiritual experience and insight. Ronald Laing also has suggested links between the anguish of a schizophrenic breakdown, with its intense experience of guilt, worthlessness and alienation from one's self and others, and the 'dark night of the soul' experienced by mystics before profound insights.

These dramas, in the form of breakdowns, are individual and personal rather than collective and social, but the immense popularity of religious evangelists, indicates the close links between individual and collective experience. The 'still small voice' that is suggested by the solitary act of self-communion and writing, seems very different from the stentorian, amplified voice of a Billy Graham in a vast amphitheatre, accompanied by organ music and massed choirs, but the continuity is there. In each case the concern is with moving through a breakdown to a breakthrough.

To return to the question of courage. There seem to be two main choices in one's life: to stay with the things one knows, feeling ever more secure as they become increasingly familiar and automatic through repetition, or to move into the unknown. If we make the latter choice, we may limit our stake by measuring our steps or our commitment. But we are taking some risk, though we hedge our bets, and it is this that needs courage. Every step into the unknown implies that we might fail, and many failures leave us worse off than we were when we started.

All professions require this courage. Doctors, architects, actors, managers are all in the kind of work that exposes them to uncertainty. The doctor stands between his patients and the frightening worlds of suffering and death. The actor has to help his audience to suspend disbelief for their delight or purgation. He faces the nightmare of drying-up or incurring primitive wrath and contempt (no wonder that actors are masters of the art of apology). Managers are familiar scapegoats and villains—tramplers of the faces of the widows and orphans, gamblers with uncertainty, inventors of organizational futures. Architects must create art works within which people can live. Doctors, it is said, bury their mistakes. The mistakes of architects are exposed to public derision for generations.

If society is to get the best value from people in these professional jobs, it must expect them to have deeper commitment than compliance or even identification can yield. It is no surprise, therefore, that selection and training for these professions place great emphasis, almost to the point of obsessive exaggeration, on personal involvement—'dedication', 'love of one's work', 'a sense of one's calling', and so on. Any more superficial relationship would waver and fail in face of the many ups and downs in the uncertain life of the members of what I think of as the 'great' professions. If you ask me why I have not mentioned lawyers and priests, it is merely because I have not worked so closely with them as the others, and have a little less interest in them. But the length and arduousness of the training for both is a byword.

Drama and form

Although I have been talking of drama in every other sentence, I have said little of the forms that drama takes, other than vague mention of tragedy and comedy, development and breakdown, and a few examples. It will be clear that I use 'drama' as a noun and not in verbal or adjectival form. A drama is a sequence of activities in time, with a beginning, middle and end. Not, of course, that these have the same clear-cut form as art works—three-act plays, three-decker Victorian novels, or the cantos of narrative poems. Though clarity of this kind would not be remarkable, because drama arises from human needs and expectations, and life (social life) notoriously imitates art, since it has to find its forms from somewhere, being human and derivative, rather than primal and divine.

Some dramas last only a few moments, and are remembered for a lifetime. This applies not only to romance—Dante and Beatrice, Petrarch and Laura. Oedipus, for example, meets an old man on his way to a foreign country, quarrels with him and kills him. Only later does he discover that this brief encounter contains his fate. Only later does Freud attempt to show that Oedipus is in all male children, who are condemned by their gender to wish the death of their fathers in order to enjoy undisputed possession of their adored mothers.

The 'Oedipal conflict' in real life is vastly different from the nightmare clarity of the Greek myth. It is a *theme* rather than a clearly recognizable pattern of events. Since human beings are able from a very early age to reflect on their experience and re-enact it (or, more disturbingly, to be compelled to re-enact it through lack of courage to reflect on it), dramas beget dramas.

A notorious failing of intellectual people, however, is that they constantly nag at life for not being completely amenable to elegant analysis, and, given half a chance, will re-write life to make it fit into their rational systems. I am strongly aware of my own inclination to do this. It is stronger than an inclination, it is more of an obsession. In the modern 'behavioural sciences', however (if the pot may call the kettle even blacker than he is himself), the search for rational analysis goes all the way to the point of ignoring or denying the reality of drama in everyday life. Personal and social life is seen in terms of conscious or unconscious routines, or breakdowns in routine (which themselves are often triumphantly claimed to have their own routine structure). In my theorizing, I have found it necessary to see three forms of coherence in life—dramas, rituals and routines. If we return briefly to the metaphors with which our discussion began, the metaphors of building and engineering can assume a manipulative approach to the person. It is only when we come to the theatrical metaphor and then transcend it by seeing the differences between a theatrical performance and the hazards of real life that we can allow the human person to be a mystery, and a source of action rather than a predictable form of reaction.

For me, then, people are at their most individual and personal when they engage in dramas. These are the growing points of their lives, their sources of personal history, the stories of their commitments. But I cannot bear, I suppose, to leave 'drama' completely mysterious. I look for its causes, its functions, its shape and content. This is, perhaps, the old story of the intellectual rejecting his own rationality and then trying to force the non-rational into a rational mould. Perhaps the truth of the matter is that people strive to shape their most powerful experiences, and the fusing of form and energy is what drama is all about. Where the ability to place a shape on the energy fails, one has the varied forms of breakdown: some so total that they cannot even be charted.

While the desire of the individual to shape his own experience in a meaningful form cannot be doubted, the decisive influence in shaping human action in drama is undoubtedly that of social traditions. In games, plays, art works, histories, biographies, the individual is put in touch with those who have responded to opportunities and failures with 'style'. If we see dramas as capable of being placed on a lengthy scale of patterned energy, ranging from relatively minor, though genuinely fresh experiences in the individual person's life, to the great moments of truth in which everything a person stands for hangs in the balance, we can say that social influences work at every point in the scale. To some readers this may seem a contradiction. How can an individual show his individuality, his personal commitment to a chosen line of action, if he has been influenced by 'society'? Perhaps I have not made myself clear. To me, individuality is what we have made of ourselves, and our willingness to be responsive and responsible. The materials on which we base our commitment are ours only because we are committed to them. Only in the most exceptional case did we *originate* them. Society is shared living, together with our commitment to the common stock. But as we shall see, in some forms of 'society', commitment is not all that common.

From dramas to rituals

I started this essay on 'three aspects of the person' by indicating the need to see people in all their diversity, in the whole range of personal and social activities. I then launched into a series of metaphors, six in all, and plumped for one of these metaphors, somewhat modified to get away from the constraints of theatrical convention. What of the other two aspects? One of them—ritual—I have mentioned already in passing. The third is routine. Together—drama, ritual and routine—the three aspects of the person connect him indissolubly with society. Drama is concerned, whether on the small-scale or the large, with novelty, importance, and the possibility of action. Ritual is a class of activities that are less novel, sometimes (though by no means always) less important. The actions associated with ritual, unlike those in a drama, are *predictable*, often very familiar.

Rituals, because of their greater familiarity and stability, provide a kind of platform below the dramas, a link with the banalities of everyday life (I mean the endless flow of *routine* activities without which we would have no sense of continuity, as familiar to us as our hearts beating and lungs drawing breath). All the major social sciences, and branches of zoology as well, have uncovered various kinds of rituals (I shall group ceremonies in with rituals from now on, as a kind of 'mini-ritual'). Zoologists have been particularly concerned with rituals of courtship and aggression. These turn out to be quite closely linked with the rituals observed by social anthropologists (as Konrad Lorenz's fascinating book, *On Aggression*, brings out so clearly). The difference between the rituals noted by zoologists and those described by anthropologists and historians is that the former are largely unlearned, springing into existence at the appropriate stage in the individual development of members of a particular species.

Zoologists like Lorenz who have undertaken the mothering of a brood of goslings have sometimes found themselves becoming a 'love-object' in another sense, towards whom the maturing birds direct their courtship rituals. In birds the ritual pattern is fixed but they need appropriate experience to respond to the right object. In higher animals, much of the behaviour may need to be learned also. Zoo animals commonly become so humanized as a result of daily contact with keepers and visitors that they cannot respond to their own kind—a very costly incapacity in the case of the London and Moscow pandas. Perhaps there are human analogues of rituals which have become misdirected. The children celebrating, for example, Guy Fawkes Night are not usually thinking of the saving of Parliament in the seventeenth century.

As you might expect, things become much more complicated when we turn to people. Most of our conduct is learned, and much of the learning is a highly individual variant on social themes. Human rituals have two sources. First, there are activities that were once dramas, but the situations that evoked them have now become recognized, and the resulting actions have started to stabilize. But for reasons we shall glance at later, they have now become automatic enough to be experienced as routines. Second, there are forms of behaviour that are socially established as rituals, and have been successfully acquired by the individual as such through a process of social learning (I know that the term 'social learning' sounds rather pretentious, but I cannot think of a better way of indicating the things that we take over ready-made from social experience, such as the form of a religious service, or a school-leaving ceremony).

There are innumerable ways of classifying rituals, each serving particular purposes. I would like to divide them into three groups, as follows: (1) rituals which have a special affinity for drama, serving to introduce dramas, or at least prepare for their eventual occurrence, to round off dramas, or to punctuate them; (2) rituals which have an enduring value in their own right, as evocations of matters of importance to a person and his society; (3) rituals which make routines more meaningful and therefore more tolerable (because human beings, although they need a measure of security, often become bored by routines).

Let us consider the first class of rituals.

I have the firm impression, looking at the speed with which most people build up habits, that dramas quickly run down into routines after a few repetitions of the relevant situation. To an inexperienced mother, a toddler's temper tantrums can be dramatic, but after a time the required restraint or comforting contact can be experienced as routine. It may be that nothing ever happens twice in the same way, but human beings, like other animals, are quick to classify events as 'the same', whenever they can get away unscathed by doing so. That is, we are usually eager to look for the leading features of situations, so that we can respond to them with an existing pattern of behaviour. Since perception is closely linked with response, our perceptions of ourselves and the world around turn into habits as quickly as our actions do.

Dramas resist becoming routines if failures occur in the process of responding to a situation. The contrary can also be true. If the underlying need met by a response is strong (like hunger or sexual passion), then successful responses often become ritualized rather than routinized. If, for instance, the temper tantrum is on the part of a husband rather than a child, and if it occurs with some frequency, then it is more likely to be accommodated by way of ritual —a ritual argument for the expression of feeling, an appeasing gesture or a cup of tea. These considerations suggest that the persistence of rituals indicates a special condition in human life, such as links with a physical appetite or strong functional need. Rituals surrounding the taking of food, including cooking itself, are everywhere recognized to be distinctively human elaborations of processes meeting basic biological needs.

One of the strongest needs of human beings is to live in a world that is comprehensible and meaningful—that makes sense to our minds and speaks to our feelings. Presumably this need originates in a straightforward need to control one's environment in order to survive. But in human beings it burgeons, becomes convoluted, and becomes a need in its own right. I have argued that dramas are the most meaningful parts of our lives, but we often fear the consequences of breakdown. Rituals provide a safer, more familiar world. The first kind of ritual stays close to drama. In one of its most pervasive forms, it is a symbolic re-enactment of an earlier drama, usually a drama relevant to our needs and involving a 'culture hero'. Religious rituals are mostly of this kind, taking key events in the life of the founder of the religion.

Where people are engaged in a long and demanding drama, it is strengthening for them to prepare by 'anticipatory rituals' (the war dance, the knight's vigil, prayer and sacrifice are examples). At the end of the drama, the need for some kind of closure can be provided by a ritual of celebration or mourning. This not only happens in warfare (except in the most modern and degraded forms of 'liquidation') but in industry and commerce. The most traditional forms of human endeavour are rich in 'closing rituals'—launching a boat, topping-out a building.

The second class of ritual is concerned with the unchanging truths of human life, birth, marriage, death, sickness, recovery, making, destroying. While it is true that many of these activities, because of their importance, are experienced by people as dramas, and therefore the rituals associated with them come into the first class we have discussed, some important social values may, nevertheless, not be associated with drama for each individual. We can see every developed form of society as having a vast repository of rituals on which the individual can draw when he is in need. If he is experiencing these rituals in relation to drama, then they belong to the first class of rituals that we have discussed. But there are many rituals which society offers us which do not speak to our condition so deeply. Yet they may be satisfying at several removes from drama. Many passionate people believe that a ritual is only meaningful if it is very closely associated with drama. They believe that the separation of ritual from drama is a clear sign of a society running down into rigidity and boredom. This may be so, but I rather doubt it. My belief is that in a rich complex society, there are many rituals which are satisfying without touching the deepest springs of action in each of the individuals engaging in them. This seems to be particularly true of British society in the later part of the twentieth century.

It is undoubtedly true, however, that many of our rituals have run down to the point at which they are merely perfunctory. Geoffrey Gorer has described, on a basis of extensive evidence, how the reduction of mourning customs has robbed the bereaved individual of his right to experience his reaction at length and in depth. This can occasion unshared inner suffering and endanger the later processes of readjustment.

This leaves us with the third class of rituals, those which remind us that routines were once dramas, and that they have some connection, however tenuous, with social necessities and social values. In modern industrial society, the lack of ritual for 'legitimizing' routine has, in my view, constituted a very serious weakness in industrial and commercial morale. I think that we desperately need to find rituals that will justify routine, where the use of intelligence and imagination does not enable us to transcend routines.

From the vantage point of a business school where so many social processes are described in terms that appear to be characteristically Western, it is salutary sometimes to ask whether experimental and other research findings would apply in a quite different form of culture—such as the Japanese. We have no need to remind ourselves of the dynamic pace of Japanese industrial advance; but perhaps we may pause to recall that the Japanese appear to be given far more to the use of ritual in industry than ourselves. Television documentaries have made us familiar with the formal greetings, the ceremonies surrounding installation of new machinery, the breaks for physical exercises, the presence of the departmental manager in a central position at his subordinate's wedding. It would be naïve to see these merely as strange customs, and more profitable to ask what part they play in Japanese achievement. We may also observe, however, that such rituals with them are not hollow as they might well become with us. I have in mind the well-known fact that joining a firm in Japan is like joining a family—the mutual obligations are expected to last through life.

A closing word on routines

It may seem ironic that I leave routines to the end of the discussion. The characteristic of modern society, often called 'industrial society', is that it has harnessed man to the machine, turned craft work into unskilled labour, and alienated man from his birthright. To the extent to which this is true, I am perhaps provided with a justification for stressing the opposite point of view. Every man starts as a child for whom everything is dramatic, finds his continuing meaning in the rituals associated with dramas, and is a creature (should I say creation?) of drama and ritual rather than of routine. In a sentence: man lives by drama, remembers by ritual, and survives by routine.

Yet I am always being shocked by my patronizing attitude to routine. As an academic of fairly regular habits, I am sure that much of my life is a model of orderly routines. For all I know, my friends set their watches by me (the only resemblance I have to Immanuel Kant). More to the point, the regularities of our social lives, on which our sanity rests, are largely formed around the routine behaviour of others. What wonders of intricate balance and order are to be found in bus and railway timetables! Even the overwhelmingly factual, alphabetical profusion of a telephone directory has a fascination of its own ('wonderfully interesting characters but not much by way of a plot' as a voracious reader was once supposed to have said, mistaking the directory for a novel . . .).

If we are wise, we pass on our routines to others when they begin to pall, arranging that the others will be less experienced than we are, so that our routines come to them as dramas. The best teachers have always been clever at doing this: in management it is called 'delegation'. It is always possible, though often difficult, to look afresh at the hoariest routine with an innocent eye, and re-kindle the sense of drama. This is what one kind of artist does for us, or a child that we love. This reminds us that the link between drama and routine is of our own devising.

These considerations suggest that routine has a wonder of its own, that its security and complexity can be a joy, and that we may resent it only because we have more of it than we want. The key question it seems is: How do we achieve a personally satisfying mixture of drama, ritual and routine? I have found it helpful to put this matter in a simple diagram, shaped like a cone. At the top of the cone, appropriately placed there because it looks like the fiery top of a volcano or the probing tip of a space rocket, are the dramas. At the weighty bottom come the routines. At the middle, linking dramas with routines, are the rituals.

At any given time, the individual can be seen schematically as a cone, with the dividing lines between the three forms of experience and behaviour at different levels. One person may have a large proportion of dramas, another may be virtually wholly absorbed by routines. With repetition of acts and situations, dramas become routines, and with a greater knowledge of one's self and one's circumstances, life may become increasingly a matter of routine. Individual preferences are likely to vary, one person enjoying a high proportion of drama in his life, another feeling the agreeable security of routine. The idea of representing the three aspects of the person as a cone occurred to me some time ago, and I have found that

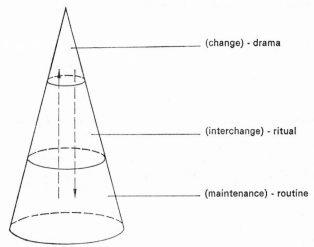

(change) - drama

(interchange) - ritual

(maintenance) - routine

Figure 4.1 Three aspects of the person

people respond very differently to it. Some see it as a rather satisfying solid object, resting comfortably on its routine base and fizzing in a lively way at the top. For others, the cone is more exciting, a space rocket on its launching-pad. I note that I tend to see the cone as symmetrical, orderly, and yet active and purposeful.

A more dynamic representation could easily be found. The important point is for us to note the attitude that we express towards these three aspects: for in these our particular balance of personal qualities is revealed. Or lack of balance! Our search throughout life is for the highest level of balance that we can achieve, with the energies, abilities and circumstances at our disposal. This search may be encouraged by those among whom we live, if we are fortunate. If we are less fortunate, we find our search being subordinated to some stock social conception of the good life for someone of our age, sex and station. The tension between our personal needs and the social roles allotted to us may be great and this denial of our right to live at our highest bent is itself a source of drama—perhaps a tragedy rather than our intended comedy.

Where all this ends no one knows. All I have been suggesting is that three common conceptions of human personality need to be brought into one more complex form—that man as seeker for security, as true believer, and as adventurer, needs to be seen as man the individual person attempting to bring all these aspects of his personality into a coherent unity.

Bibliography

Abegglen, J. (1958), *The Japanese Factory*, Chicago, Free Press; London, Asia Publishing House (1959).

Burke, K. (1969), *The Grammar of Motives*, University of California Press.

Goffman, E. (1959), *The Presentation of Self in Everyday Life*, New York, Doubleday; London, Allen Lane (1969).

Goffman, E. (1961), *Encounters*, Indianapolis, Bobbs-Merrill.

Gorer, G. (1965), *Death, Grief and Mourning*, Cresset Press.

Heider, F. (1958), *The Psychology of Interpersonal Relations*, Wiley.

Kelman, H. C. (1961), 'Processes of opinion change', *Public Opinion Quarterly*, vol. 25, pp. 57–78.

Laing, R. D. (1961), *The Self and Others*, Tavistock.

Lorenz, K. (1966), *On Aggression*, Methuen.

Russel, L. C. & W. M. S. (1961), *Human Behaviour*, André Deutsch.

5 Conditions of personal identity

Ralph Ruddock

Introduction and summary

An attempt to study the human individual in depth rapidly reveals the extent to which his personality and behaviour are dependent upon his relationships, and indeed, have arisen out of relationships in early life. An attempt to study human relationships equally reveals the extent to which they are dependent on individual characteristics. There is a common field of interest which groups of scholars approach from opposite directions. On one side we have psychologists and clinicians, psychiatrists and psycho-analysts concerned with the individual in the first instance. On the other side sociologists and anthropologists are primarily concerned with the systematic properties of human relationships.

Encounters between these groups are now occurring with some frequency. For the most part, however, they tend to miss one another, while proceeding deeply into each other's territory along parallel tracks. Psychiatric social workers, for instance, are very much concerned with family relationships but the concepts they use, such as identification, dependence, projection, rejection, introjection, are based on individual psycho-dynamic models. On the other hand, sociologists are prepared to discuss any aspect of an individual and his behaviour in terms of socialization and inter-action.

This essay explores some areas where these two approaches might come together. An attempt is made to construct a model, using concepts derived from each. Six component concepts necessary for such a model are identified: self, personality, identity, role, perspective and project. Identity is seen as chosen by the self for the purpose of organizing and integrating the other components. The consequences of locating identity at one or other point in the personality or role system, and of a lack of congruence between the components are illustrated, with examples.

A brief account of some psycho-analytic approaches to relationships is followed by a consideration of the treatment of the self in sociology. The term 'role-tree' is proposed as an organizing concept for the personal role-system. A discussion of inter-personal perception, and a short section on 'the project', follow. The final section presents the model, examines some of its possible uses and offers a very tentative visual representation.

If, under stress, a man goes all to pieces, he will probably be told to pull himself together. It would be more effective to help him identify the pieces and to understand why they have come apart.

Psychology should help one to do this, but in the event its resources are usually disappointing. It has done something to identify the pieces. The clinical psychologists, especially the psycho-analysts, have done more. However, both are weak when dealing with the central integrative processes—the self, as distinct from the ego. Academic psychology is often open to the critical comment of David Cooper: 'the reductive approaches end in a specifically inter-related aggregate of inert totalities . . . the point of intersection of a series of abstract theoretical lines is proposed as the (more or less) irreducible reality of the person.' In terms of personal reality, as he says, most of us feel this to be beside the point, or to be a point about something else.

A self, on the other hand, must be thought of in terms of subjective experience and a sense of continuing identity. It is a 'centre of re-orientation of the objective universe' (Mounier). This re-orientation is an active process. One is constantly working on it. Adjustment is more a matter of initiative than of passive reaction. Orientation in the human being is not that of the floating compass card, but rather that of the pilot who reads the compass, selects the course and controls the energy supply. Orientation requires not only that we identify what lies around us, but that we integrate it into a coherent pattern.

Cooper writes of human reality as 'a movement of progressive synthetic self-definition which cannot be grasped by a method that would arrest it'. The question becomes 'what the person does with what is done to him, what he makes of what he is made of'.

The Freudian psycho-analysis is rightly attacked for its reductive and deterministic assumptions. Freud spoke of the person as being lived by the forces within him, before which he was helpless, though he liked to think otherwise. Neuroses, dreams and all thinking were seen as necessary outcomes of the inter-action of mental components. A more sophisticated critique says that Freud found it heuristically valuable to make these assumptions. It helped him to discover that every strange item in a dream world made sense if the patient could trace what led up to it; 'sense' means *meaning*, however, and in so far as psycho-analysis is a psychology of meanings (of dreams, symptomatic acts and so on) it contradicts its determinist basis. Meaning cannot be attributed to inert processes. Further, Freud's treatment of patients was clearly based on assumptions that they were capable of choice and responsibility.

Only now, perhaps, is psycho-analysis resolving this contradiction, although many of the early secessionists felt it necessary to correct Freud's backward-looking reductionism with a forward-looking integrationism. The first was Jung, who came to see life as a struggle to achieve by progressive integration one's unique identity. Freud had said that anyone who asked what was the purpose of life was ill. (See J. W. Shaw's chapter in this volume.) Freud required the sense of identity to be unconscious, or at least, pre-conscious. Only the neurotic person was self-conscious. He might have given a simple psychological meaning to the statement that one must lose one's life in order to find it. For Jung, on the other hand, identity was bound up with existential consciousness.

It has not been sufficiently recognized, however, that the sense of identity is tentative and mobile—perhaps 'labile' is the word. It can embrace much of the personality or a small part of it, and the part selected may be changed in an hour or a minute. Such changes appear to be recognized in common speech, e.g.:

'I don't always know which is my real self.'

'I like to show my best self.'

'He wasn't quite himself yesterday, but he's his old self again today.'

'He was beside himself with rage.'

'I like to get out of myself sometimes.'

It would seem that 'I' can be related to 'myself' in various ways that everyone understands but no one has fully explored: It is possible to feel that the locus of one's identity shifts around within the personality as one's situations and feelings change. One is aware of choosing to become a somewhat different person: few experiences can be more familiar than that.

Psycho-analytic approaches to relationship

Games People Play by Eric Berne is probably the most meaningful attempt during the last thirty years to offer a relational psycho-analysis. Berne employs contemporary American speech, with the intention of capturing the emotional impact of everyday encounters. The book is written with great concentration, however, and economically develops the system presented in his earlier clinical text, *Transactional Analysis*.

Where classical theory presents id and super-ego locked in conflict and ineffectively refereed by ego trying to get both of them to take more notice of reality, Berne replaces id, super-ego and ego by *Child*, *Parent* and *Adult*. Berne cites the brain stimulation experiment of Penfield, regression phenomena under hypnosis and other evidence in favour of the Freudian postulate that the past is always present, in that under certain conditions we re-assume the earlier identities of childhood, including that of the internalized parent. We thus have three possible selves, or 'ego-states' as Berne calls them, as basic modes of relating to others.

In the 1940s Karen Horney (1942, 1946) proposed a four-fold typology based on relationship disposition, including a relationship to the self. Her four primary dispositions were:
    moving towards people (because of a dread of conflict);
    moving against people (because of a dread of love);
    moving away from people (because of a dread of involvement);
    moving away from self (because of a dread of realizing one's supposed imperfections).
The 'dread' is an anxiety of a kind that all human beings are subject to, but raised to a degree of neurotic intensity. *Relationships* are seen as shaped by anxiety, whereas the Freudian scheme represented anxiety as shaping the individual personality.

Moving towards, against and away from, might be seen as Child ego-states. Moving away from self is likely to be a Parent ego-state. In a social-identity perspective, a mode of adaptation between inner anxieties and social requirements will prompt the assumption of an identity, such as:
    I am a person who gets on with everyone;
    I am always ready to take on anyone;
    I keep myself to myself;
    I live by the highest standards.

Horney's discussion of the extent to which the 'centre of gravity' lies in the self or in the expectations of others offers a psycho-dynamic approach to problems of identity and relationship.

These problems are central to the work of R. D. Laing and his colleagues; and in different ways, to the work of Goffman and other 'micro-sociologists'.

R. D. Laing's first book, *The Divided Self*, is a study of the split between the *true self*, which is inward and pre-occupied with feeling, fantasy and thought, and the *false self*, which is put forward to meet the demands of others. Most of us experience some tension between these two selves. The schizophrenic is a person who has opted out of both; the split has become unbridgeable. He is a person who comes to feel less and less real in his social behaviour, and finally withdraws all investment of his identity from it. The normal person, on the other hand, finding social adjustment (work, family) more satis-factory may withdraw his sense of identity from his inner world. He moves into a condition of 'normal alienation' and becomes a hollow man (most of us are, by this account). Laing acknowledges his debt to the existentialist philosophers, and has used this approach for the understanding of schizophrenia.

The split between the true and false self, the dangers of losing touch with one's real self, of behaving inauthentically, are set out in varying terms in the writings of Kierkegaard, Heidegger, Sartre; and in psycho-analysis by Binswanger, Rollo May and Winnicott.

In later writing Laing affirms the existence of a *transcendental self*. This has its own modes of experience, mostly different from those of 'egoic' life, being far more significant and varied. One may experience it when out of the ego, due to sleep, drugs, trance or religious exercise. It is Shakespeare's 'glassy essence', the world of the 'lunatic, the lover and the Poet', who are 'of imagination all compact'.

Social pressures require us to extinguish awareness of this ultimate self. Any discovery of it is dangerous, and exposes us to hallucina-tion, as well as to disturbing visions of other orders of reality. A doctrine of this kind is, of course, central to many religious tra-ditions, which see 'the world' as endangering or extinguishing 'the vision'.

Laing's recent writings have presented the social processes in which we are all engaged as a form of violence against ourselves and especially against children. Wordsworth posed the problem in his ode, 'Intimations of Immortality from Recollections of Early Child-hood'. The child is seen as the true philosopher. Not only the teaching of Jesus on this point, but Wordsworth's own experience was enough for him to know the blessedness of childhood. The child saw the world with 'the glory and the freshness of a dream', 'apparelled in celestial light'. Why does the 'visionary gleam' fade? Why do the 'shades of the prison-house . . . close upon the growing boy'? Wordsworth could not answer the question. He saw the child rehears-ing in play his future adult roles, and could not understand why he should thus 'be blindly with thy blessedness at strife'. Shakespeare reaches a position near to Laing's in five famous lines:

> Man, proud man,
> Drest in a little brief authority,
> Most ignorant of what he's most assured,
> —His glassy essence—like an angry ape,
> Plays such fantastic tricks before high heaven
> As make the angels weep.

There is a further aspect of self which is best touched on in the context of Laing's writing. This is identification with *the body*. The schizophrenic may provide the most striking manifestation of the breakdown of this identification. He may appear to regard his body as an alien thing, whose well-being is a matter of indifference to him. He may tear bandages from wounds, stub a cigarette on the back of his hand or cut himself without apparently feeling pain. It is fairly generally agreed, following the work of Melanie Klein, Winni-cott and others, that the infant has to learn what is his own body, to discover its boundaries, his powers over it and progressively to identify with it. This identification is indicated in common speech in such phrases as:

'Don't push me.'

'It doesn't fit me.'

'I'm getting too fat.'

Illness reveals the extent of the identification. There is ample evidence that much illness, perhaps most, can be seen as a kind of behaviour in which the whole person is implicated. There is a 'lan-guage of the body', in expression of psychic content through the malfunctioning of bodily organs. There is psycho-somatic illness, in which the functions of breathing, circulation or digestion become disordered due to psychic stress. Identification is involved here, in that if it had been more complete, if the person had been fully 'embodied' in Laing's term, he would have been sensitive to the continuous signals of organic distress, instead of over-riding them for egoic reasons. There is a constant stream of sensation from the body pressing towards consciousness. Yoga techniques direct attention towards this stream, with a view to neutralizing it (J. Clark, this volume; D. Wright, 1970).

The authorities cited so far have derived their views from clinical experience. Some have not been specially interested in problems of identity, and would prefer the whole issue to be absorbed into a discussion of ego function. Others have described forms of behaviour and experience suggesting that the sense of identity has taken up a position within the personality. None, until recently, has taken sufficient account of relationship factors as determinants of the self-image. The sociologists have studied relationships, more recently in face-to-face settings. They observe the pressures on individuals to accept *roles*, and to adopt an identity that has in the last analysis been forced on them. The gap between psychology and sociology is thus closing. A worker in one field must be familiar with ruling concepts in the other field and ready to incorporate them in his own work.

Sociologists have avoided the term 'behaviour' as descriptive of their field of study, and so have escaped some of the problems of one school of psychology. Generally they prefer to speak of 'social action', which makes possible the attribution of *meaning* to action in social terms. This brings them nearer to the position of the psychoanalyst. No doubt the meaning of 'meaning' in the two cases is somewhat different; but not widely so. 'Meaning' asks for subjective assent: so that, to take the case of formal sociology, relationship properties susceptible of objective validation by statistical processes become meaningful for the individual only on the basis of his experience. This is perhaps central to the argument of Michael Polanyi in his major work, *Personal Knowledge*.

Neither meaning nor knowledge can be stored in a computer. Only a person can 'know'. Meaning requires understanding. Sociological enquiry may in the first instance be concerned with data and the validation of hypotheses, but in the last instance, with intelligibility. The ultimate objective is subjective.

The self in sociology

In our day we see some concentration of sociological interest on the subjective self. Perhaps the first major influence was that of the personality-in-culture school—Benedict, Kardiner, Linton, Margaret Mead, Wolfenstein and others. Most of these anthropologists had some sophistication in psycho-analysis. One of the contradictory features of classical Freudian theory, now well recognized, is that on a basis of philosophical monism was erected what is essentially a social psychology. Freud's model of personality based on instinctual drives contained by a structure of ego and super ego is recognized to be inadequate. However, his work directed attention to the way in which personality arises within the mother–child relationship. His own and subsequent observations showed personality to be the product of a social situation. Recording of child-raising practices became a requirement for anthropologists, and cross-cultural studies in this field prompted much shrewd speculation on, for instance, sex roles or the inhibition of aggression. The cultural variability of the human species had long been demonstrated. These studies traced significant pathways along which the children were led to acquire, not merely an identification, but a basic personality structure like that of their own people.

A second major influence has been the development of role theory. The concept of role has turned out to be of real use for psychiatrists, social workers, management theorists, counsellors and psychologists, as well as for anthropologists and sociologists. It is a concept common to all the social sciences. Roles are the units from which social structures are built up. Few limits could be proposed for the concept of role, as all action can be seen as role behaviour. This is to say that all social action is action shaped by awareness of relevant relationships, and the expectations of other people. A man's speech, movements, feelings, perceptions and ethical standards change as he moves from his role as husband to his role as father, then as employed person, then as customer and so on. From this it is a short step to argue that his actions when alone are also shaped by his social awareness; and hence to say that one is never out of a role. Role-occupancy is synonymous with being a member of society.

It is not, however, the universality of application of the role concept that interests us here so much as the claims that are made for the internalization of role expectations in the structuring of personality. The contemporary sociologist likes to view the individual as a social construct, the product of a socialization process; and moreover, to see him as open to re-structuring as his roles change. The present writer has pointed out that the view of man presented by Jacques in *As You Like It* is exactly similar. Surely we are intended to understand that the sighing lover with his woeful ballad, the soldier jealous in honour, sudden and quick in quarrel, the justice full of wise saws and modern instances are not only three of the many parts we may have to play, but that these are played in turn by the same person at different stages of life. A radical change of identity appears to be involved.

If all action can be subsumed under the concept of role, and if child-raising is seen as a form of conditioning for adult role performance, it becomes possible to degrade the concept of personality to the status of a highly dependent variable, and to see the psychoanalyst or personality theorist as engaged in a solipsistic struggle with reified abstractions. Peter Berger, and somewhat differently, Erving Goffman, come near to this position.

What for others is personality, however, for the self is identity. One's very sense of being, one's ontological security, in Laing's term, is shaken by this sociological perspective. One is invited to see oneself as relative, mutable and contingent. This is a part of the shock treatment intended to promote the development of a sociological consciousness. Berger writes:

'Normally, one becomes what one plays at.'

'We become that as which we are addressed.'

'Every act of affiliation entails a choice of identity.'

'In a sociological perspective, identity is socially bestowed, socially sustained and socially transformed.'

'The person is perceived as a repertory of roles, each one properly equipped with a certain identity.'

'The self is rather a process, continuously created and re-created in each social situation that one enters, held together by the slender thread of memory.'

Goffman's interest is indicated by the title of his first book, *The Presentation of Self in Everyday Life*. He studies in fine detail the selection of what is to be presented from one's total resources, how the presentation is staged and performed, how the performance relates to role and situation, and the degree of identification between the person and his role. He takes the view that identity is formed by role.

S A P—H

'A self, then, virtually awaits the individual entering a position: he need only conform to the pressures on him and he will find one ready-made for him. In the language of Kenneth Burke, "doing is being".'

'It is well appreciated that in small, long-standing social circles each member comes to be known to the others as a "unique" person. This term "unique" is subject to pressure by maiden social scientists who would make something warm and creative out of it, a something not to be further broken down, at least by sociologists.'

Elsewhere he speaks of this attitude as 'arising from a touching concern to keep a small part of the world safe from sociology'.

We know that, in fact, both Berger and Goffman are very much concerned to enlarge the scope for individual autonomy within society. Much of Goffman's work can be taken as a minutely descriptive account of means both devious and deviant whereby individual identity expresses itself through the cracks and interstices of imposed institutions. It should be stressed, lest the claims of the sociologist appear to be pitched too high, that the dependence of personality on role is powerfully documented. It has been observed, for instance, that prolonged unemployment often leads to a deterioration of moral character. An unemployed man may at first be active and enterprising in job-seeking. Then his determination begins to give way to anxiety. After the anxiety phase comes depression. His family roles change. He is no longer the breadwinner and perhaps is no longer accorded the respect he formerly had. He has lost his role as a worker among colleagues; and because he has less money and less to talk about, cannot maintain a social life with former friends out of working hours. Financial weakness may make him dependent. He may come to be grateful for a drink and a cigarette. These may come to be such welcome interludes in a drab day that he centres hope and feeling upon them: he feels himself becoming a cadger. His habits of early rising and daily shaving begin to seem pointless. He becomes slack and lazy. He can no longer invest pride in his appearance, and begins to neglect his clothes. What adjustments to his self-image does he make during this slow sequence? His family may well run into a problem, and if the social worker calls she may assess him as an immature and inadequate personality. (This danger is now recognized, and the needs of the man for money and for support in re-adjusting to either work or permanent unemployment is better realized.)

The delinquent and the criminal are commonly diagnosed in psycho-dynamic terms; but it becomes apparent that these are often people for whom society has no use—that is to say, offered no satisfactory roles. This, of course, is often true of old people, the handicapped and mentally disordered and the poorest families. There is abundant evidence that irresponsible and deviant behaviour on the part of such people is related to lifelong experience of rejection and isolation. A supportive approach can often bring impressive changes in social adjustment and personality.

Much of the brutality formerly directed towards social outcasts has abated. This, however, has not led to a position where they can be accepted. The number of the rejected is probably increasing, and in general they are accorded the non-person treatment. They are ignored if they behave well. Identity becomes involved. To have one's existence ignored is tantamount to having it denied. A healthy child will provoke a teacher or parent to an act of discipline rather than be ignored. A criminal identity may be preferred to becoming a non-person, perhaps in a mental institution.

Some highly literate persons have recorded their experience of becoming non-persons. Philip O'Connor is a writer who has described his early life as a 'public baby' and later spells of vagrancy when he found himself 'unable to cope with the demands of respectable living'. The stages the neophyte tramp may expect include relief, adventure, depression, fears,

> the awfulness of authority, its abstraction . . . a tighter and
> diminished sense of self . . . immense afflatus in heart and soul
> towards evening . . . daylight predatoriness, the rancid irrita-
> bility at the stupendous elaborations of the respectable person-
> ality in towns—its complacent complexities, its weird
> indirectness, its sumptuous self-feeling . . . a still augmenting
> loss of identity, terrors of unmanageable abstraction of self,
> akin to non-existence; interrupted by the sheer debauchery of
> a cup of tea or of any human communication . . . the utter
> awareness that we are total strangers; and a fury of hatred at
> the morbid privacy of individual lives . . . Tramping, even my
> gentle kind, introduced me to a totally new kind of reality,
> and gave me a viewpoint from which our culture looked like
> a top-heavy wedding-cake, and our so-called polite manners the
> gestures of insane skaters performing before mirrors. It gave

me also a clue to the insubstantiality of identity, to its frightening dependence upon the existence of cliché thinking and behaving. Without familiar supports, it broke in no time, and until through grim desperation I learned to distinguish self from identity (if you like, to distinguish what I more or less always *am* from all the things I am temporarily *said* to be), this insecurity of identity felt like imminent death-in-life. It positively introduced me to the profound sociality of man, a fact which our silly cults of noble isolation and caricatured individuality try to undermine . . .

Let us accept the evidence that personality is forced into existence and forced to maintain itself, by the inter-action requirements of role-relationships. The sociologists have further perceived that self-image and identity are bound up with roles. This has led them, however, towards much too simple a view of the identity problem—the view that one changes one's identity, as one might change one's clothes, with every change of role. To quote Berger again: 'The self is rather a process, continuously created and re-created in each social situation that one enters, held together by the slender thread of memory.' From the same position, Goffman is prepared to concede more to a central agency of some kind.

It is a basic assumption of role analysis that each individual will be involved in more than one system or pattern, and, therefore, perform more than one role. Each individual will, therefore, have several selves, providing us with the interesting problem of how these selves are related. The model of man according to the initial role perspective is that of a kind of holding company for a set of not relevantly connected roles: it is the concern of the second perspective to find out how the individual runs this holding company.

The assertion that we change ourselves as we change our roles is unlikely to meet with general assent. Most of us feel ourselves to be somewhat different in different roles, but not absolutely. There is a central sense in which we feel ourselves to be more than a thread of memory on which roles are strung. Objectively, we observe behaviour changes in others as they move from role to role, but not to the extent that we think of them as different people. Indeed, if a person presents himself as differently as that, we have a sense of discomfort. Normal personality can be seen as an incapacity to play some roles.

People who change their personalities with their roles may be diagnosed as hysterical. A hysteric is said to be a person who plays at being what he is. Such people are ready to become whatever the immediate situation requires, often in a style somewhat larger than life. There are Greek legends about beings who, if you manage to catch them, metamorphose into a sequence of startling guises. Only if you hold on firmly will they eventually re-assume their basic identity. Psychiatry has always regarded such behaviour as pathological, early psychiatry speaking of 'dissociation', and contemporary post-Kleinians of 'splitting' and 'attacks on linkages' characteristic of schizoid processes.

Psychology has hardly come to terms with the dependence of personality on role, so it is not to be expected that any model for a central integrative agency, which might be the locus of a central identity, will have been worked out in that discipline. Goffman's metaphor of a holding company is much more promising, but he did not develop it. We do not know what attributes and powers he would have assigned to it. Presumably Goffman's selves *experience* their roles: does the holding company also experience? Is it in fact subjective? Is it another kind of role?

In an earlier book (Ruddock, 1969), I proposed the term 'role-tree' as an organizing concept for the articulation of the personal role system.

A father takes his family to the sea and while bathing, warns his son about the ebb tide. What is his role at that moment? That of disciplinarian, perhaps. A bather, also a holiday-maker, a father, a man? If, a few seconds later, he is teaching his daughter to float, in what sense has he changed roles? What sense does it make to say he plays five roles at once? Can they be considered as separate roles? If so, how are they related to each other? . . .

Banton (1965) proposes the terms basic, general and independent roles. 'Married woman' is a basic role, determining most of the way of life of the person; a general role might be that of a minister's wife, a role which extensively influences behaviour in many social settings. Independent roles are freely chosen, and do not influence other roles very much. The parson's wife for instance, might spend what free time she has in growing cacti. It would be possible to add to this classification a fourth category of transient roles, meaning those positions we occupy in conversational exchanges, often changing from minute to minute as we explain something, ask for help, give an order or make a joke.

Instead of referring to a person's 'role-repertory', which is an unsystematic term, we might speak of his 'role-tree'. This would be a branching net-work concept, familiar in the field of computers and teaching machines. The trunk would correspond to the basic role: say, a middle-aged man; the main branches would be his general roles—husband, father, probation officer; the secondary branches would correspond to special roles belonging within the general roles, such as a probation officer's roles in court, in home visiting, in seeing probationers and in office work; Banton's independent roles, would also belong here. The transient roles would be represented by the leaves, which are in fact the organs by which a tree interacts with its environment. We should have to suppose that the tree bore a variety of leaves, a phenomenon not unknown in nature. The fact that a man might take a supportive role as probation officer, as parent and as husband in turn would correspond to the growth of similar leaves on different branches.

A role-tree would grow from small beginnings in infancy. It might be possible, with systematic observation, to record growth and differentiation, and to compare the role trees of different people. Some would prove to be strong in the basic role, but poorly developed in the branching system. Some might be one-sided, as with a man who can only proliferate roles at work. Some would appear to be maintaining inter-change on a minimum of roles, with some branches bare. The balance between expressive and instrumental roles would be related to feminine or masculine basic roles . . . Suppose, however, the question is put, what is the relation between the personality and the role-tree? At first it might seem that they are the same since the role-tree is a way of describing the person's total capacity for relationships of various kinds, and this is near to a definition of personality. It is true that at present much description that would be appropriate to the role-tree is sub-sumed under the heading of personality. It is not possible here to enter into all the ramifications of this question, but we can say that the concept of personality includes configurations and

structures of needs, wishes and fears (old-style 'complexes')
derived from past adjustments to experience. These immensely
complex structures within the personality will not be fully

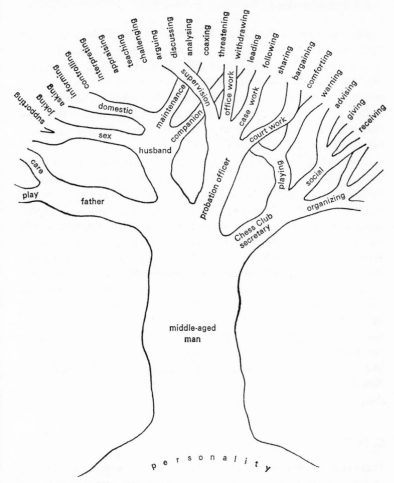

Figure 5.1 The role tree

expressed in any role-tree. They will however, in total and in
relation to the total environment of the person, determine the
growth and shape of the role-tree. The role-tree can be viewed
as the visible outgrowth of personality, and as its means of
expression. The role-tree would be open to interpretation in

terms of personality. It might be said that a cluster of roles appeared to be used as defences against anxiety; or that a predominance of aggressive and of dependent roles indicated a deep ambivalence.

The question is further complicated by the findings of social psychologists, who have shown that when people are placed among others whose views differ from their own, they show a tendency, over time, to change their views and move towards the majority position. Perhaps this is not surprising, but what is rather disconcerting is that the subjects of these observations report that they were not influenced by the views of others but changed their own views after private re-consideration.

It seems that in order to become ourselves, we have to take things from others, forget where we took them from, forget that we did in fact take them from someone else; and finally forget the process of forgetting. (This is, in essence, R. D. Laing's description of 'repression'; Laing, 1967.) In this sense, personality development may be seen as appropriation. We start perhaps with a nuclear collection of items that have been given to us, assimilate items taken from others and present to the world as our own an assemblage of *objets trouvés*.

This is a concept of personality as acquisition and accumulation. The material will be organized around roles. Experience of playing former roles will not be lost, but be carried forward into new roles and differently patterned. A geological metaphor suggests itself. Personality is the accumulated deposition of material from successive roles, precipitated always on the contours of earlier roles. Personality is thus past role experience expressing itself in a present role.

G. H. Mead on 'I' and 'me'

There is no escape, it appears, from the need to explore the interior systems of personality, and to attempt some generalizations of interest to sociologists. Of this kind, the work of G. H. Mead has been the most notable, and perhaps exercises an increasing influence after forty years. Mead is as absolute as any contemporary on the social constituents of the self:

'A self can arise only where there is a social process within which this self has had its initiation. It arises within that process.'

'The self is not initially there at birth but arises in the process of social experience.'

This reminds one of R. D. Laing's formulation: 'One's identity is in the first instance conferred on one. We discover who we already are.'

This discovery presumably occurs at the point where brain and social development permit self-awareness. Mead says: 'The reflexive character of self-consciousness enables the individual to contemplate himself as a whole', and: 'It is in addressing himself in the role of another that his self arises in experience.' This leads to his famous distinction between the 'I' and the 'me'. 'The "I" is the response of the organism to the attitudes of others: the "me" is the organized set of attitudes of others which one himself assumes.' Action is in principle indeterminate: 'Well, what is he going to do? He does not know and no one else knows.' Mead speaks of the unpredictable 'I' as 'getting the situation into his experience', when it becomes past and a part of the me.

However Goffman might see it, Mead sees the 'I' as something warm and creative and safe from sociology. It is the 'me' that is the rightful province of the sociologist who must, however, recognize the interference of 'I'. The 'me' is not simply planted into the person, in the sense of a required internalization of imposed role expectations. On the contrary, the 'me' is built up out of the reactions to situations of the unpredictable 'I'. This model appears to be much nearer to experience, and less likely to involve over-enthusiastic sociologists in an attempt to 'get empirical reality to conform to their own scientific conceptions of it' (Roland Robertson). Mead writes:

> Human society, we have insisted, does not merely stamp the pattern of its organized social behaviour upon any one of its individual members, so that this pattern becomes likewise the pattern of the individual's self: it also, at the same time, gives him a mind, as the means or ability of consciously conversing with itself in terms of the social attitudes which constitute the structure of his self, and which embody the pattern of human society's organized behaviour as reflected in that structure. And his mind enables him in turn to stamp the pattern of his further developing self (further developing through his mental activity) upon the structure or organization of human society, and thus

in a degree, to reconstruct and modify in terms of his self the general pattern of social or group behaviour in terms of which his self was originally constituted.

Interpersonal perception

Mead has a paper written in appreciation of Cooley, whom he quotes as follows:

> I do not see how anyone can hold that we know persons
> directly except as imaginative ideas in the mind. I conclude that
> the imagination which people have of each other are the *solid* ...
> *facts* of society, and that to observe and interpret these must be
> a chief aim of sociology.

This statement is perhaps the starting point for a phenomenological sociology. As an insight it is not specially original. Are not the plays of Ibsen, Chekhov, Pirandello intended to reveal that a social system, a family and then a personality are stable only so long as people believe what they claim to be. Hamlet had already discovered that there is nothing either good or bad but thinking makes it so. Shakespeare is in fact constantly concerned to show how contingent the social order is (especially in so far as it depends on the authority of a ruler) on the view people have of it.

These are significant matters in the understanding of social behaviour. One's view of other's view of oneself has been discussed over the centuries in terms of 'honour'; one's self-view in terms of 'pride'. There was much to debate. While parents, teachers and military commanders stressed pride and honour as virtues, religious philosophers warned against them as sins, temptations and illusions. Pascal writes of man that he wants to be great, and sees himself small. He wants to be happy, and he sees himself miserable. He wants to be perfect, and he sees himself full of imperfections ... He devotes all his attention to hiding his faults both from others and from himself, and he cannot endure either that others should point them out to him, or that they should see them . ..

> Il arrive de là que, si on a quelque intérêt d'être aimé de nous,
> on s'éloigne de nous rendre un office qu'on sait nous être
> désagréable; on nous traite comme nous voulons être traités:

nous haïssons la vérité, on nous la cache; nous voulons être
flattés, on nous flatte; nous aimons à être trompés, on nous
trompe. . . .
C'est ce qui fait que chaque degré de bonne fortune qui nous
élève dans un monde nous éloigne davantage de la vérité,
parce qu'on appréhende plus de blesser ceux dont l'affection
est plus utile et l'aversion plus dangereuse. . . .
    Ce malheur est sans doute plus grand et plus ordinaire dans
les plus grandes fortunes; mais les moindres n'en sont pas
exemptes, parce qu'il y a toujours quelque intérêt à se faire
aimer des hommes. Ainsi la vie humaine n'est qu'une illusion
perpétuelle; on ne fait que s'entre-tromper et s'entre-flatter.
Personne ne parle de nous en notre présence comme il en parle
en notre absence. L'union qui est entre les hommes n'est fondée
que sur cette mutuelle tromperie; et peu d'amitiés subsisteraient,
si chacun savait ce que son ami dit de lui lorsqu'il n'y est pas,
quoiqu'il en parle alors sincèrement et sans passion.
    L'homme n'est donc que déguisement, que mensonge et
hypocrisie, et en soi-même et à l'égard des autres. Il ne veut
donc pas qu'on lui dise la vérité. Il évite de la dire aux autres;
et toutes ces dispositions, si éloignées de la justice et de la
raison, ont une racine naturelle dans son coeur.

The main points of the above may be set out in translation in the
following sequence:
'Is it not true that we hate truth and those that tell it to us, and
that we like them to be deceived in our favour? . . . We desire flattery
and they flatter us. We like to be deceived and they deceive us. So
each degree of good fortune that raises us in the world removes us
further from the truth. . . .
Human life is thus only a perpetual illusion . . .
No one speaks of us in our presence as he does of us in our
absence. Human society is founded on mutual deceit . . .
    Man is then only disguise, falsehood, and hypocrisy, both in him-
self and in regard to others. He does not wish anyone to tell him the
truth; he avoids telling it to others.'
Pascal's assertion that 'man is only disguise' bears directly on our
theme, the nature of personal identity.
    Laing, with his colleagues A. Phillipson and A. Lee, has explored
identity-for-the-other and identity-for-oneself in a sequence of

perspectives. They acknowledge the original analysis of another religious philosopher, Martin Buber, from whom they quote:

> imagine two men, whose life is dominated by appearances,
> sitting and talking together. Call them Peter and Paul. Let us
> list the different configurations which are involved. First, there
> is Peter as he wishes to appear to Paul and Paul as he wishes
> to appear to Peter. Then there is Peter as he really appears to
> Paul, that is, Paul's image of Peter, which in general does not
> in the least coincide with what Peter wishes Paul to see: and
> similarly there is the reverse situation. Further, there is Peter
> as he appears to himself, and Paul as he appears to himself.
> Lastly, there are the bodily Peter and the bodily Paul, two living
> beings and six ghostly appearances, which mingle in many ways
> in the conversations between the two. Where is there room for any
> genuine inter-human life?

The Inter-Personal Perspective Method developed by Laing, Phillipson and Lee explores a person's view of the other; his view of the other's view of him; his view of the other's view of his view of him; his view of himself; the other's view of that; and all the reciprocal views within a dyad. Without doubt this method throws a flood of light on the relationships of two people. In fact, the quantity of information it yields is so great and so immediate that a computer-like process is called for in tabulating, analysing and interpreting it.

Laing goes a long way towards asserting that such hierarchies of reciprocal perspectives *are* the substance of relationships. On first examination one might suppose that this analysis leads towards infinite regress and increasing abstraction.

Quite simple examples are sufficient to show, however, that perspectives of the second and third order commonly govern major decisions. It further appears that normal socialization is enough to render us capable of making and expressing, such discriminations, though not, of course, enough to enable us to formulate them in abstract terms.

Suppose we have the following situation: A man frequently tells his wife he loves her. She finds this insincere and tiresome, although in fact she loves him and he loves her. He thinks she likes to be told he loves her, though in fact she does not. She knows he thinks this. He, of course, does not know she does not like it, and she knows he does not know. Although he loves her, he does not always feel sincere in his expressions of love. Again, she knows this and he does not know that she knows. She thinks he knows she knows that, however.

Now let us suppose she tells him she does not like his telling her he loves her, as she feels his words are not always sincere. He may then think she thinks he does not love her. Further, he may decide she does not love him. Both these conclusions are mistaken and there could be major consequences.

For our purposes, however, the question is, what effect does her revelation and his subsequent mistaken assumptions have on his self-image? He may feel:

(a) that he cannot give love to another;
(b) that others cannot love him;
(c) but that he can still love another.

This condition will be painful, but not hopeless as long as (c) is in some balance against (a) and (b). If he loses (c) by ceasing to feel love, his 'personality' and correspondingly his identity, is likely to undergo a significant deterioration.

Analysis of a dyadic relationship by this method may reveal a situation of the following kind. A mother frequently criticizes her son. He thinks she thinks poorly of him and can find nothing right with him. In fact, she thinks very highly of him. He thinks she is very self-righteous. In fact she can find little right in herself. (For this reason she prefers to provoke others into behaving badly to her: she prefers quarrelling to depression.) Here there is a discrepancy between the social persona of the mother as presented to others and her inner sense of self: and between the way she is generally responded to by others and what she feels herself to be. This is a point of theoretical significance for sociology. The simple assumption so often made in sociology is that what is reflected to the person by others *becomes* the whole person. Sociologists need to recognize that the self-as-presented may be a defensive construction, a personality built on a 'defence mechanism'.

Even so distinguished an authority as Harry Stack Sullivan, who did more than anyone of his generation to re-build psychiatry on a concept of the person as a meeting point of social relationships, expresses himself incautiously on this point. 'The self may be said to be made up of reflected appraisals. If these were chiefly derogatory . . . then the self dynamism will itself be chiefly derogatory. It will facilitate hostile disparaging appraisals of other people and it will entertain disparaging and hostile appraisals of itself.' What Sullivan describes here is certainly common and of great importance, but it is not a universal consequence of disparagement. There are alternative modes of reaction, one of which is the aggressive response. If this is reinforced and becomes successful it can lead to a high self-valuation, maintained by intimidating others. In middle-class settings where a child may grow in a climate setting infinite aspirations in all directions, he may react to total parental approval with feelings of guilt. The following instances may serve as a warning against a simple assumption that the views others have of a person come to constitute his self-image. A student of high ability is suffering from a depressing conviction of his own worthlessness. At the same time he knows that he has high ability, and consistently refuses research opportunities he feels to be below his powers. What is the identity of this student? It appears that no one has any influence on his self-image. Praise and criticism are uniformly discounted. The struggle inside this person is strictly private: no one else is allowed to join in. The struggle is between the two selves, and neither can vanquish the other. The identity question is not resolved.

A girl may have every endowment to make her attractive except that she cannot feel herself to be so. A man may not be able to accept the clearest hints that he is not wanted by a group he aspires to join. A person of mildly paranoid disposition may not be able to accept any gesture of goodwill, even a smile, as spontaneously meant for him. Coriolanus, who rated himself very highly, could not bear to be praised.

One might indeed ask if anyone is able to receive the cues from others without distortion. What we are is for each of us a loaded issue: the ultimate issue, in temporal terms at least. Can we be expected to receive information about ourselves without the greatest trepidation? Further, cognitive studies reveal the extreme complexity of perceptual processes, and the extent to which all signals are interpreted in terms of pre-existing schemata.

The project; and the 'real' self

It is necessary to refer again at this point to the position taken by Cooper, Jung and many others, that human action is not intelligible if seen only as pushed from behind, as deterministically caused; but that it has to be understood in terms of a person's project for himself.

All action is intentional, and has a future reference, but the *project* is something more than that. It might be seen as the fantasy of a future self or future state. It is argued by Marxist existentialists, followers of the early Sartre, that we choose ourselves, choose what we are to become, and have no option but to choose. Marxists generally reject postulates about human nature, and charge psychologists with a failure to recognize that their human subjects, and their findings about them, are findings about members of a specific society at a given historical moment. Man has no fixed nature; what appears as his nature is, in fact, his history. On the basis that man is at present alienated from his human potentialities, the Marxist can argue that man must become the author of his own nature—'man is the future of man'. Nietzsche announcing the death of God and the consequent transvaluation of values, similarly requires that man transcend his historical condition and become the superman.

The working out of such views would involve an understanding of the ways in which individuals and societies derive their projects out of their past. It requires an account of how we transform and integrate our experience—surely the central process of mind?

The psychologists for whom self-actualization is the central process see the processing of experience as occurring in relation to the need of an ultimate self to find expression, to develop and manifest its unique pattern. 'Self-realization' is a term frequently used in this connection. It enables us to speak of the postulated innate unique self when realized in this way as the *'real' self*.

The location of identity

It is now possible to order the concepts presented so far along a temporal series, and to impose upon them the concept of an identity capable of selection and movement between different locations. For this model, the self is the continuing sense of individual being. It is subjective, that which experiences; it is the origin of intention, action and choice. It is unpredictable, not determined. Its relation to the temporal dimension and to the social personality are problematic. This self corresponds to G. H. Mead's 'I'. I shall call it the original self.

Identity arises from the need to integrate the personality. The achievement of a measure of integrity is a requirement for participation in any society. To say one thing and do another, to break promises, to take contradictory attitudes from day to day is to invite sanctions. Continuing relationships require consistency over time. The degree of integrity achieved by a person may be seen as a major psychological variable, but in fact it is a concept so loaded with moral overtones as to present problems of operational definition. Integrity is even expected of the 'criminal'; a part of his problem is that people treat him as if he is *all* bad, and are confused to discover he is not. Evidence of the strong inner drive towards integration is the acute discomfort experienced in states of conflict. In these respects the human individual is like other biological and social entities. All have systems required to be self-maintaining, adaptive, goal-oriented and integrative. These four functions are interdependent. The goal will largely determine the modes of adaptation and integration, and the pattern to be maintained. The entity then becomes characterized. The goals chosen, with the modes of adaptation and integration, will characterize the person. The subjective aspect of the achievement of a degree of integration is the sense of identity.

The need to discover and develop a viable identity is fundamental in the sense that other choices depend on it. Roles and project can only be selected on the basis of an established identity. Powerful drives maintain the search for identity if it is not securely possessed. It is well known that some adopted children make great efforts to discover the detail of their early life. Foster children may experience identity confusion due to the change of home. Robert Holman tape-recorded interviews with twenty foster children to test the extent of their knowledge about themselves. He reports that his questions aroused a great deal of painful emotion, indicating the importance of knowledge to the child. He found that a lack of knowledge was profoundly disturbing, 'because the past is a part of oneself, without it there is a feeling of incompleteness'. He then writes,

> the work of Weinstein indicates that a foster child needs to identify predominantly with either his parents or his foster parents. It was the child who had a mixed identification who did less well in the foster home, presumably because being uncertain where his loyalties and feelings lay he was unable to take the foster home for what it was. It may follow that the more a child knows about his past the more easily he can identify with one or the other, the less he knows the more likely he is to have mixed identification.

These observations suggest that love, security, acceptance and understanding are not effective in a child's family setting until his identity problem is resolved; that he is likely to be 'disturbed' if he lacks knowledge about his past; and that given knowledge, some choice is possible between alternate identities. When the choice is made, the personality can be organized and relationship accepted.

It is in accord with our experience that the sense of identity can move around to select a position from which to attempt to organize the components of personality and life-style. We experience this possibility as inner freedom of choice. Existentialists insist that we choose ourselves, within the limits of our constitution at any given moment. The sense of identity is dependent on social experience, social possibilities and projects. It is moved around by the self, which is independent of all social experience. It may be conveniently thought of as moving along a spectrum, throwing up different colours. The original self is white light.

The sequence I propose is developmental, extending from the present past, through the present present to the present future. (These terms will, it is hoped, explain themselves: Mead's essay on temporality (1965) provided the basis.) The positions listed are taken from the authorities named. Movement along the sequence is from inner to outer, and then towards integration. Events in each of these locations are to some extent dependent on events in the earlier locations.

> The model requires
> *an original self*
>
> choosing
>
> *an identity*
> on the basis of alternative positions within
> *the personality*
> *the role-tree*
> *the perspectives* of self and others
> *the project.*

The present past is the personality. The role-tree and the self-perspectives are the present present. The project is the present future.

The psychiatrist works on the personality—it is sometimes said to be his function to correct the past. Counsellors and consultants—in business, family life, education—work upon the future. They are concerned with policies, strategies and decisions. Social workers work upon the present, and are concerned with roles. The situations they are required to enter into are *always* matters of role performance and relationship.

This model can be conceptualized, but also experienced. As with the Freudian 'mechanisms'—projection, displacement, rationalization and others—one should feel that it accords with experience. It should be possible to recognize that one (original self) did progressively adopt what seemed the most favourable identity available within the resources of one's childhood personality; that at a later stage one developed it or changed it for another identity that seemed possible; that this became actual in role behaviour, which was in turn always subject to the views one had of one's personality and one's roles, and to the views of others. The whole system came to be oriented by one's project for the future. (See further on p. 204.)

Uses of the model

The model has three possible uses. First, it offers the possibility of giving an intelligible account of certain inner states without reducing the person to part systems. Second, it offers an elucidation of reflexive sentences, such as, 'He was trying to alter his attitude to his past behaviour.' Third, it brings the central components of the person (self, identity) into dynamic connection with relationship, in roles and reciprocal perspective systems.

The first and second of these applications may be considered together, because the intelligibility of inner states will depend on the verbal accounts we are able to give of them. In particular, it will depend on the meanings we can assign to 'I' and 'myself'. Paradoxically, 'I' usually refers to the 'self'; 'myself' usually does not—it more often means my personality-in-role. (Personality can only be seen, or expressed in role, as has been said above.) A sentence such as 'I am disappointed with myself' expresses a perspective on personality-in-role taken by the self. 'I like to show my best self' suggests that the speaker has a number of ways of organizing his personality for role-performance. The reflexive use of 'self' in 'myself', 'my best self' indicates a possibility of identification with personality-in-role. A person who says, 'I am disappointed with myself', may be preparing to withdraw from an identification, and later may say, 'I can't go on like this. It's not really me to behave like this at all.' Such a person is seeking to separate the real-me from the role-me.

Personality is shaped by the body, heredity, sex, age, experience and roles. The real self is aware of all such factors, but does not share the attributes of personality. In one sense, it knows itself to be 'the same' at forty as at four. Though it is itself enduring, it is the agent of change. It may reject an inadequate personality, in order to constitute a new one. The realized self requires a total identification of self, personality and role; but the two last modes of being must be subject to the first.

On the basis of these propositions the 'spectrum' which follows has been elaborated. Concepts taken from the authorities cited are arranged in the order: Mead, Berne, Laing, Goffman, Horney, Maslow, Jung. A symbolic notation is offered.

Given	B	the body
	S	the original self
	SB	the embodied self
The present	c	the child one was
past	pa	the internalized parent
	P	the personality
	SP	identity-in-personality
The present	R	role
present	PR	personality-in-role
	SR	identity-in-role
	SPR	identity-in-personality-in-role
	SpS	perspective of self
	SpP	perspective of personality
	SpPR	perspective of personality-in-role
The present	Spr	the project for the self
future		
	SS	the real (ized) self

The spectrum permits mental constructions long recognized and described to be re-stated in terms of identity:

The false self—PR (no 'S')
the idealized self—SPpa
the self one thinks one presents—SpPR
the self one tries to present—SRpr

Such a usage should make possible some degree of precision in the understanding of complex sentences employing personal pronouns, especially reflexive pronouns. In most such sentences, if 'I' 'myself', 'you' 'yourself' are taken to refer to the totality of the person, the result is a nonsense. In 'Don't push me or you will make me angry'—the two 'me's' can hardly have an identical reference. We must understand 'Don't push SB or SPR will become angry.' 'I'm feeling better now' refers to SB. 'I've improved all round recently' probably refers to SP; 'my golf is better' to SPR. 'I force myself to be submissive to rich customers' refers to PR. 'I despise myself for it', describes SpPR. 'I never allow myself to . . .' might be SpaSc. 'I live for the day when I can . . .' is Spr. SS could be at the centre of 'I must be free, or die.'

Identity-choice is an existential concept. It is a choice made by the self and is not open to prediction. Whatever hand of cards we have picked up at the point of conception in consequence of the sexual re-shuffling of the genes, and however we have played and improved upon the cards we hold, however predictable the chances of the deal and the game situation are as probabilities, the nature of the life-game is that events repeatedly turn upon the identity assumed by the joker. That choice will determine strategy and the way the rest of the hand is structured for roles in partnership and encounter (see chapter 7). A final example will illustrate the use of the model in bringing psycho-dynamic interpretation into the understanding of relationship. The mechanisms of defence described by Anna Freud (1937) included identification with the aggressor, a form of altruism, and restriction of ego. Everyday expressions of these defences might be:

identification with the aggressor—

'If you can't beat them, join them.'

a form of altruism—

'If I stay at home and look after our invalid mother, you will be able to go to university. I shall enjoy hearing about your experiences.'

restriction of ego—

'Don't get too fond of anyone; then you can't get hurt.'

Tendencies to react defensively in these three modes are universal. Each of them, however, involves a choice of identity. Granted that the disposition is there, the decisive moment occurs when self lends itself to the disposition, confirms the defensive reaction and builds upon it. The psycho-analytic treatment invites self to free itself from commitment to this unprofitable location.

This requires a change of perspective. The possibility of this change however turns upon events in the past which have been built into the personality. Early psycho-analysis correctly identified processes in the personality. Advances in understanding now require a recognition that in working upon the ego, the analyst is engaged with the self, the perspectives, the location of identity and the project.

A re-phrasing of these three defensive modes in terms of identity means that they cease to be 'mechanisms'—a term that must always be repugnant to the subjective self. They become modes of relationship based on aggression, sacrifice and withdrawal—as described by Karen Horney (1942, 1946). The choice of identity converts the components of personality into components of relationship and becomes the central reference for role function. The location of identity thus becomes basic for an existential sociology. This would require that inter-personal relations are not seen as the inter-action of indifferentiated individuals. They are to be seen as involving the component sub-systems as organized on the basis of identity choice. Where behaviour is largely constrained by role, as in some military or industrial transactions, role-analysis may suffice for most purposes. 'Personality variables' may manifest themselves at any point, however, in styles of role performance, in role-distance or in the resolution of role conflict. If, after completion of a role, a shop assistant enters into a more 'personal' discussion with the customer, then both have changed roles and entered into a different role-relationship. We can speak of a personality-in-role relationship, and we may guess this is desired because it offers a chance for the expression and confirmation of identity—a basic need, as said earlier. It is unlikely that in a situation of this kind the perspectives would come into play, though they easily might if, for instance, the two started to exchange views on 'what suits me'. If the transaction between two people involves a proposal of marriage, case-work, therapy or a selection interview, the mutual and self-perspectives may well be the central components. In relationships described as encounters, confrontations, or intimacy, identity itself is likely to be at stake.

The model thus offers a four-level system for the classification of inter-personal relationships. For instance, there are role-relations with little involvement of personality and identity (which may indeed be antipathetic to the required role performance). Second, there are personality-in-role relations, with more or less involvement of perspectives and identity. Third, there are relationships primarily concerned with perspectives, and fourth, there are those where identity is central. By far the largest proportion of relationships belong in the first two classes. These will accommodate John Morris's categories of routine and ritual.

Relationships which bring perspectives and identity into question belong in his third category—they are dramatic, fraught with consequences, uncertain in outcome.

The relationships as classified above are thought of as complementary. There will also be crossed relationships, as when one person attempts to personalize a transaction while the other wishes to confine it strictly to business. A radical or a religious person might wish to challenge the other person's identity choice, who might counter by attempting to establish a more comfortable personality-in-role relationship. Probably it will appear that in most transactional sequences there is a rapid move towards one or other option, but the system would also facilitate analysis of conflict.

A visual representation

Some people find it helpful to think of concepts visually. They develop three-dimensional images of models as systems of forces. It is not necessary to do this, but a possible gain is in the direction of clarity, and for this reason this essay ends with a schematic diagram.

The original self is without form. Experiences are unco-ordinated.

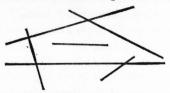

The mother–child role relationship and later role training establish the foundations of a personality;

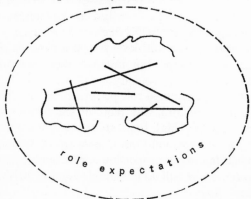

later the child can look at himself, and look at the way others look at him.

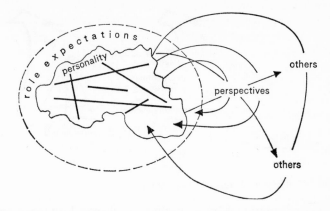

He makes an identity choice, usually finalized on becoming adult. Here the model becomes three-dimensional, and is in movement towards the project.

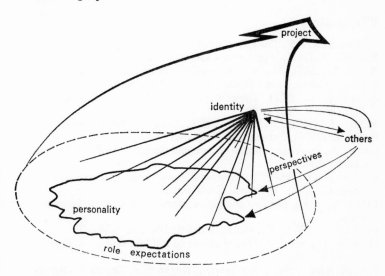

This permits a representation of the four classes of relationship.

This representation is of course static and it does not reveal the possible conjunctions, separations and oppositions of personality, role and identity. A representation might be attempted with a series of diagrams in colour, and it is hoped that some readers will be stimulated to develop their own. Such readers will probably accept

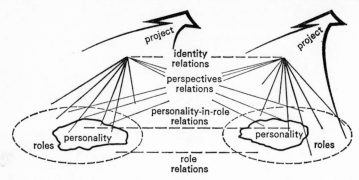

Figure 5.2   The four levels of relationship

the value of model-making, as outlined in chapter 1, in that a main function of models is the suppression of data in order to throw into sharp relief a few significant components.

Bibliography

Banton, M. (1965), *Roles*, Tavistock.

Benedict, R. (1935), *Patterns of Culture*, Routledge.

Berger, P. (1966), *Invitation to Sociology*, Penguin.

Berne, E. (1966), *Games People Play*, André Deutsch.

Binswanger, L. (1958), 'The existential analysis school of thought', in *Existence*, R. May *et al.*

Buber, M. (1959), *I and Thou*, T. & T. Clark (2nd British edn).

Burke, K. (1970), *University of California Press*.

Cooley, C. H. (1902), *Human Nature and the Social Order*, New York, Charles Scribner.

Cooper, D. G. (1967), *Psychiatry and Anti-Psychiatry*, Tavistock.

Erikson, E. (1968), *Youth and Crisis*, Faber.

Freud, A. (1937), *The Ego and the Mechanisms of Defence*, Hogarth Press.

Goffman, E. (1961), *Encounters*, Indianapolis, Bobbs-Merrill.

Holman, R. (1966), 'The foster child and self knowledge', in *Case Conference*, March.

Horney, Karen (1942), *Self Analysis*, Kegan Paul, Trench & Trubner.

Horney, Karen (1946), *Inner Conflicts*, Routledge & Kegan Paul.

Kardiner, A. (1945), *The Psychological Frontiers of Society*, Columbia University Press.

Klein, M. (1948), *Contributions of Psycho-Analysis 1921–1945*, Hogarth Press.

Laing, R. D. (1967), *The Politics of Experience*, Penguin.

Laing, R. D. (1967), *The Bird of Paradise*, Penguin.

Laing, R. D., Phillipson, H., and Lee, A. R. (1966), *Interpersonal Perception*, Tavistock.

Linton, R. (1947), *The Cultural Background of Personality*, Routledge.

May, R. (ed.) (1961), *Existential Psychology*, New York, Random House.

Mead, G. H. (1934), *Mind, Self and Society*, University of Chicago Press.

Mead, G. H., ed. Anselm Strauss (1965), *Social Psychology*, University of Chicago Press.

Mounier, E. (1948), *Existentialist Philosophies*, Rockliff.

O'Connor, P. (1963), *Vagrancy*, Penguin.

Pascal, B., ed. Lafuna (1958), *Pensées*, Paris, Le Club du Meilleur Livre.

Polanyi, M. (1962), *Personal Knowledge*, Routledge & Kegan Paul.

Robertson, R. (1970), *The Sociological Interpretation of Religion*, Blackwell.

Ruddock, Ralph (1969), *Roles and Relationships*, Routledge & Kegan Paul.

Shaw, G. B. (1952), *Selected Prose*, New York, Dodd Mead.

Sullivan, H. S. (1953), *Conceptions of Modern Psychiatry*, New York, Norton.

Weinstein, E. A. (1960), *The Self-Image of the Foster Child*, Russel Sage Foundation.

Winnicot, D. W. (1965), *The Maturational Processes and the Facilitating Environment*, Hogarth Press.

Wolfenstein, M. & Mead, M. (eds) (1955), *Childhood in Contemporary Cultures*, University of Chicago Press.

Wright, D. (1970), 'Meditating', *Listener*, 12 November.

6 The personal imperative: a study of the evidence for self-actualization

John W. Shaw

Introduction

Psychology has already made an extensive contribution to our knowledge of emotional and intellectual development in childhood and youth. Some acquaintance with studies in this field is considered part of the necessary equipment of professional workers in many fields.

There is a growing body of work, stemming from both academic and clinical sources, which seems to show that these developmental processes point towards the larger concept of 'self-actualization'. These studies, if satisfactorily replicated and widely accepted, will place the idea of individual development into a lifelong context and call for a considerable shift in our view of the human person.

The following quotation (Kahn, 1969) illustrates the point:

> We have been accustomed to thinking that all growing stops at the end of adolescence. It is true that height cannot increase once the bony structure is complete. Perhaps it was on the analogy of this that it was thought that intelligence reached its maximum before the beginning of adult life. Psychologists are now prepared to think of further stages of intellectual development, and there is no structural limitation for this such as there is for physical growth. Ideas about *emotional* growth have never been able to be expressed in precise language, but it seems credible that every relationship with another individual can add something to one's personality. This is part of the process of growing-up which can continue even into the stage of life when we must admit to growing old.

Adult life, however, has a variety and complexity about it that makes the choice of the crucial parameters of adult development difficult. A survey, for example, which Marie Jahoda (1958), made of the many ideas associated with the concept of 'mental health' led her to formulate six major categories of human functioning. These were acceptance of oneself, realizing one's potential, integration of one's various mental functions, a relative independence of social pressures, adequate perception of reality, and adequacy in love, work and play. There are also important lists of personality factors, obtained by factorial analysis of hundreds of traits and preferences, which must surely include crucial parameters.

Alternatively, we may turn, for our insight into adult functioning, to psychological research which is narrower in its focus, for example, Rokeach's studies (1960) of open-mindedness and closed-mindedness. The open-minded individual in contrast to the closed-minded person, has a greater ability to form new systems, whether perceptual, cognitive or aesthetic. He does not set as high a valuation on external authority. His beliefs are not compartmentalized to the same extent. Nor does he hold oversimplified views about beliefs held by others but not shared by himself. Rokeach also found that open–closed-mindedness was a more fundamental characteristic about belief systems than left of centre/right of centre in politics, religion/atheism, intelligence/dullness. For Rokeach found that a highly educated expert might equally likely be open-minded or closed-minded.

In searching for the parameters of adult development and functioning, it may be useful to look in yet another direction. The way the adult performs his major professional social roles has been recognized as a crucial index of satisfactory functioning. Jourard (1964) has described the phenomenon of stereotyped role-behaviour, that is, performing a role in a standard procrustean manner which involves the suppression of one's spontaneous self. The ill-effects on the performer seem even greater than the ill-effects on the client, for Jourard argues that the individual does violence to his own needs, through failing to be aware of them and hence to give them expression.

Jourard feels that satisfactions all round are increased and personal growth is facilitated when people perform their roles spontaneously, according to the needs of the client and the demands of the situation.

Turning to the question of motivation, we find that the most influential theory of motivation among psychologists is a need-reduction theory. This is the model of the organism as possessing an inbuilt capacity for homeostasis. When satisfaction of certain needs falls below a certain safe level, the organism is impelled to take action to restore the deficiency. The overall picture of man here is of a well-constructed system with feedback mechanisms to enable certain levels of input and output to be kept constant. But the kind of motivation implied by self-actualization would be more dynamic and would include an impulse within an organism to transcend the *status quo* and move towards higher levels of functioning.

Two related questions

There are two questions that require an answer. First, is there evidence that human motivation is more than the protection of the developmental *status quo*, as the theory just mentioned describes? Second, if the motivation question is settled, do we have any parameters of optimal human functioning? To a consideration of these two questions we now turn.

The most penetrating analysis of motivation theory published in recent years is that by A. H. Maslow (1954). Basic to his analysis is the following complaint:

> Current conceptions of motivation proceed on the assumption that a motivational state is a special, a peculiar state, sharply marked off from the other happenings in the organism.
> Sound motivation theory should, on the contrary, assume that motivation is constant, neverending, fluctuating and complex, and that is an almost universal characteristic of practically every organismic state of affairs.

He adds that this error combined with the lack of serious attempts to integrate into a system 'atomistic lists of drives', plus the failure to recognize the crucial role of long-term unconscious goals, make a new theory of motivation urgent.

Maslow, having diagnosed the need, formulates a theory to meet it. He argues that the basic human needs are organized into a hierarchy of relative prepotency. The physiological needs (e.g. for food, water, warmth and sleep) occupy the bottom level in the hierarchy. If they are ungratified, all other needs are non-existent.

But when well gratified, the next level in the hierarchy comes into play. This level consists of the 'safety needs' which are satisfied for the normal adult when he finds himself in a peaceful, stable, smoothly running society. But these needs become dominant again in natural and political emergencies. When physiological and safety needs are regularly being gratified, a yet higher level of needs becomes potent, the 'belongingness and love' needs. At a higher level still are the 'esteem needs'. Finally, if all the previous four levels are regularly gratified, the need to actualize oneself emerges.

Maslow's own description (1954) may help to fix for us the meaning of this perhaps strange term.

> Even if all these needs (of the first four levels) are satisfied, we may still often (if not always) expect that a new discontent and restlessness will soon develop, unless the individual is doing what he is fitted for. A musician must make music, an artist must paint, and poet must write, if he is ultimately to be at peace with himself. What a man *can* be, he *must* be. This need we may call self-actualisation.

Lest it be thought that Maslow's 'need to self-actualize' is only found in those with artistic abilities, he stresses the desires to know and to understand as a vital part of human functioning at an optimal level. The human organism if not cognitively involved falls into boredom, self-dislike and general depression of bodily functions. For such conditions, Maslow advocates 'cognitive therapy'. For example, taking up an intellectually more demanding job or immersing oneself in something more worthy of one.

If Maslow's hierarchy seems unduly rigid, it must be pointed out that he makes a number of important qualifications to his theory. First, there can be exceptions to the hierarchical order. For example, there are some people for whom self-esteem is more important than love. Second, the higher needs emerge gradually out of the growing satisfaction of the lower needs. One hundred per cent satisfaction of any need is extremely unlikely. But the higher needs become stronger as the lower needs are more generously satisfied. Third, all behaviour is multi-motivated and is usually the expression of a variety of needs. Fourth, Maslow makes the interesting statement that levels of needs, once very fully gratified, cease to play an important part in a person's motivation. A need with a long history of gratification ceases to be a motivator. Fifth, a related point, aspects of people become functionally autonomous. For example, loss of popularity and love can be withstood by one whose basic needs are gratified. Such a person can live without it. Its absence is not a totally threatening experience.

The term 'self-actualization' and its synonyms seems now to be fully established in the literature of psychology. Cofer and Appley, writing in 1964, list ten major theorists who have placed the notion, or something very like it in a central position. Their list is as follows:

Kurt Goldstein	Self-actualisation
Erich Fromm	The productive orientation
Prescott Lecky	The Unified Personality
Snygg and Combs	The preservation and enhancement of the phenomenal self
Karen Horney	The real self and its realisation
David Riesman	The autonomous person
Carl Rogers	The fully functioning person
Rollo May	Existential being
A. H. Maslow	Self-actualisation
G. W. Allport	Creative Becoming

If one, therefore, regards consensus and convergence as providing some grounds for assuming the correctness of a principle, then this is a very powerful case, especially when one realizes that these users of the concept are from very different disciplines, e.g. psychiatry, psycho-analysis, sociology and academic psychology. In a survey of the evidence, Cofer and Appley conclude that it is as yet inadequate. But I believe that a detailed study of the case made out by Maslow and a comparison of this case with parallel arguments from, say, Rogers and Allport, would leave the reader convinced. It would leave him feeling that life can be, under certain conditions, the continuous unfolding of unrealized potentiality.

Self-actualizing people

We turn, then, to our second question, viz. the characteristics of those people who are experiencing the 'self-actualizing' motivation of which Maslow speaks. He offers the beginning of an answer to this. He set out to find a group of individuals who could be identified as self-actualizing people and from a study of whom he could find the characteristics of optimal functioning. His negative criterion for inclusion in the group was an absence of neurosis, psychopathic personality or psychosis; and, positively, they should seem to be fully using their talents and capacities and doing the best they are capable of. His final group numbered forty-five people and included acquaintances, friends and public and historical figures.

The outcome of Maslow's study may best be summarized by listing the fifteen characteristics which, as he admits, is the analysis of his overall impression of these people and not a quantitative conclusion. The analysis is as follows:

1. They have a more than usually efficient perception of reality and more comfortable relations with it. That is, they perceive others more accurately and they tolerate uncertainty better.

2. They show acceptance of self and others. That is, they have relatively little guilt, shame or anxiety. They are not defensive about their shortcomings.

3. They live spontaneously. But they are not unconventional for its own sake and will suppress unconventionality for the sake of others' feelings.

4. They are not ego-centred. Rather are they oriented to solving problems outside themselves. They often have a mission in life.

5. They do not avoid privacy and actually seek it. They can detach themselves and look at things objectively.

6. They are autonomous. That is, they are able to be relatively independent of the general social environment in which they live.

7. They continually derive ecstasy, inspiration and strength from the basic and ordinary experiences of life.

8. They often have peak experiences. These are quasi-mystical experiences involving the feeling of being outside time and space. And following these experiences they have the conviction that something extremely important and valuable has happened.

9. The term '*gemeinschaftsgefuhl*' best describes their feelings for mankind. That is, they have a feeling of identification, sympathy and affection for mankind, although they are realistic about the shortcomings of the species.

10. Their inter-personal relationships can be very deep but usually with a few rather than with many individuals. They are capable of expressing hostility, but such hostility is re-active rather than chronic.

11. They have a democratic character-structure. That is, they can learn from, and relate to, people, irrespective of class, education, race and religion.

12. They feel it important to differentiate between means and ends. But, while they never lose sight of the end within the means, they can enjoy the means without impatience.

13. They are characterized by a sense of humour which is philosophical and non-hostile.

14. They are creative in the sense that one can be a creative carpenter or clerk. This creativity appears in their everyday life as an expression of a personality which is perceptive, spontaneous, expressive, childlike and which shows no fear of the unknown.

15. They are not well-adjusted in the naïve sense of approving of, and being identified with, their culture. They can relate satisfactorily to their culture in various ways but they maintain, in a profound way, a certain inner detachment from the culture in which they are immersed. (A. H. Maslow (1954), pp. 199–228, contains a full account of methods and findings in this study of psychological health.)

These characteristics are not a description of ideal people, written from a particular moral standpoint. They are a description of what Maslow found when he looked at certain people who were living life to the full, who were happy and who were finding fulfilment in life. Maslow (1954, p. 228) emphasizes that these people are not perfect. They have many ordinary human failings and can, on occasion, be ruthless, can alienate others, and can be indifferent to others' needs.

Maslow concluded that the self-actualizing person does not *need* love, hence his approach to the 'other' is not as a means to some end but is rather an end in itself. So that enjoyment, admiration, delight, contemplation and appreciation, rather than *use*, characterize the expression of love in the self-actualizing person. Maslow calls this kind of love, B-love (i.e. love for the other person's being) as opposed to D-love (i.e. deficiency-love, or selfish or neurotic love) (Maslow, 1954, ch. 13).

On the transcendental, or 'peak experiences', referred to above, Maslow points out that such experiences can come to anyone at any time. But he adds that, perhaps, they are more frequent, intense and perfect in the self-actualizing person than in the average person.

I believe that in this work of Maslow we have the broad outline of our parameters of optimal human functioning. No other writer has analysed the nature of the self-actualizing person with the same amount of detail as Maslow has. But there is considerable support from other psychologists for many of the characteristics he describes.

Allport (1961) defines psychological maturity as follows:

1. There are specific enduring extensions of the self (i.e., relationships with individuals and groups, loyalties and interests) (cf. Maslow's list, no. 10).

2. There are dependable techniques for warm relating to others (cf. Maslow, nos 9 and 11).

3. There is stable emotional security or self-acceptance (cf. Maslow, no. 2).

4. There are habits of realistic perception (cf. Maslow, no. 1).

5. There are skills and problem-centredness (cf. Maslow's nos 4 and 14).

6. There is established self-objectification in the form of insight and humour (cf. Maslow, no. 13).

7. There is a unifying philosophy of life, including a differentiated religious sentiment and a personalized conscience (cf. Maslow, nos 8 and 12).

Allport's description is not derivative from Maslow, but stems from his own work on 'creative becoming'.

Further support is to be found in the writings of Carl Rogers. His description of the 'fully functioning person' (1967, pp. 183–99) consists of the following:

1. Openness to experience, i.e. has self-awareness and self-acceptance (cf. Maslow, nos 1 and 2).

2. Existential living, i.e. living fully and in each moment (cf. Maslow, no. 7).

3. Organismic trusting, i.e. relying on the spontaneous decision rather than on the rigid pre-conceived category as a basis for decision (cf. Maslow, no. 3).

4. Experiential freedom, i.e. experiences himself as someone who feels free in his choices (cf. Maslow, no. 6).

5. Creativity, i.e. the ability to produce new and effective thoughts, actions and things (cf. Maslow, no. 14).

Such a list hardly does justice either to Rogers's descriptions of the fully functioning person or to its similarity to Maslow's self-actualizing person. His descriptions are very rich and detailed. And his composite picture of the fully functioning person (ibid., pp. 195–6) is one of the most exciting passages of modern psychology.

The contribution of depth psychology

I think one would expect to see a contribution to this subject from psycho-analysis. For the 'man in the street' is surely right in thinking of 'analysis' as a means to self-development. However, Freud himself thought of analysis as a medical matter, a means of removing the conflicts that produce neurotic symptoms. This was his goal and when it was achieved, the analysis was over. He, at least, did not claim that 'analysis' had a larger role than this.

Jung, however, went beyond the notion of analysis as a medical exercise. He says, 'psychotherapy has to spread far beyond the confines of somatic medicine and psychiatry into regions that were formerly the province of priests and philosophers' (C. G. Jung, 1954, p. 122). He was faced with numbers of patients who, although successfully treated for their neuroses, wanted to continue in analysis to try to understand the senselessness and aimlessness of their lives. This led Jung into areas of experience denied to others who took a strictly medical view of analysis. It led him to concepts of motivation and fulfilment similar to those already discussed, although expressed in a different phraseology.

He discovered a basic human motivation towards wholeness, called by him 'individuation'. His teaching is not systematic, but a number of points can be made by way of clarification of the concept. It is not an urge to perfection, but towards completion. It is a modest striving to fulfil ourselves and to be as complete human beings as possible. This is deliberately vague, for he says 'Since life only exists in the form of living units, i.e. individuals, the law of life always tends towards life individually lived' (1934, p. 179). But Jung did, on a number of occasions, expound his ideas more fully.

In his lectures at the Tavistock clinic in 1935 (published in 1968), Jung indicated four stages in the treatment of the transference, i.e. the subjective factors which the patient projects upon the analyst:

1. the realization by the patient that he is projecting the authority figures of his early experience on to the analyst and that he has to recognize the projections as parts of himself to be assimilated.

2. personal and impersonal projections have to be distinguished; personal projections are dissolved by realization (as in 1 above); but impersonal projections are not dissolved, rather they are to be transferred from the analyst to a more suitable receptacle. Jung gives the

example of a 'saviour complex'; a Saviour is a reasonable expectation but the analyst cannot fill the bill.

3. a natural gratitude towards the analyst must be distinguished from a tendency to worship him. The problem of the transference which is based on impersonal factors is solved if the patient can join a church or adopt a religious creed. But if the patient cannot do this, then he falls back on the transference again and again. And the relationship with the analyst is vitiated by unreasonable demands and expectations.

4. individuation, therefore, is, in Jung's view, the only way possible for coming to terms with the 'impersonal images' for those who cannot objectify them through religious or spiritual belief of some kind.

As Jung says of these images, 'they have to take a form, they have to live their characteristic life, otherwise the individual is severed from the basic function of the psyche, and then he is neurotic, he is discontented and in conflict with himself. But if he is able to objectify them and relate them, he is in touch with his vital psychological functions' (1968, p. 187).

So, in Jung's view, 'religions are psychotherapeutic systems' (ibid., p. 181), because they give form and expression to deep psychological needs, and in so doing give to an individual depth and stability. But the problem for many modern individuals is that they find our traditional religions archaic and unacceptable. Hence, Jung's concern with finding a method for the modern individual of giving form and expression to these needs.

The method is based on *creative play* with the spontaneous fantasies of the unconscious mind. As Jung said, 'My aim is to bring about a psychic state in which my patient experiments with his own nature—a state of fluidity, change and growth where nothing is eternally fixed and hopelessly petrified ... I learned this from Freud's method of free association and I regard it as a direct extension of that' (C. G. Jung, 1954, p. 46).

The natural starting-point for individuation is dream-analysis, but Jung asserted that his aim was to wean the patient from this dependence on the analysts' interpretative powers and to initiate in him the process of *active imagination*. This begins, first of all, in the subject being urged to paint, draw or model particularly vivid dreams. But, fundamentally, *active imagination* is a waking method of getting in touch with the unconscious through drawing, painting, modelling, dancing, playing a musical instrument, weaving and, of course, writing.

Jung gives many examples of how the process may start for an individual, for example, a poster, a photograph, a painting, a dream or a hypnogogic image may impress itself upon him. As one looks at the picture, it begins to move and the characters come to life. Or one, as it were, steps into a painting and one can, according to many reports, have experiences that have a force or vividness quite distinct from that found in fantasies of one's own invention. Or, as one concentrates on a mental picture, it begins to stir, the image becomes enriched by details, it moves and develops and a series of images are given which add up to a complete event. (For an example of *active imagination*, see Field, 1950, p. 21.)

The effects of this process are manifold:

1. the images anticipate one's dreams and the dream material begins to peter out.

2. the material produced is better than dream material, being far richer in feeling, visibility and logical cohesion.

3. the images contain a large amount of archetypal material. What these archetypes mean must be pointed out to the individual, for in order to benefit from these images he must see them not as queer subjective experiences, but as typical, ever-recurring expressions of the objective processes of the human psyche (C. G. Jung, 1968, p. 195).

4. the products of 'creative imagination' are artistically worthless and should be considered so; for the question at issue is not art, but an attempt to give form, however crude, to the inexpressible, and thus to give it a living effect upon the individual.

5. the struggle to express one's phantasies concretely increases their effect upon one: for 'the concrete shaping of the image enforces a continuous study of it in all its parts . . . this invests the bare phantasy with an element of reality which lends it greater weight and greater driving power' (Jung, 1954, p. 49).

6. the individual is made autonomous, more mature, for he finds that unpleasant moods can be brought under control by working at his symbolic pictures and so he has a means of obtaining release when it is needed.

7. the individual becomes aware that there is a living force working within him and that it is not the personal ego; for the personal ego itself is the object (not the subject) of this living force. He realizes

that by giving form to these phantasies he is, in fact, shaping himself. He becomes fascinated by the motive of this interior agent, but discovers that it cannot be captured or known. Practical discovery, through painting and other methods, of this interior force and its developmental urge, shifts a person's centre and standpoint. 'The ego is by definition subordinate to the self and is related to it like a part to the whole' (C. G. Jung, 1951, p. 5).

8. In sum, 'it would seem to be some kind of centring process, for a great many pictures which the patients feel to be decisive point in this direction. During this centring process what we call the ego appears to take up a peripheral position. The change is apparently brought about by an emergence of the historical part of the psyche . . . Exactly what is the purpose of this process remains at first sight obscure. We can only remark its important effect on the unconscious personality' (ibid., p. 51).

Freud's view of the unconscious was that it largely consisted of disagreeable aspects of consciousness which had been repressed or forgotten. Jung believed that if Freud's view of the unconscious were right, then a normal ego would be synonymous with wholeness, since little of importance would have been lost to the unconscious. It is fundamental to Jung's view, however, that the process of individuation is the process that makes an individual a 'whole man' by uniting the knowledge and skills possessed by the ego with the historical meanings that he finds in his deepest unconscious.

Jung told his students that the systematic elaboration of his ideas was a task that they would have to take on, if there were to be any progress in the science of analytical psychology. Jolande Jacobi (1967) has attempted to systematize Jung's ideas and some of her distinctions are important for our understanding of the *individuation* process.

There are two kinds of individuation. First, the natural process, occurring more or less autonomously and without the participation of consciousness. And, second, there is the artificial process (Jacobi's term), which is aided, for example, by analysis, and which is developed by definite methods and is consciously experienced.

In both forms, the same power is at work, striving for maturation and self-realization. But the two forms are as different as, say, a wild fruit and a highly cultivated one. Of the natural process, she says, 'there are people who, entirely by themselves, without using special methods or needing any guidance, let alone the help of analysis, win

to that wholeness and wisdom which are the fruit of a life consciously experienced and assimilated, all its battles fought' (ibid.,
p. 17).

But she adds that in many cultures, forms of discipline have
existed to facilitate the process. Jung does not call in question the
natural individuation process, no more than do any of the other
disciplines, from all parts of the world, that are now coming to light.
He seeks only to supplement and deepen the natural process.

Jung does not have a sequential pattern of the complexity of
Maslow's hierarchy of needs, but he does recognize that there is a
logical chronology of development through human life. In the first
half of life, as Jung refers to the period of young adulthood, the
aim of individuation is adaptation of the person to outer reality—
work, the family and society. A Jungian analyst would see neurosis at
this stage of life, in terms of the goals of individuation, i.e. a neurotic
person is one who has started along the wrong road and is trying,
therefore, to develop in a quite inappropriate way.

The goals of individuation in the second half of life, i.e. from
middle age onwards, attracted most of Jung's attention. He believed
that it was at this point in life that the need for self-realization
assumes its greatest importance. If the need is recognized by the
individual and the methods which assist the process are taken up,
then life can be given fresh meanings and the characteristic sense
of loss in middle age, of which depression is a symptom, can be
overcome. Jung also taught that individuation includes a psychic
preparation for death.

The course of individuation, leading to wholeness, is not linear;
it is more like a spiral. And in analyses in the first half of life, the
preoccupation is with the *shadow*, Jung's term for the repressed
disagreeable aspects of oneself. In the second half, the preoccupation
is with the anima/animus, Jung's terms for the unconscious contra-
sexual characteristics. Beyond these figures lie others essential to
development, but unconsciousness is not broad enough to accommodate them until the *shadow* and the *anima* have been accepted and
assimilated.

The goal of the process of individuation is a synthesis of all
psychic aspects of both conscious and unconscious. This synthesis is
called the self. The ego stands to the self as the moved to the mover,
or as object to subject. If the process succeeds an ego-self axis is
established. The dynamic function of this axis is to give the in-

dividual an inner certainty and a feeling of security, as though he were contained in an all-embracing whole.

Jung sums up what people have to say about their experience of becoming individuated. 'They came to themselves, they could accept themselves, they were able to become reconciled to themselves; and thus were reconciled to adverse circumstances and events' (1958, p. 81). This is the phenomenon of self-acceptance, which was also found by Maslow to be a common characteristic of his self-actualizing people.

A search through Jung's voluminous writings reveals a number of other characteristics of *individuated persons*.

a. They live their own lives, rather than seeking mainly to adapt.

b. Being individuated is a form of human dignity, which is not simply based on recognition by the mass.

c. They strike a balance between being true to themselves and being a member of the collective.

d. They are not outstandingly intelligent nor necessarily talented in any other way. Anyone can with the right determination achieve relative wholeness.

e. They can tolerate isolation, for they are not totally dependent on the value-judgments of their fellows.

f. Despite their capacity for isolation, they are not recluses. Their relationship to their fellows becomes more tolerant, deeper, more responsible and more understanding. They can open themselves with greater freedom, since they need not fear that the other will take possession of them, or that they will lose themselves in the other.

g. The 'individuated person' does not suffer from the characteristics of individualism, namely ego-centredness and eccentricity. He recognizes his obligations and yet remains a whole self.

I believe that the reader will find substantial agreement between Jung's description of the 'individuated person' and Maslow's description of 'self-actualizing people'. Perhaps the only notable difference in the two lists presented is Maslow's emphasis on 'peak experiences' and their absence of mention in the statements I have taken from Jung's writings.

Maslow asserted that peak experiences occur in a variety of circumstances, such as 'in the B-love experience, the parental experience, the mystic or oceanic, or nature experience, the aesthetic perception, the creative moment, the therapeutic or intellectual insight, the orgasmic experience, certain forms of athletic fulfilment'

(1959, pp. 44–5). And about such experiences, individuals use such words as wonder, awe, unity, perfection, timelessness and meaningfulness. Jung's ambivalence towards religion and his fears of becoming involved in mysticism led him to play down this aspect of experience. But in his 'autobiography', published posthumously (Jaffe, 1967, ch. 10), there is a chapter entitled 'Visions', which indicates both the recurrence of such 'peak experiences' in Jung's own life and the profound impression they made upon him. He, in fact, regarded mystical experience as experience of archetypes (Jung, 1968, p. 110).

Practical implications

What are the implications of the discovery of the drive towards self-actualization and the type of personal adjustment it produces? I think the first implication is a practical one, i.e. it provides an empirical basis for a variety of agent–client relationships, which were previously justified mainly in moral or religious terms.

The teacher in the school situation has been provided by psychological research with an empirical basis for his work. For example, the primary teacher envisages himself as collaborating with the on-going process of maturation in the child. He can see himself as facilitating, and combining with, this process. The notion of a fixed intelligence has given way to the idea of potentiality, which can be restricted or fostered by the poverty or wealth of intellectual stimulation at appropriate times and in appropriate ways. Similarly, emotional development may be fostered or restricted. Thus the teacher's role is enhanced.

The university teacher, similarly, is able to set as his goal for his student the development of his understanding towards certain definable, and in some cases, attainable limits. With what processes, however, can the probation officer, the community development worker, the adult educationist, or a worker engaged in the rehabilitation of meths drinkers, be said to be combining?

Not all those in the 'helping professions' lack an empirical basis of some kind. Many of them can define certain behavioural goals which when achieved mark a successful outcome for their activities with a certain individual. But they need, one would think, more than this. They perhaps need to feel that they are facilitating certain organic processes within individuals, if their work is to be more than a well-intentioned attempt to 'sell' the average way of life to alienated people. I believe that the concept of self-actualization provides precisely this basis.

The adult educationist, especially, has the need for an empirical basis. His students are often the normal, well adjusted members of the community. His role is educational but it is not exactly the same role as that of his colleague who teaches undergraduates. He can see the minds of his students develop and their knowledge grow but he is also struck by their insistence on the practicality and relevance of what he teaches them to everyday life. They are often impatient with knowledge for its own sake. Here the role of the development of the intellect in self-actualization would seem to be crucial, what Maslow calls 'cognitive therapy'.

It is likely that the social worker whose main concern is with helping socially maladjusted clients to take a regular job, accept family responsibilities and become a normal member of society will see difficulties in the notion of self-actualization. For one is struck, in reading the evidence for self-actualization, by the independence and autonomy which it fosters in individuals. Self-actualization, if widely experienced, might begin to overturn social norms and prevailing values, the very goals that the social worker has for his clients.

But, in fact, normal social adjustment is usually the foundation upon which the self-actualizing person builds his further development. He does not deny normal social values but has a drive to transcend them. There is, however, in modern urban society, the problem of 'alienation', a term used by Marx and also by the existentialists to describe the experience of separation from fellow man, society, nature and oneself. The evidence from the self-actualizing person holds out hope that individuals in a modern urban society may be able to 're-appropriate' these relationships. It is the experience of self-actualization which could give the social worker more confidence in rebuffing the assertions of some clients that normal social adjustment is simply the road to deadness, unreality, or the treadmill of normal working life.

Personal development

The implication of the concept of self-actualization for personal development is obvious. The question one naturally asks is, 'how can one become a self-actualizing person?'

Therapy, especially as practised by existential, Jungian or eclectic psychotherapists is one way, albeit expensive, laborious and time-consuming. As one psychotherapist says, 'Psychotherapy is an attempt to assist people to cross a bridge between two worlds—the world of what we have been calling the "false self" and the world of the "true self"' (Doel, 1970, p. 132). Here the 'true self', as this writer uses the term, can be equated with the freer, more realistic, more complete self-insight and self-acceptance enjoyed by self-actualizing people.

Existential therapists assert that the transition from 'false' to 'true' self entails a dying to the old self, and a rebirth to the new self. And that this process is usually mirrored in a symbolic way in the spontaneous phantasy-life of the subject. The following spontaneous phantasy, recounted by a patient in therapy, is an example of this:

> I realised that the animal was my soul and that it was dying.
> God was there. I couldn't see him, but I could feel His
> presence. He burned the animal with such intense heat that
> even the ground became molten. I thought, 'He has destroyed
> me'. Then the ground healed over and all across the moor as far
> as I could see, there sprang up golden-headed wheat, which
> moved gently in the breeze. I thought, 'He has healed my soul,
> I am not sick any longer' (ibid., p. 133).

The client goes on to report changes in vision, a heightened awareness of life, and ecstasy in the simple perception of physical nature (ibid., p. 134). So that one has here the feeling of greater autonomy, a peak experience, the heightened perception, the ecstasy derived from ordinary experience—all of them characteristics of the self-actualizing person as defined by Maslow and all experienced within, and as a result of, a therapeutic relationship.

Unfortunately, therapy is ineffective with many people whose 'resistance' is so strong that the 'free association' method of traditional analysis is not able to bring to light repressed traumatic incidents or uncover crucial complexes. Nor, even when uncovered, can the insights of the therapist be accepted or self-acceptance be achieved. In the terminology of existential therapy, the ego is unable without assistance to make the perilous journey towards the authentic self.

It was for this reason that the availability of psychedelic drugs, before they were made illegal, proved a boon. Psycholytic therapy (using LSD in low dosage) became widely practised in Europe. *Rapport* was more rapidly established with the client; restricting defences were overcome; transferences were quicker; the core of the client's problem was more rapidly reached; insights were more readily accepted; and progress was more rapid and cures more striking (see Newland, 1963).

Naturally, the use of these drugs as psychedelic agents has attracted most attention. This consists in giving a larger dose of the drug and often results, for the subject, in a single overwhelming experience. It is, in our terminology, a drug-induced 'peak experience'. And it seems clear from the evidence that the 'peak experience' is a rather crucial phenomenon. For it is not only, as Maslow found, one of the characteristics of the self-actualizing person, but seems in itself the sort of experience that is likely to *lead to* the other behavioural characteristics associated with the self-actualizing person.

The utterances of those who undergo drug-induced peak experiences are no different from those who either have such experiences while in therapy (without drugs) or those to whom peak experiences simply occur. There is some disagreement among authorities as to whether there is any difference between 'drug-induced' and 'genuine' mystical experiences. Professor R. C. Zaehner (1957) concluded that drugs create merely a minor kind of 'preternatural experience'. But W. T. Stace, the Princeton philosopher and author of *Mysticism and Philosophy* (1961) is reported as replying, when asked about the authenticity of the drug-induced peak experiences that he had studied: 'It is not a matter of its being similar to mystical experiences. It is mystical experience' (Stafford and Golightly, 1969, p. 149). In other words, the natural and the artificially-assisted processes are at one in this respect, as, indeed, Jacobi says they are in all respects. These subjects say that life has meaning; they have been reborn; they have a new outlook on life; their conscious self is only a small function of the whole self; they have a feeling of well-being; colours and shapes astound them by their clarity; and so on. The possibility of drug-induced peak experiences is certainly very important; especially if we can feel more certain about the causative role of the peak experience in bringing about the total syndrome of behaviour associated with self-actualizing people.

Maslow makes use in his theorizing of the concept of a 'personality syndrome', a complex of thought, behaviour, drives and perception that has a common unity and a common purpose (1954, chapter 3). Because personality is organized in syndromes, particular aspects of individuals, such as radical beliefs or religious observance, will often have different significance in different people, depending on the total syndromes of which they are part. This applies equally to the characteristics of self-actualizing people, if taken in isolation. Non-hostile humour, for example, would have a different significance in a 'dependency' syndrome than in a self-actualizing syndrome.

Developing the notion of a syndrome further, Maslow goes on to argue that one-to-one, cause–effect relationships do not really help us to make sense of psychological change. Syndromes have a built-in resistance to change, but when change does take place, it tends to be change in the syndrome as a whole. External influences, if effective and significant, tend to change the whole human being and not just a bit or part of him. Small influences change the personality as a whole, albeit by only a small amount; large influences, like a peak experience, for example, may make a large impact and produce a radically different personality.

It is the phenomenon of the syndrome, its stability and persistence, but also its tendency to change as a whole, which can make the search for the peak experience meaningful (whether the methods used are the traditional ones of the mystical tradition or the modern chemical ones). A significant experience can reverberate throughout the psychic structure producing effects of a most unexpected, and apparently unrelated, kind. This phenomenon would, for example, explain the results obtained in changing the whole life-style of alcoholics by the use of drugs as psychedelic agents (Stafford & Golightly, 1969, pp. 104 ff.).

It has long been recognized that religious conversion has powers of character transformation. So the use of large doses of LSD with alcoholics, preceded by a carefully planned sequence of preparation and counselling, is intended to create a 'religious experience' which will propel the client into personality reformation. This technique is now well-developed, with the 'props' so well organized that the client invariably surrenders to the impact of the drug. Users of the technique with alcoholics report that the effect of the experience is to create in the subjects new feelings of compassion, tenderness, sensitivity and concern for others, in place of hardness, cynicism and rigidity. In the new state of perception fostered by the drug, the subject seems to be open to suggestions that can have long-lasting effects on behaviour. The relapse rate is reported as being low and the reason given is that the subject now seems to possess a resilience that enables him to cope with regression constructively.

In the light of evidence like this, and much more of a similar kind from other areas, there seems little doubt that the 'self-actualizing personality' is going to be sought by wider numbers of people. Whether the legal prohibition on the use of LSD and other chemical agents will lead to a resurgence of the methods used through the centuries by the mystics of achieving 'peak experiences' or to the methods of meditation favoured in the East, or to the continual growth of the black market in drugs, is not known. But the drive towards ego-transcendence is now perhaps more marked than ever before and will make itself felt.

It may well be, as Jung once suggested, that the growth of affluence and the overcoming, for many people, of the physical and social obstacles of want and poverty deprives the individual of an external arena into which his internal conflicts can be projected. As a result conflicts become more and more internalized, with a consequent increase in stress, neurosis, and their physical and social accompaniments. In short, in this sort of situation, self-actualization may become a prerequisite to survival.

One of the important implications of this research into self-actualization is the place it gives to creativity as one of the distinguishing features of optimal human functioning. What Maslow says is this:

> This creativeness appears in some of our subjects, not in the
> usual forms of writing books, composing music, or producing
> artistic objects, but rather may be much more humble. It is as if
> this special type of creativeness, being an expression of
> healthy personality, is projected out upon the world or touches
> whatever activity the person is engaged in. In this sense there
> can be creative shoemakers or carpenters or clerks (Maslow,
> 1954, p. 223).

This generalized creativeness noted by Maslow is very similar to a characteristic that Carl Rogers referred to in his description of the 'fully-functioning person'. Of them, Rogers (1967) says that they discover to an increasing degree that if they are 'open' to their experience, doing what feels right proves to be a competent and trustworthy guide to behaviour which is truly satisfying. They are surprised at their own intuitive skill in finding behavioural solutions to complex and troubling human relationships. It is only afterwards that they realize how surprisingly trustworthy their inner reactions have been in bringing about satisfactory behaviour.

It has been increasingly recognized that rigidity in, say, role-behaviour is a form of defensiveness designed to protect the individual from situations that he fears he may not be able to cope with, but which has, in fact, the long-term effect of increasing the strains on the organism and predisposing it to disease and disorder. The question for us here is whether a deliberate fostering of openness and creativeness in, say, professional role-behaviour would lead to other aspects of the self-actualizing syndrome, as the evidence seems to indicate is the case with the deliberately sought 'peak experience'.

Rigid interpersonal behaviour was called by Wilhelm Reich (1969) 'character armour' and he made it clear that the neurotic personality could deal with its central conflicts by developing a certain rigidity of behaviour rather than by manifesting symptoms. Reich proceeded in therapy with the intention of loosening the client's 'character armour'. This he would do by concentrating on the behaviour of the client, e.g., his silence, or his submissiveness, his complaints, or his tendency to provoke the analyst. Reich's aim was to try to arouse the client's interest in his own character traits in order to be able ultimately to explore analytically their origin and meaning. He aimed, therefore, to make the client self-conscious of his own behaviour; to confront him with a trait until he saw it as a harmful symptom and wanted to be rid of it. So, a submissive client, for example, when made fully aware of his submissiveness, tended to react with the aggression that the submissiveness had been designed since infancy to protect him from. Thus, the hidden conflicts which the character traits were designed to cover come to light and can be explored and, hopefully, dissolved.

Out of this insight into the importance of character armour, a whole 'technology' has developed of sensitivity training, of T-groups and process-groups—all situations, broadly, in which individuals can be made aware of their defensive character traits and of their function in the psychic economy. The experience of this type of training has confirmed Reich's view that the destruction of a character neurosis temporarily creates a condition which equals a breakdown of personality. But, as Reich also said, the method is highly potent, even if very unpleasant for the client.

Reich went on to develop the view that character armour could be expressed not only behaviourally but also in terms of bodily tension or muscular tension. He, therefore, began to introduce *doing* or *activity* into therapy. He himself worked at deepening the breathing of the client and at breaking down the muscular armour. And when these techniques led to the release of emotions, as they usually did, the client was encouraged to assist their release by hitting, kicking or yelling.

Out of all this pioneering work have emerged new kinds of group techniques which, doubtless, will be used more and more as a means of breaking down interpersonal rigidity. In such groups which are already functioning (e.g. the Esalen Institute, Centre 48 and C. R. Kelly's Interscience Work Shop), one may, through mutual assistance, arrive at a knowledge of one's own armourings as they are revealed in one's facial characteristics, gestures and posture. Again, the object is to move towards the syndrome of the self-actualizing person.

One might ask why do there seem to be so few self-actualizing persons? Society, it has been claimed by some, blocks the road to individuation by its false goals and the conformity on which it insists. Others, notably Theodor Reik, have seen the role of the parent as crucial in the destruction of their children's individuality. Quite clearly too, the dominance of the lower needs of the hierarchy leaves small opportunity for the higher needs to become salient. In many ways, therefore, man's alienation from his true self is accomplished, whether by education, religion, socialization or political systems of various kinds. But there is more to the issue than the finding of scapegoats of this kind.

The desire for ego-transcendence is very widespread and is expressed through the wide use of drugs, alcohol, revivalist religion and mass-participation of various kinds. But whatever traditions may have existed in the past in our society for channelling this desire in the direction of developing the 'authentic self' have become moribund or have disappeared without trace. Such knowledge as we now have relates largely to the extraverted side of man's nature. It is knowledge about how to exploit nature successfully, or to transport ourselves, or to communicate with each other, or it is knowledge of physical disease. There is no living tradition in the West, in any central position, of knowledge which is to do with ego-transcendence and self-development. The research referred to in this paper is as yet fairly peripheral in our consciousness.

The current emphasis by the younger generation on the transcendental, as expressed through the drug scene and the underground, represents a complete reversal of what was held to be, by the authorities on the life process, the true order of priorities throughout life. Youth and young adulthood was for adaptation to social reality, work, family and the laying of economic foundations, they said (see p. 138 above). Middle age and old age necessitated a growing preoccupation with the spiritual component of life—the transcendental element. But the reversal of this process now seems to indicate that there is a reaction by youth against the neglect of the ego-transcendent needs of man, especially at a time of change when man needs to be at his most flexible and creative. On the other hand, their parents can only point out that they are neglecting the more compelling concerns peculiar to their stage of life.

How can society organize itself so that the demands of the individual and of the collective can be reconciled? How, in short, can a harmonious social order still provide opportunities for the individual to actualize himself? B. F. Skinner, the experimental psychologist, described in *Walden Two* (p. 76) a fictional experiment in ordered community life. The community has no private property or money and strictly avoids all uncreative and uninteresting work.

> What we ask is that a man's work shall not tax his strength or
> threaten his happiness. Our energies can then be turned
> toward art, science, play, the exercise of skills, the satisfaction
> of curiosities, the conquest of nature, the conquest of man
> —the conquest of man himself but never of other men. We have
> created cuisine without slavery, a society which neither sponges
> nor makes war.

He describes a society in which there is complete equality of the sexes; the family unit is less important; and group care of children is recognized as an improvement on parental care. Each individual has eight or ten hours of leisure per day which can be spent in cultivating one's friendships, enjoying family relationships, being artistically creative, or simply resting. Crime is largely non-existent. In short, it is a utopian society in which man shall be able to realize himself fully. Additionally, it is a science-based utopia; for many of the strategies and techniques are derived from the behavioural psychology that Skinner practises.

There seems little doubt that people will want to set up the sort

of community in which the undoubted effectiveness of positive rein-
forcement can be applied in a total social setting. But membership
of a sheltered community, however effectively organized, will always
fail to appeal to certain types of person, who will see it as a form of
extended dependence that must be rejected.

On the other hand, the advocates of LSD envisage great opportunities for individuals to realize themselves, even without radical
changes in society, but provided that the new agents become legally
and socially acceptable (Stafford & Golightly, 1969, p. 255).

> Assuming that the stringent laws against responsible
> LSD use will be relaxed and that public sentiment will eventually
> appreciate the psychedelic's positive features, it can be
> assumed that the quality of life as we now know it has a
> first-rate chance of changing for the better.
>
> It is safe to predict that if LSD treatment of alcoholics is
> allowed to resume and is expanded, alcoholism will be dealt a
> crippling blow, bringing it within bounds as T.B. was curbed
> with isoniagid and polio with the salk and sabine vaccines.
>
> If organised religion decides to avail itself of LSD's efficacy in
> spiritual matters, the church may once again be a strong
> spiritual force.
>
> If guidance centres for those struggling with personal and
> psychological burdens are able to use the LSD in restructuring
> programmes, the nation's mental health problem could be vastly
> reduced.
>
> If gifted people in our schools and industries were allowed to
> participate in LSD programmes aimed at making the most of
> their creative abilities and stimulating peak production, we could
> anticipate a periclean age of achievement in all fields.

Both these authors and Skinner, in the previous section (see p. 148
above), claim for their visions the status of universal panaceas; but
this is no more than has been claimed many times in the past,
though usually by religious prophets or radical politicians.

It should be remembered that these two authors are not without
evidence for their conclusions. And as Dr S. C. Krippner (Director,
Dream Laboratory, Maimonides Medical Centre, Brooklyn, New
York), one of their academic authorities, points out: 'The currently
available data suggest that, under the proper conditions, psychedelic
drugs can enable the individual to cultivate those creative and

spiritual facets of his personality that so often remain unexplored' (Stafford & Golightly, 1969, p. 267).

In drawing the threads of this paper together, some comment is called for regarding the connection between (a) the scientific study of psychology, (b) the characteristics of the self-actualizing person and (c) the impact of these findings upon the whole science itself.

While scientific knowledge is usually sought for its own sake, the upshot is a technology leading to practical improvements, e.g., in improved transport, or engineering or in the making of artefacts, or the cure of diseases, etc. The science of psychology, as practised in universities, has already generated a technology of better selection methods, interviewing, educational approaches, diagnosis of mental patients, etc. All this is quite apart from psychoanalysis, begun by Freud and carried on in a variety of forms by Adler, Jung and others, which can be included here under the heading of psychological technology.

If one reminds oneself what the scientific subject-matter of psychology is, one knows quite clearly what the likely developments in the technology of psychology will be. If the optimal functioning of the person is the concern of psychology, then the technology which will inevitably be generated more and more, may be expected to lead to improved ways of using the mind, for example, in practical situations. For technology is, above all things, practical.

In the realm of the mind we have lived so far largely in a pre-technological era. And the dawn of any technological era is always greeted with dismay and anxiety; just as the first flying-machines were regarded as blasphemous, so similar reactions can be expected and have been expressed about modern psychology. Argyle, who has extensively studied 'eye-contact', refers in his book, *Social Interaction*, to some of the fears his book has generated. One of his friends told him after reading its analysis of interaction, 'I'll never be able to look you in the eye again' (1970, p. 432). Similarly, it will take us some time to accept that the artificially-induced 'peak experience' is as valid as the spontaneous one. Or that there is nothing blasphemous in defining self-actualizing behaviour and in seeking ways to compensate for the fact that spontaneous growth towards self-actualization usually only happens to a fortunate few.

If the person is an embodied mind, then the technological

approach which is now accepted towards the body, needs to be extended towards the mind and towards individual development and functioning at all stages of life. I think that the importance of the work on self-actualizing persons is that it highlights further the need for this acceptance. This technological or scientific view means a refusal to accept that, for example, problem-solving should be laborious and time-consuming; that failure (either through neurosis or psychosis) to develop towards self-actualization has just got to be accepted; that the alcoholic is just stuck with his problem; that 'writer's block' (or any other hindrance to creativity) is insoluble; that our central beliefs (even when out-dated) cannot really be changed; or that genuinely multi-racial communities cannot be created. In short, the study of optimal human functioning is not a threat to freedom, but a contribution to it. Though, as we are discovering with other technologies, any technology can be abused.

Consider the following description of the 'creative individual' (Dr F. Barron, quoted in Stafford & Golightly, 1969, p. 59):

> The thing that *was* important was something that might be
> called a cosmological commitment. It was a powerful motive to
> create meaning and to leave a testament of the meaning
> which that individual found in the world, and in himself in
> relation to the world. This motive emerged in many ways, but
> we came across it over and over again when we compared
> highly creative individuals with those of equal intellectual ability
> as measured by the I.Q. tests, but of less creative ability. The
> intense motivation having to do with this making of meaning—
> or finding meaning and communicating it in one form or
> another—was the most important difference between
> our criterion and control groups.

The technological approach to the person, as I have called it, would I think, be characterized by a refusal to accept that the differences between these two groups, the creative and the not so creative, was permanent or fixed.

Potentially, the technology of psychology could cause the greatest anxieties of all, besides which the fears about the atomic or hydrogen bomb would look small. How this can be avoided remains an important problem for the technology itself to solve.

Summary

The evidence for the possibility of lifelong psychological development is now strong. Crucial questions remain, however, regarding the nature of this development and how success or failure in this development can be measured.

The hierarchy of needs of Maslow gives a pattern for the optimal course of human development and this analysis is substantiated by others, for example, in the life-maintenance/life-enhancement distinction dream by Kurt Goldstein (1939, p. 197). In the fifteen characteristics of self-actualizing people of Maslow, in Allport's description of psychological maturity, and in Rogers's description of the fully functioning person, we have substantial agreement on the parameters of optimal human functioning.

Jung's concept of 'individuation' is expanded at length because of its chronological significance. For, as Hall and Lindzey say in *Theories of Personality*, Jung was the first to use the phrase 'self-actualization'. One of his important conclusions is that the process lends to the emergence of the 'self' and the ego moves to a peripheral position in the economy of the psyche.

The implications for teachers, social workers and the individual are explored. Modern forms of psychotherapy are possible means of self-actualization. But what of other techniques? Can the deliberate creation of 'peak experiences' by chemical means make the sort of impact on a personality that will lead to radical progress towards self-actualization? Much of the evidence seems to give a positive answer and the signs are that the search for ego-transcendence, especially among the young, will continue to grow.

Another way of facilitating self-actualization in individuals lies in the rapid growth of groups devoted to helping individuals to break down interpersonal rigidity by providing one with feedback about facial expressions, gesture, posture, mannerisms, etc. Rigid and stereotyped interpersonal behaviour is not normally found in self-actualizing people, and experiences resulting from these techniques may well provide a breakthrough for individuals towards optimal human functioning.

Forms of social organization are obviously crucial in fostering self-actualization. For it is clearly impossible in certain sorts of social environment to practise the openness to experience which is fundamental to self-actualization. Utopias derived from the findings of the behavioural sciences are proposed by some as the answer to the need for suitable social milieux. Others believe that even if our social structure remains broadly the same, enormous progress could be made in reducing the incidence of certain social problems if there were wider availability of LSD to doctors and therapists.

In conclusion, some consideration is given to the thought that society has always had its saints and sages and, to a large extent, has shown appreciation of their achievements in personal development. But the creation of a psychological technology for self-development is likely to be much less acceptable. Nevertheless, this is a practical possibility in the light of modern developments.

Bibliography

Allport, G. W. (1955), *Becoming: Basic Considerations for a Psychology of Personality*, Yale University Press.

Allport, G. W. (1961), *Pattern and Growth in Personality*, Holt, Rinehart & Winston.

Argyle, M. (1970), *Social Interaction*, Methuen.

Cofer, C. N. & Appley, M. H. (1964), *Motivation: Theory and Research*, New York, Wiley.

Doel, D. C. (1970), 'Alienation', in *Faith and Freedom*, vol. 23, part 3.

Field, J. (1950), *On Not Being Able to Paint*, Heinemann.

Fromm, E. (1941), *The Fear of Freedom*, Routledge & Kegan Paul.

Goldstein, K. (1939), *The Organism*, American Book Company.

Hall, C. S. & Lindzey, G. (1957), *Theories of Personality*, New York, Wiley.

Horney, K. (1950), *Neurosis and Human Growth*, New York, Norton.

Jacobi, J. (1967), *The Way of Individuation*, Hodder & Stoughton.

Jaffe, A. (ed.) (1967), *C. G. Jung: Memories, Dreams and Reflections*, Collins, Fontana.

Jahoda, M. (1958), *Current Concepts of Positive Mental Health*, New York, Basic Books.

Jourard, S. M. (1964), *The Transparent Self: Self-disclosure and Well Being*, Van Nostrand.

Jung, C. G. (1933), 'Aims of Psychotherapy', *Modern Man in Search of a Soul*, Routledge & Kegan Paul.

Jung, C. G. (1934), *The Development of Personality*, Collected Works, vol. 17, Routledge & Kegan Paul.

Jung, C. G. (1951), *Aion*, Collected Works, vol. 9. part 2, Routledge & Kegan Paul.

Jung, C. G. (1954), 'Fundamental Questions of Psychotherapy' in *The Practice of Psychotherapy*, Collected Works, vol. 16, Routledge & Kegan Paul.

Jung, C. G. (1958), *Psychology and Religion*, Collected Works, vol. 11, Routledge & Kegan Paul.

Jung, C. G. (1968), *Analytical Psychology: Its Theory and Practice*, Routledge & Kegan Paul.

Kahn, J. H. (1969), *Human Growth and the Development of Personality*, Pergamon Press.

Lecky, P. (1945), *Self-Consistency: A Theory of Personality*, New York, Island Press.

Maslow, A. H. (1954), *Motivation and Personality*, Harper & Row.

Maslow, A. H. (1959), 'Cognition of being in peak experiences', *Journal of Genetic Psychology*, vol. 94.

May, Rollo (1953), *Man's Search for Himself*, New York, Norton.

Newland, C. (1963), *My Self and I*, Muller.

Reich, W. (1969), *Character Analysis*, Vision Press.

Riesman, D., Glazer, N., & Denny, R. (1950), *The Lonely Crowd*, Yale University Press.

Rogers, C. R. (1967), 'A therapist's view of the good life: the fully functioning person', *On Becoming a Person*, Constable.

Rokeach, M. (1960), *The Open and Closed Mind: Investigations into the Nature of Belief Systems and Personality Systems*, New York, Basic Books.

Skinner, B. F. (1962), *Walden Two*, Collier-Macmillan.

Snygg, D. & Combs, A. W. (1949), *Individual Behaviour*, New York, Harper.

Stace, W. T. (1961), *Mysticism and Philosophy*, Macmillan.

Stafford, P. G. & Golightly B. H. (1969), *LSD in Action*, Sidgwick & Jackson.

Zaehner, R. C. (1957), *Mysticism, Sacred and Profane*, Oxford University Press.

7 A Map of Inner Space

John H. Clark

Man has his country, the geography of his personal self.

Rabindranath Tagore

Introduction

The attempt to understand ourselves

Perhaps the attempt to understand ourselves is the most important enterprise of the immediate future. Our artefacts may well be ready to feed us and to control our population, but mankind is locked in its own conceptual systems which prevent the action which is required for us to avert disaster. We are trapped in a series of Stafford Beer's interlocking and nesting 'esoteric boxes' (1970) whose main function appears to be to preserve their own existence. Typical examples of 'esoteric boxes' are the cabinet, the various ministries and the civil service. All professions tend to be 'esoteric boxes' and, in particular, medicine and law. New professions try vainly to emulate the older ones but the latter have centuries of box-building expertise up their sleeves.

Unless we can be sure to avert the ecological disaster which is looming so near at hand, then we had better make haste to preserve a few mementoes of our culture, somewhere in the universe. I have suggested elsewhere (1970a) that as a first step we should send Mozart to the moon. However, I hope that this drastic step won't be necessary.

The present chapter presents a new theory of the mind and I hope it will be a contribution to the above attempt to understand ourselves.

'Inner Space'

My approach to the person is via a new model of the mind. This model has been embodied, literally, in a three-dimensional structure which might be compared, in appearance, to a terrestrial globe but which I call, in contrast to that, 'A Map of Inner Space'. (The phrase 'Inner Space' is one that I first encountered, used in this context, in the work of J. G. Ballard.)

Much of my argument depends upon my analysis of the mystical literature and upon the analogies which I draw between mystical states and other altered states of consciousness, particularly certain mental illnesses and certain drug-induced states. Should the reader have previously *not* encountered the mystical literature or even realized its existence, then at this point in my chapter I would urge him to dip into those riches. They are readily available in the anthologies mentioned below (p. 164) and until he has done so the meaning of my analysis may remain somewhat obscure. People vary greatly in their natural response to mystical literature, but I would urge the reader to have a look at it if he has not previously encountered it.

Using the Map I can trace out the path taken by a person as he travels through his own Inner Space. I can plot many different mental states, healthy and unhealthy, dreaming and waking, happy and sad. Some of these states are commonplace and well known; others are extremely uncommon. In between, there are unusual states of mind which a person may only experience once or twice in a lifetime. The experience of 'falling in love' can, for example, be a rare but very powerful experience and, as such, it has been celebrated often by novelists and poets, the latter including 'Pop' lyric writers.

Among literary descriptions of 'falling in love' a most vivid example is contained in the first chapter of D. H. Lawrence's novel, *Women in Love*, where Gudrun watches Gerald enter the church at his sister's wedding. Gudrun experiences a 'transport', a 'paroxysm' at the sight of him, although, as if to emphasize the fragility of this experience, Lawrence mingles with it a quality of anxiety on Gudrun's part, as if she were experiencing not only joy but also a sharp emotion of 'nostalgia' (one might even say 'instant nostalgia'), a fear that she might never see Gerald again.

That was a description of an intense and rare experience, quite outside the routine of everyday life and yet an experience which, perhaps, many people have at one time or another. Then again, with the recent popular interest in the hallucinogenic drugs, such as cannabis and LSD, drug-induced alterations of consciousness have become more widely known and written about (Tart, 1969). These experiences also, are very far from the world of everyday life.

Mental illness is another way by which a person may travel to unusual places—or indeed get quite lost—inside his own mind. In particular the manic-depressive, in his alternation of blissful and miserable states, treads a parallel path to the dedicated mystic, who may find himself oscillating between the mystical state proper and its horrific complement, the dark night of the soul. (The mystical path is yet another way to these unusual states of mind.)

Psyche and person: a metaphysical excursion

My concept of the person, derived from a study of mental states, usual and unusual, is I think rather a traditional one—not far, in fact, from that of Aristotle. The first point to be faced is that we all have minds and that we all have bodies. However, what the relation between them is, nobody can say. *In other words, the mind–body*

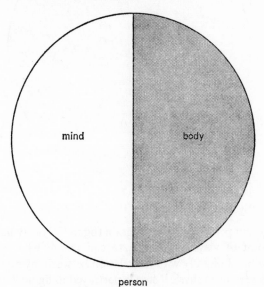

Figure 7.1 Mind/body: the person

problem has not yet been solved. This awkward fact leads the psychologist into difficulty. In the past many psychologists used to concentrate on their minds, whereas now the emphasis is going the other way and most psychologists pay a great deal of attention to behaviour. Some try to observe both kinds of data at once, mental and behavioural. This method is what most people (including doctors) do most of the time in ordinary life and it has many advantages. However, it is necessary to repeat again that the relation between the two kinds of data is unknown.

Nevertheless, in everyday life we begin many sentences with 'I' and I (for one) like to think that, when I say 'I', I am speaking for both parts of 'Me' as a person, for my mind and for my body. Then my mind and body together constitute, or better my mind/body

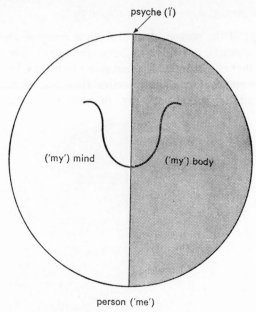

Figure 7.2   Psyche and person

constitutes, my person. A little diagram (figure 7.1) may help to sum up this point of view. I also like to call the 'I' who speaks, my 'psyche', which I identify with the relation between my mind and my body. This very metaphysical step is portrayed in figure 7.2, in which the reader may recognize the form of the Greek letter ψ (psi).

Apart from this explicitly metaphysical section, the rest of this chapter is scientific. Where I present a theory of mysticism I do so in a scientific and non-mystical meta-language.

My metaphysical assumptions, which lie behind figure 7.2, are that a mind and a body are linked in a mysterious way: and that psyche bears to mind/body the same relationship that Tao does to yin/yang or that the Cheshire cat's grin does to the Cheshire cat. (A most elegant expression—'. . . mathematics is a way of saying less and less about more and more'—of the viewpoint I am advocating is to be found in chapter 12 of G. Spencer Brown's *Laws of Form* (1969).)

The subjective dimensions of the Map

Having made my metaphysical excursion I must now return to the matter in hand and try to develop a theory of the person in terms of my 'Map of Inner Space'. The Map of Inner Space is a map of the mind. At any moment the state of the mind can be plotted on it in

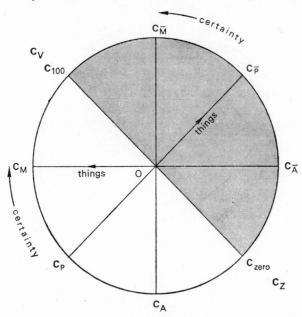

Figure 7.3 Certainty

terms of three variables. Just as you can find a street in a street-map by looking along the two dimensions (letters and numbers) which define the sides of the map so, in the Map of Inner Space, you can locate a particular mental state by looking along the three dimensions to the appropriate place. These three dimensions form a solid map which has a volume rather than the mere area of a two-dimensional map. This three-dimensional *volume* of the Map of Inner Space can be seen in figures 7.4, 7.5 and 7.9. It will help the reader to 'get the feel' of the Map if he looks at figures 7.4 and 7.5 and imagines the triangular upright section to be a sort of gate which can swing all around on its vertical pivot.

At any moment a particular mental state is defined, on the Map, as being a certain distance along the 'things' dimension from the central origin O, and a certain distance along the 'attention' dimension—those two distances define a particular place on the triangular upright section—and finally, as being at a certain point along the

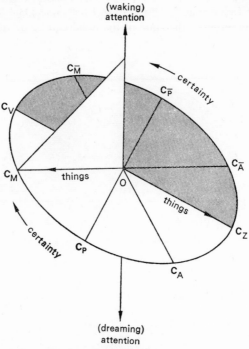

Figure 7.4   Things, attention and certainty

angular 'certainty' dimension which forms a complete circle, as shown.

The meaning of a particular point, so defined by these two linear distances and by that angle, will gradually become apparent as this chapter proceeds. I hope then that the reader will compare different places on the Map and relate them to one another. The usefulness of the Map can then be assessed. Let me therefore begin again.

The Map of Inner Space has three main dimensions, all of them subjective, as follows: things, attention and certainty. Certainty is an angular dimension in the horizontal plane and is, in fact, an *intensity* factor. The term 'certainty' as a name for this factor seems appropriate when analysing the mystical literature, where certainty is a highly valued prize, for part of the mystical path at least; but in other fields, such as the drug-induced states, it may be less appropriate.

The dimensions, things and attention, form the horizontal (radial) and vertical axes of the Map respectively, thus forming a vertical plane which swings around on the attention axis to all points on the angular certainty dimension (see figures 7.3 and 7.4). These are all subjective dimensions, which I cannot measure, but about which I can make comments—as to their limits and as to the order in which places on them occur. Certainty, for example, runs from a value of zero at Z to a maximum value of 100 at V, passing through A (average, everyday life), P (peak experience) and M (mystical state proper) on the way.

The reader has by now been plunged into what may be very unfamiliar territory. Moreover, he has already been presented with several diagrams, several letters of the alphabet and with the hint of mathematics. I hope he will pause at this point and let me re-assure him that once my ideas have become a little more familiar he will find my terminology helpful rather than abstruse and my notation a convenient shorthand rather than a repellent jargon. I base this claim on my experience with many varied lecture-audiences, many having little or no mathematical training, who have quite quickly assimilated the Map.

Before moving on please look carefully at figure 7.4 again and I will point out its salient features. Once this figure has become familiar the next part of this chapter will fall into place. Figure 7.4 consists of a horizontal circle labelled 'certainty' seen as from above and to one side. This accounts for its oval appearance in the figure. There is a central point called the origin, O. The origin, O, is pierced by a vertical axis which is the dimension I call 'attention'. The more attention a person is paying at any moment the further away along the attention dimension from the origin, O, will his representative point, p (shown in figure 7.5), be plotted on the Map. In this chapter I shall be mostly concerned with states of waking attention which are plotted above the horizontal circle. However, below the circle the attention axis can also be seen, in figure 7.4, labelled 'dreaming attention'. This enables me, in theory, to plot the states of mind encountered in our dreams as well as those encountered when we are awake.

Next, please look again at the horizontal circle, labelled 'certainty'. This is divided into two halves, one of which is shaded, by the line VZ which also passes through the origin, O. This line VZ is an extremely important landmark in the Map and is one which gives the Map many of its paradoxical properties. On each side of the VZ line the certainty dimension, which is an angular dimension, runs from a value of zero certainty at C_Z to a value of complete, or absolute, or 100 per cent certainty at C_{100} (or C_V). On its way from zero certainty to 100 per cent certainty this angular dimension passes through C_A, C_P and C_M. Each of these represents a greater degree of certainty than the preceding one. Hence C_V is greater than C_M, or in mathematical notation $C_V > C_M$. Continuing, we can write

$$C_V > C_M > C_P > C_A > C_Z.$$

Moreover, since the certainty dimension runs from C_Z to C_V on both sides of the circle we can also write $C_V > C_{\overline{M}} > C_{\overline{P}} > C_{\overline{A}} > C_Z$.

Note that on the shaded side of the circle the places marked out on the circumference are the same as on the other side apart from having a 'bar' placed over the latter, thus: $\overline{A}$, $\overline{P}$ and $\overline{M}$. This bar and its meaning will be explained later. At this point it is sufficient to consider the unshaded side of the map as happy or optimistic and the shaded side as sad or pessimistic.

The letter A stands for the A-state, the average everyday state of mind. I take this to be on the optimistic side but please notice that the level of certainty I attach to this average state of mind is quite low. Indeed I do not think we notice our state of mind much at all in average everyday healthy states. We only notice the A-state when we leave it. If we then move in the direction of a P-state we experience an unusually *high* state of certainty. This is the euphoric state of joyful certainty, encountered in states which have been called peak experiences. Mystical states proper (M-states) are known by their extremely high levels of certainty which are still moreover on the optimistic side.

The meaning of the other places on the circle of certainty may now be emerging and I hope the reader will try to puzzle them out a little for himself at this point.

The sources of the Map

The sources of the Map are fourfold, as mentioned above on p. 156. First, there is the ancient and worldwide literature of mysticism. Second, there is evidence from psychiatry and, in particular, the descriptions we have of manic and depressive states. Third, there is the growing literature on the experiences caused by the various hallucinogenic drugs. These three types of mental state, mystical. psychiatric and drug-induced, have a number of similarities. They also differ in some very important ways. Fourth, there is the evidence from those rare but unforgettable experiences such as 'falling in love' which perhaps happen to many people from time to time.

The map relates these four kinds of states to each other and to everyday states of ordinary health. Moreover, in addition to the above descriptions of mental states, the map can also be interpreted in terms of the brain. Other interpretations may also occur to the reader—such as theological and philosophical ones.

Previous maps of the mind

Before and after proposing my own map of the mind I looked around to see who else had attempted the same task. This led me to scrape a rather empty barrel, for although many writers have described the mind, few have been cartographers.

For example, in all the writings of Sigmund Freud there seem to be only one or two very sketchy little diagrams (Freud, 1961, p. 24) which reveal hardly any of the splendid complexity of his dynamic model of the mind.

The next map I came to was that of Jung. This is very much like one of Professor Tolkien's fairy tales, full of good wizards and sinister shadows. The actual topography of Jung's map is however not very clear. (Hermann Hesse's novels traverse a similar dark forest.)

From Jung one naturally passes on to a study of alchemy, which Jung (1953) believed to be a psychological system as much, or even more, than a chemical one. Here, in alchemy, we touch gold indeed, as, for example, in the mental map of Robert Fludd. Two more veins which might yield a rich ore are the Cabbala—with its tree of life— and the 'Vision' of W. B. Yeats (1937)—with its interlocking cones.

Still casting around for maps I came upon the fascinating

topological diagrams of Kurt Lewin (1936). These are without doubt and explicitly, maps.

Finally in the course of my reading among the mystics I naturally came upon Plotinus who, like many mystical writers, certainly puts forward a map of the soul, if not a map of the mind. In particular, Plotinus (O'Brien, 1964) has a very detailed, though purely verbal, hierarchical map of the soul, in its upward and downward relations with the divine and natural worlds.

Mystical language

Content analysis

My method of investigating mystical language was to immerse myself in as many examples of it as I could find. In doing this my task was made easy by the many excellent anthologies which are available. These cover the world literature of mysticism, ancient and modern, and, where necessary, provide translations into English. Such anthologies, which I can recommend to the interested reader, and which are all available in paperback, are those edited by Stace (1960), Happold (1964) and Fremantle (1964). In my reading I was first guided by the work of William James, whose chapter on mysticism I had encountered in his classic—one of the very few classics that the still-young science of psychology has so far produced—*The Varieties of Religious Experience* (1960). Later I read Marghanita Laski's book, *Ecstasy* (1961), and her content analysis of mystical literature encouraged me to look myself for what might seem to be the essential features.

For those unfamiliar with the mystical literature let me give a brief explanation. The mystics are people who have experiences which, when they try to write them down, they describe roughly in the following way. They have had, they say, an almost ineffable (indescribable) experience. Often it came on suddenly and often it came unbidden, although sometimes it came as the response to their eager and persistent entreaties (meditation and the like).

They say that they had a sense of overwhelming certainty, as to their knowledge of the truth, meaning and significance of the world. They express a sense of unity with everything and a sense of timelessness or eternity. All this is accompanied by the most intense joy, and often by a sense of light, sometimes seen indeed as a flash of lightning (even on a bright summer day). What is more they feel a glorious freedom, so that all decision-making becomes easy.

Following these experiences the mystics return to the ordinary world of everyday once again, but now they feel changed or reborn, as if all things were new.

The above description can only serve as an introduction to the mystical literature, for I must press on now with my analysis of it.

I eventually emerged from my reading with the conviction that the basic ideas were extremely few, and were, indeed, only seven in number, as follows: certainty, knowledge, unity, eternity, light, joy and freedom. For convenience, I started to use their initial letter to refer to them thus: C, K, U, E, L, J and F. This very short list of ideas needs some qualification. Under each of these headings I have collected lists of subsidiary ideas which, I can reasonably argue, have a strong link with the main idea. Thus, under the heading light, L, I include: light, fire, sparks, rays, illumination, enlightenment, and even more remote concepts such as the dawn.

Literary devices

Similarly, by the application of negation to these ideas one can generate lists of related ideas which provide the mystic with a large vocabulary, in spite of its limited range of meaning. Thus, from light L, we can get darkness $\bar{L}$ (I use the notation of a 'bar' to denote the negation of an idea and, for example, call the above term $\bar{L}$, 'L-bar'). We can also get ashes (from fire), shadows and the concept of the light being extinguished. I hope my reader will feel, by now, tempted to apply the same sort of rules to the other main ideas. In addition to listing associated ideas and negations, we can move on to double negation and redundancy. Double negation (which I denote by a double-bar, thus: $\bar{\bar{J}}$, which I call 'J-double-bar') leads us back again to the original idea and is much used in mystical literature to add variety to the language. For example, from the idea of eternity E, we can move to $\bar{E}$, which stands for time, mortality, birth and death. But by applying double negation we can say with John Donne, 'Death, thou shalt die' (or $\bar{\bar{E}}$). Please note that the 'bar' is being used here to reverse the meaning of an idea. Light L becomes darkness $\bar{L}$, and so on. I have already introduced the use of the 'bar' in a slightly different way. In that case it was used to turn a peak experience on the optimistic side of the Map, P, into the complementary version on the gloomy side, $\bar{P}$. These two usages of the bar are quite similar.

Redundancy is simply the method of saying the same thing twice or, even better, thrice. To enliven such repetition we can also use double negation. So a redundant phrase about light might be represented say, by $LL\bar{L}$, which could stand for 'Illuminated by the flame which dispels the darkness'. I am, personally, ashamed to coin such a banal phrase but, fortunately, among the mystics are to be

Table 7.1 Literary devices used by the mystics

Symbol	Idea and associated ideas	Negation	Double negation	Redundancy	Paradox
X	X	$\bar{X}$	$\bar{\bar{X}}$	XX	$X\bar{X}$
K	KNOWLEDGE Reality Truth Significance	IGNORANCE Illusion Falsehood Pointlessness	Unveil the truth Dispel illusion	Real knowledge Absolute reality	Learned ignorance
U	UNITY Perfection Infinity Completeness	DISUNITY Imperfection Finiteness Boundaries	No boundaries No divisions	Complete unity	Multiplicity in unity
E	ETERNITY	TIME Mortality Birth and death	Timelessness Immortality Deathlessness	Eternal timelessness $(E\,\bar{\bar{E}})$	The timeless moment $(\bar{\bar{E}}\,\bar{\bar{E}})$
L	LIGHT Fire Spark Ray	DARKNESS Shadows Ashes	Shadowless Rekindle the flame	Brilliant light	Dazzling obscurity Darkness visible
J	JOY Bliss Delight	MISERY Despair	Relieved of misery	Blissful joy	Joyful pain
F	FREEDOM Liberty	BONDAGE Servitude	Released from bondage Unchained	Free and at liberty	'. . . Whom to serve is perfect freedom'

numbered some great poets. For example, the English poet and seventeenth-century divine, Thomas Traherne, when he wants to say that everything is eternal, says in fact that 'The corn was orient and immortal wheat, which never should be reaped . . .' (see Happold, 1964).

The point has now come where I can summarize my ideas by a very condensed little table of the literary devices used by the mystics, who tell us about their experiences in language which, although very limited in content, nevertheless can delight us by its variety and exuberance (table 7.1).

I have said nothing yet, by the way, about paradoxes, which are a most prominent feature of mystical writing. What is more, the mystics use more than one kind of paradox! However, a commonly occurring one is the juxtaposed contradiction or oxymoron. I denote this by an idea and its negation placed side by side, thus $L\bar{L}$, $J\bar{J}$, $K\bar{K}$, which could stand for 'dazzling obscurity', 'joyful pain' and 'learned ignorance', respectively.

The role of certainty

Please note that certainty C is not included in table 7.1. This is not to imply that the same games cannot be played with it: for they can. For example, we can get $\bar{C}$, uncertainty, doubt; $\bar{\bar{C}}$, doubtless; and

Table 7.2 Basic ideas

Basic idea	Symbol	Psychological function
Certainty	(C)	
Knowledge	(K)	cognition
Unity	(U)	
Eternity	(E)	
Light	(L)	perception
Joy	(J)	emotion
Freedom	(F)	volition

CC, certain sure. Nevertheless, I have not included certainty in table 7.1 because it seems to play a rather different role to the others. It seems to be used to indicate degree, to be an index of intensity. Thus certainty *about* knowledge, unity and eternity can be present to a greater or lesser degree. Also, in the opposite state to the mystical state, the desolate 'dark night of the soul' (where the description seems to be the reverse of the mystical state, thus, C, K̄, Ū, Ē, L, J̄ and F̄), the only idea that does *not* seem to change is certainty, C, which adds all its force to the mystic's desolation.

It may be interesting, at this point, to look at my list of basic ideas in a different way. Table 7.2 analyses the seven ideas according to their psychological function.

A network of mental states

The different mystical states

I now wish to put forward a notation for describing, in an economical manner, the various mystical states—for there are at least six of them—and also for showing their various inter-relations. The method is to allot a symbol to each of the mystical states and then to show how a person can pass from one to another of them. The path between the states is represented by an arrow. Please note that I am *not*, in this section, using the Map of Inner Space (as already studied and as already displayed in figures 7.4, 7.5 and 7.9). It is true that I am using diagrams in this section but they stand, at first, in their own right. (Some of them are, technically speaking, network diagrams.) They indicate, by their arrows, the pathways along which a person can pass from one mental state to another. The letters A, P, M and so on should be familiar by now. They stand for the average state, the peak experience and the mystical state proper.

Gradually, however, as the networks gain in complexity the reader may detect a pattern emerging with which he is also already familiar. (This is my intention.)

Let us start by considering the everyday state of ordinary life. Let us call it the average state, or A-state, and abbreviate this to the letter A standing by itself. The A-state is not a *mystical* state at all; it is the ordinary, normal, 'healthy', common-or-garden state in which most people, presumably, spend most of their waking hours. Now, from A we can consider a step towards one of the mystical states, such as the state I call the P-state. I represent this step thus:

$$A \rightarrow P \tag{1}$$

The letter P, for P-state, is taken from the term coined by the American psychologist, Maslow, who talks about 'peak experiences'.

These are euphoric states, but they are less intense than the fully developed mystical state proper, which I call the M-state. All the features of the M-state are present in the P-state, but to a lesser degree. I intend the term P to stand for many of the sort of states described by Marghanita Laski (1961).

From P it is easy to assume the mystic may pass into the more intense M-state and I show this by the symbols:

$$A \to P \to M \qquad (2)$$

I also assume that these transitions are reversible, along the same path, and so I next write:

$$A \leftrightarrow P \leftrightarrow M \qquad (3)$$

Beyond the M-state we enter even stranger territory, and the mystical writers become even more paradoxical than before. In particular, they tend to fall back on the assertion of the absolute ineffability—that is to say, of the absolute inexpressibility—of the next stage on the path.

However they *name* it, sometimes calling it the Void and sometimes (I think) Nirvana, I use the term V-state for it, which I abbreviate to V. So now I can write:

$$A \leftrightarrow P \leftrightarrow M \to V \qquad (4)$$

Note that my last arrow, between M and V, is not a reversible one. This transition, between M and V, is called, in some mystical traditions, contemplation and it is said to be passive, in contradistinction to the active and energetic procedure of meditation, which is the path from A to M.

The step from M to V leads to the V-state which I can only describe by the following deliberately cryptic equation:

$$V = \{ \ \} \qquad (5)$$

For I 'describe' the truly ineffable V-state by a pair of empty brackets, representing the null class—the empty set—of descriptions; whereas the M-state can still be described, and for that I write:

$$M = \{(C_M[K, U, E]) L, J, F\} \qquad (6)$$

Note that the bracketing is an attempt to keep the cognitive functions together and to show certainty as an intensity factor.

Let us pause here awhile to give the reader time to assimilate my notation. The above quasi-mathematical equation (6) brings together two different sections of my argument. First of all, notice that it starts off with the letter 'M'. This means that I am going to describe the M-state and that the large outer brackets contain the description. Similarly, the reader will find below other such equations, describing $Z(7)$, $\bar{M}(9)$ and so on.

Now, within the large outer brackets are a set of letters of the alphabet some of which are enclosed within two further sets of brackets, round and square respectively. The letters inside the large outer brackets are the letters already encountered above (p. 165). They are my set of basic ideas: C, K, U, E, L, J and F (see also tables 7.1 and 7.2).

The square brackets are intended to group together three of the 'thinking' or cognitive functions K, U and E, while the round brackets are intended to portray the fourth cognitive function, certainty C, as an intensity factor or 'operator', which acts upon the contents of the square brackets. The particular value taken up by certainty C, in the M-state, is denoted by the subscript M which is attached to C, thus C_M. Finally the remaining functions, L (perception), J (emotion) and F (volition), are grouped loosely together within the outer walls of this nest of brackets.

The rest of this section explores this notation and in the course of this exploration stumbles upon some rare specimens.

But now we must get ready for another step and one which is quite as strange as the last. From V, the next step goes to a state which is also somewhat ineffable, but whose ineffability is of yet another kind. This is the Z-state where the letter Z is taken from the word Zen (and the word zero). The Zen tradition speaks more eloquently about this state than does any other and so I use the letter Z for it, and imply by this a state of exact neutrality with regard to certainty. Anything written about Zen is liable to sound like the most complete nonsense. One is reminded of the lady who asked Louis Armstrong what jazz was. He replied, 'Ma'am, if you gotta ask, you won't never know.' But Alan Watts (1962) refuses to adopt this attitude and he tries as hard as he can to explain what Zen is (perhaps also what Jazz is?). Of course, you will be told that Zen cannot be put into words, but I reject that counsel of despair. This chapter is, after all, an attempt to put Zen (among other things) into a *meta-language* at least.

It is a state where nothing is certain, where everything is equi-probable, and indeed, a state where words can hardly be spoken

(Watts, 1962), for to speak implies choice and choice implies preference. In my notation the Z-state can be shown as follows:

$$Z = \{(C_{Zero}[K, U, E,]) L, J, F\}$$
$$= \{(C_{Zero}[\bar{K}, \bar{U}, \bar{E},]) L, J, \bar{F}\} \tag{7}$$

Now I can write:

$$A \leftrightarrow P \leftrightarrow M \rightarrow V \leftrightarrow Z \tag{8}$$

This completes the 'main line' of the mystical path. However, it is not nearly so simple as that straight line would imply. Moreover, as we investigate the complexities which turn that line into a labyrinth we shall come into contact with mental states of great medical interest.

Desolate states

To start with the most dramatic of the forks in this path, let us consider the famous dark night of the soul. This is the state of the most utter desolation which the mystic may encounter. It is the polar opposite to the M-state and, to indicate this, I write $\bar{M}$-state (which I call the 'M-bar state'). In my notation the $\bar{M}$-state can be described as follows:

$$\bar{M} = \{(C_{\bar{M}}[\bar{K}, \bar{U}, \bar{E}]) L, J, \bar{F}\} \tag{9}$$

Note that certainty is of the same degree as in the M-state, that is to say it is a very high degree of certainty indeed ($C_{\bar{M}}$). For the desolation ($\bar{J}$) of the dark night of the soul is felt with the same certainty ($C_{\bar{M}} = C_M$) as is the joy (J) of the M-state. However, all the other elements appear reversed: ignorance ($\bar{K}$), disunity ($\bar{U}$), time ($\bar{E}$), darkness ($\bar{L}$), misery ($\bar{J}$) and bondage ($\bar{F}$).

There is however a very curious fact about the $\bar{M}$-state and one of great importance to this theory. Spiritual directors are able to reassure their mystical pupils that the $\bar{M}$-state, although terrible, is only a branch of the mystical path and that, given patience, the $\bar{M}$-state like the M-state may lead them on to the V-state. This can be represented as follows:

$$\tag{10}$$

The next state to consider is the polar opposite to the P-state, the $\bar{P}$-state. This is equivalent to the P-state in that it is similar to, but less intense than, the $\bar{\text{M}}$-state and in the fact that all the elements of it are reversed, except again for certainty. So we can write out the formulae as follows:

$$P = \{(C_P[K,\ U,\ E])\ L,\ J,\ F\} \tag{11}$$

and
$$\bar{P} = \{(C_{\bar{P}}[\bar{K},\ \bar{U},\ \bar{E}])\ L,\ \bar{J},\ \bar{F}\} \tag{12}$$

We have now entered medical territory, for my terms, the P-state and the $\bar{P}$-state, especially when distorted by over-activity and underactivity of the brain respectively, are meant to describe states which are very close to the manic and the depressive states. Consider therefore the possible pathways of a patient who suffers from the manic-depressive illness. These can be shown as follows:

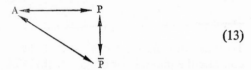

$$(13)$$

Using this diagram one can trace out some of the different sequences, which different patients display, such as: A, P, $\bar{P}$, A; A, P, A, P, A; A, $\bar{P}$, A, $\bar{P}$, A; A, $\bar{P}$, P, $\bar{P}$, A; and so on (Mayer-Gross, Slater & Roth, 1955).

Still pursuing this medical approach to the pairs of polar opposites among the mental states, there is an even more commonplace pair to be considered. It bears however the same general pattern. This pair is the A-state and its complement the $\bar{A}$-state. By the $\bar{A}$-state I mean to indicate the mild state of depression which, for example, quite often follows influenza. The pathway can be shown quite simply like this:

$$\begin{array}{c} \text{A} \\ \updownarrow \\ \bar{\text{A}} \end{array} \tag{14}$$

The labyrinth

At this point it is helpful to pause for a moment and reflect upon an interesting fact that has now emerged. Of our initial set of states which comprised the 'main line', A, P, M, V and Z, we have discussed the way in which three of them, M, P and A, are all members of pairs, M and $\bar{\text{M}}$, P and $\bar{P}$ and, finally, A and $\bar{A}$. However, the other two states, V and Z, do not occur in pairs. They are, both, mysterious and unique in their strange properties. The V-state cannot be described at all and the Z-state can only be described by two sets of equi-probable and opposite elements. There is no hint anywhere, however, that either the V-state or the Z-state are members of pairs—except, and this is also interesting, that one could regard the V-state and the Z-state as themselves making up a pair. However, the polarities of this pair cannot be expressed by the simple application of the bar symbol, as in M, $\bar{M}$ and so on.

The reason for this, I suggest, is because the V-state and the Z-state stand, themselves, on the boundary which separates the other three pairs. To express this I must now draw a diagram in which all the previous and partial maps are combined to form a single comprehensive map of the mental labyrinth:

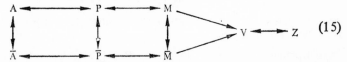 (15)

To bring out even more strongly the idea that the V-state and the Z-state form the axis of the map I will re-arrange it again, thus:

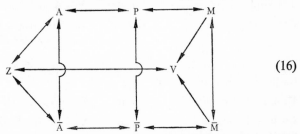 (16)

The mysterious Z-state is now shown to be linked back to the everyday states of A (and $\bar{A}$).

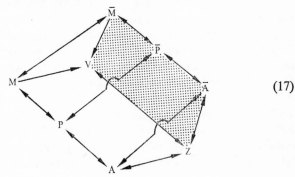 (17)

This fits the experience of the mystics, who find that they eventually return to the everyday world (although, when they do so, they see it *differently* as a result of their cycle of personal experience).

Network (17) is merely the previous one rotated, so as to show how it relates to the plane of certainty (figure 7.3 and 7.4).

In the last diagram it was also possible to bring out more clearly yet another feature of these states. The dotted area is only one half of the labyrinth, the 'gloomy' half. It is seen to be an exact reflection

Table 7.3   Mental states

Mental state	Term	Description in terms of the seven basic ideas
Average state (of ordinary everyday life)	A-state	$A = \{(C_A[K, U, E]) \, L, J, F\}$
Peak experience	P-state	$P = \{(C_P[K, U, E]) \, L, J, F\}$
Mystical state proper	M-state	$M = \{(C_M[K, U, E]) \, L, J, F\}$
The void	V-state	$V = \{ \ \}$
Zen state	Z-state	$Z = \{(C_{ZERO}[K, U, E]) \, L, J. \, F\}$ $= \{(C_{ZERO}[\bar{K}, \bar{U}, \bar{E}]) \, L, J, F\}$
Dark mystical state proper (or the dark night of the soul)	$\bar{M}$-state	$\bar{M} = \{(C_{\bar{M}}[\bar{K}, \bar{U}, \bar{E}]) \, L, J, \bar{F}\}$
Dark peak experience	$\bar{P}$-state	$\bar{P} = \{(C_{\bar{P}}[\bar{K}, \bar{U}, \bar{E}]) \, L, J, \bar{F}\}$
Dark average state (of ordinary everyday life)	$\bar{A}$-state	$\bar{A} = \{(C_{\bar{A}}[\bar{K}, \bar{U}, \bar{E}]) \, L, J, \bar{F}\}$

of the other half and, in many mental illnesses, we can trace the patient's progress from side to side.

A field of research which has recently become prominent is that of drug-induced altered states of consciousness. The colourful terminology of the 'good' and the 'bad trip' can also be interpreted in terms of states similar to P-states and $\bar{P}$-states. In the case of drug-induced states however, various elements of perceptual distortion must be added. Moreover, I think that these states sometimes move into the eerie locality between A and $\bar{A}$ (including Z). Here there is *less* certainty than in everyday life but, in its place, a sense of increased 'awareness'. This is the region explored by Walter de la Mare,

Edgar Allan Poe, H. P. Lovecraft (1970) and Hammer films. (I call these states 'Runic states'.)

At this point it may be helpful to summarize the whole family of mental states so far described. This is done in table 7.3. (Note that $C_M = C_{\overline{M}}$, $C_P = C_{\overline{P}}$ and so on.)

The Map

The plane of certainty

Let us now relate network (17) again to our dimension of certainty, and place each state in the network at a particular degree of certainty, which has been shown as an angular variable (figure 7.3 and 7.4). Having done this we can also interpret the length of the radius of the horizontal plane as the variable 'things' (starting with zero things at the origin O, the 'still centre' of the plane).

Attention

By adding a third dimension, attention, to the Map we transform it into a double-cone and can distinguish between the waking state above the horizontal plane, and the dreaming state below it.

The halves of the Map

Furthermore, the halves of the Map, 'light and dark', or 'optimistic,' and 'pessimistic', can now be seen clearly. The line C_Z to C_V, C_{zero} to C_{100}, separates these two halves. This line links two places on the network of states, the Void or V-state V, and the Zen-state, or Z-state Z. These carry maximum and minimum Certainty respectively and have strange and paradoxical properties.

Brain-switches

It is now possible to translate the model of the mind so far pictured in terms of the Map, into a simple brain theory. I have been urged however, by colleagues, to present my Map of Inner Space as primarily a map of the mind. It was, after all, the attempt to impose a meaningful structure upon the variety of mental states which first led me to construct the Map and it stands or falls by its success in so doing. Having made this *calculus* in terms of the mind I am, however,

tempted to *interpret* it in other ways and the most obvious interpretation to a psychologist is one that leaps across the mind/body
gap.

The basic idea is that of a brain-switch. Starting with two assumptions, first, that the brain is a computer of finite size, and second
that the brain can store information—as is clear from the fact of
memory—I envisage the basic element of the brain to be a single
binary switch. This can retain 1 bit (binary digit) of information. (It
can be represented by an arrow, pointing either to zero or to 1.)

I assume that whatever techniques are in fact used by the brain,
to store and manipulate information, all such techniques could be
reduced, for descriptive purposes, to a set of binary switches.

Mindwork

The effect of concentration, which will be discussed later, seems to be
to reduce the number of 'things on the mind' but, at the same time,
to increase the attention being paid to them. I can represent this
change by a diagram (see figure 7.5).

The small letter p stands for a person (accompanied, I like to
think, by psyche) who is, in this case, at the average state, A. The
point p is the 'representative point' mentioned earlier, which represents a person's mental state at any time. The representative point is
plotted on the two linear and the one angular dimensions of the
Map. The position of p′ represents the person during concentration.
The line labelled MW, for 'mindwork', has the property that all
rectangles under it, such as the two rectangles with the letters p and
p′ at their top right-hand corner respectively, have the same total
length of sides. By using this diagram I represent an assumption that
I make, that a person can move up and down such a mindwork line
(and thus continue to do the same amount of mindwork), although
varying the amount of attention being paid to a varying number of
things. Should the level of mindwork increase or decrease it can be
represented by a family of other lines, as shown in figure 7.6.

Note that in figure 7.6 the proportion of attention to things
remains the same at the three points marked p_1, p_2 and p_3. This
constancy is shown by the line labelled 'concentration = 1'. By
concentration, I mean the ratio of attention to things. That is to say:

$$\text{concentration} = \frac{\text{attention}}{\text{things}}.$$ Thus, when the ratio rises, there is a

surplus of attention per thing, and this, I take it, corresponds to our subjective feeling of an increase in concentration. In figures 7.5 and 7.7 there is just such an increase, between p and p'. I must hasten to add here that my usage of the terms things, attention, certainty and concentration conforms to ordinary speech. In so doing I am appealing to the reader's own observations of the workings of his mind.

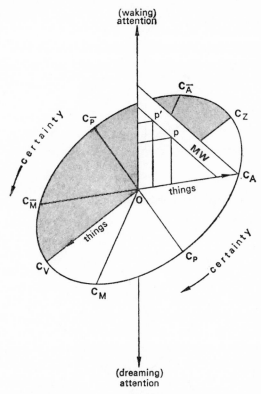

Figure 7.5 Concentration

I have kept as near as possible to ordinary English for, like G. Spencer Brown (1969), I believe that ordinary language is very deep.

Moreover, I must distinguish my ordinary English usage from the more specialized usages of words, like 'attention', to be encountered in modern experimental psychology. In that field such words will be found to be defined in terms of particular experimental methods. I

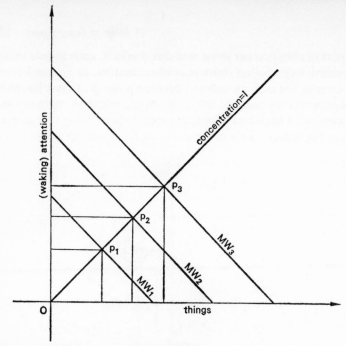

Figure 7.6 Mindwork and concentration

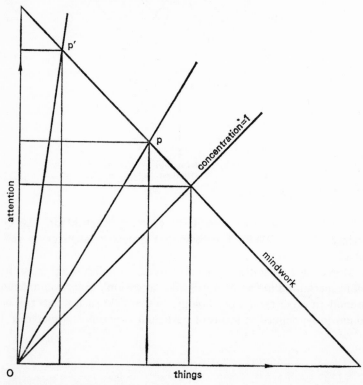

Figure 7.7 Rise in concentration

must therefore emphasize once again, that my usage is taken from ordinary English, with the possible exception of my neologism 'mindwork', which corresponds closely to the more familiar word 'brainwork'.

Internal agreement

The next important step is to see how certainty and concentration are linked on the Map. My basic idea is that certainty *sometimes* rises when there is a persistent and repeated surplus of attention, in other words, when concentration repeatedly rises above 1, as in regular meditation. However, as we all know, concentration itself is

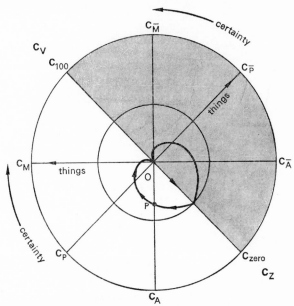

Figure 7.8 The mystical path

not *usually* enough to produce a rise in certainty; the mere act of thinking very hard about a few things does not, in itself, ensure a rise in our 'sense' of certainty. My explanation of the rise in certainty that does sometimes occur, in the presence of a rise of concentration, is as follows: I envisage that there is, in this case, an increase in a third factor. This factor is one concerning the internal agreement of some of the computing elements of the brain.

Thus, a surplus of attention implies some sort of surplus of some of the computing elements. I suppose that this surplus is arranged at random in ordinary concentration, but that when certainty starts to rise as a result of repeated concentration then some of the computing elements of the brain have become not only surplus but also mutually in agreement. I suppose that this agreement in the brain is felt as a

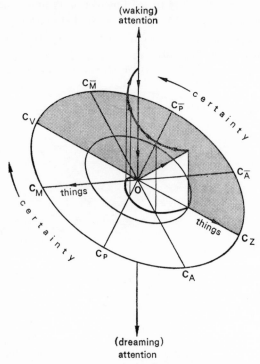

Figure 7.9   The mystical path seen as an ascending spiral

rise in certainty by the mind. This idea of an internal agreement arising between surplus computing elements can also be expressed by an analogy of a super-saturated solution, which suddenly crystallizes. Concentration is only one of the ways by which this strange and somewhat unattached 'sense' of certainty may be raised. However, it is perhaps one of the most controllable ways and, as such, it has been treasured by many quite different cultures. (Other states where there *can* be a rise in certainty are those due to hallucinogenic drugs such as LSD, and those occurring in some mental illnesses, particularly mania.)

We can now imagine the mystical path to be a spiral, as shown in figure 7.9. Assuming the level of mindwork remains at its everyday or average level, then, as concentration increases, things will decrease and attention will increase.

As things diminish, the point p moves in towards the origin and the mystical path swings round and up and inwards (see figure 7.9). Finally p reaches V, the plane of absolute certainty C_{100} but this plane is only reached at the axis, which passes down through the origin O.

A cosmic joke?

This seems, to me, to be a cosmic joke. It would appear that the mystic can only achieve absolute certainty when he reaches the axis of the map, where there are all degrees of certainty (and none): in other words, where the concept of certainty, along with all other concepts and indeed, with all other things, has disappeared.

Upon reaching the plane of C_{100}, at the axis, I imagine that p drops to the origin O, since I take it that attention cannot be 'paid' to zero things. We have now reached the V-state, the Void, and we have done so at the origin. We have reached the Void, which is so mysterious that the only thing that can be said about it is that *nothing* can be said about it. I symbolize this paradox by the following equation (seen already, above):

$$V = \{ \quad \}$$

The pair of empty brackets represent the null class—the empty set—of descriptions. This is true ineffability.

The journey to the East

From the Void a person can return to the world of things again by re-emerging, from the origin, into the strange plane of zero certainty C_{Zero}, where everything is just the same as before but also, somehow, quite different. Here the 'doors of perception' (Huxley, 1971) have been 'cleansed', time has changed its character, and the will is found to be free.

This, in the language of Zen, is *Satori* or enlightenment.

Mystical procedures

The control of certainty

We have discussed, above, the idea that an increase in certainty can be due to an increase in internal agreement, in the brain. Although these high certainty states sometimes occur 'spontaneously', the ability to experience them more or less at will appears to be a skill that is learnt by the mystic.

The mystic may use a variety of procedures to achieve these states, as listed in table 7.4.

Table 7.4   Mystical procedures

Type of Procedure	Examples
Orientation	Desiring to change Studying mystical literature Following ethical rules Attempting non-attachment
Physically calm	Solitude Absorption in nature, music and so on Systematic meditation (see Fig. 7.10)
Physically active	Singing Dancing Ritual Snake-handling
Biochemical	Breathing exercises Hunger and thirst Exposure to the elements Drugs

Meditation

The key method, however, which occurs in all mystical traditions, is that of meditation. A classic example of such a method is the yoga meditation method of Patanjali (circa 200 B.C.) (Stephen, 1957; Clark, 1970b). This method can be analysed using a flow diagram (figure 7.10).

The 'preliminary yoga' referred to in this figure is the essential orientation procedure of the person towards the mystical states. It involves, in all religious mystical traditions, a withdrawal of personal attachment to 'the world' and the sense of a 'greater goal', which lies ahead. After the orientation procedure the various mystical traditions then use calm procedures such as meditation or active procedures such as dancing.

An additional and optional procedure is the biochemical one, in which the body chemistry is modified by such methods as hunger and thirst, exposure to the elements and, sometimes, the ingestion of various drugs, such as are contained in 'peyote, datura and mushrooms' (Castaneda, 1970). In relation to this biochemical procedure we should mention the various mental illnesses which sometimes resemble, or caricature, the mystical states (and, in particular, the manic-depressive illness).

Finally, we should note again that mystical states, particularly the minor ones I call 'P-states', may occur 'spontaneously' in persons who have not deliberately set out to experience them. Such spontaneous states may follow one of the many 'triggers', such as absorption in music, nature or sexual love, which have been listed by Marghanita Laski in her book, *Ecstasy* (1961).

Although the procedures leading to mystical states are of a diverse nature it is possible to isolate the most central and widespread method. This is the combination of meditation and orientation, as found in Taoism, Buddhism, Western Christianity, Eastern Christianity, Islam and other traditions (Stace, 1960; Happold, 1964; Fremantle, 1964).

The flow diagram of yoga meditation shown below in figure 7.10 shows the way in which the number of 'things on the mind' are reduced by the systematic closing down of thinking, first about the outside world and then about the inside world of sensations, emotions and finally of thoughts themselves.

Delusions and hallucinations

Drugs such as cannabis and LSD, and illnesses, such as manic states, can produce states of high certainty but without the person having first produced a surplus of attention by meditation. I try to explain this by supposing that drugs and manic states produce in some *other* way a marked rise in agreement which is independent of there being a surplus of attention.

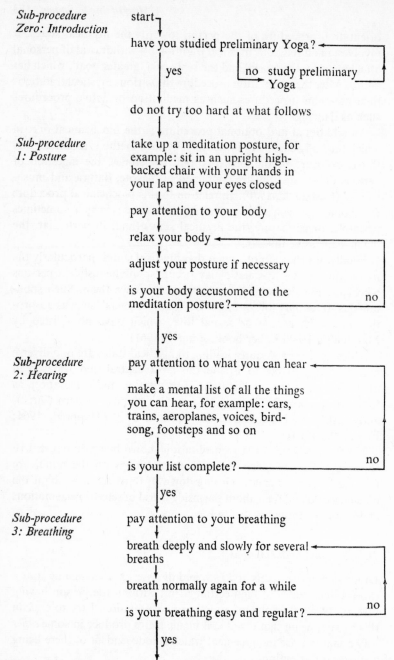

Sub-procedure Zero: Introduction

start

have you studied preliminary Yoga?

yes   no study preliminary Yoga

do not try too hard at what follows

Sub-procedure 1: Posture

take up a meditation posture, for example: sit in an upright high-backed chair with your hands in your lap and your eyes closed

pay attention to your body

relax your body

adjust your posture if necessary

is your body accustomed to the meditation posture?   no

yes

Sub-procedure 2: Hearing

pay attention to what you can hear

make a mental list of all the things you can hear, for example: cars, trains, aeroplanes, voices, bird-song, footsteps and so on

is your list complete?   no

yes

Sub-procedure 3: Breathing

pay attention to your breathing

breath deeply and slowly for several breaths

breath normally again for a while

is your breathing easy and regular?   no

yes

Figure 7.10 Flow diagram of Patanjali's yoga meditation

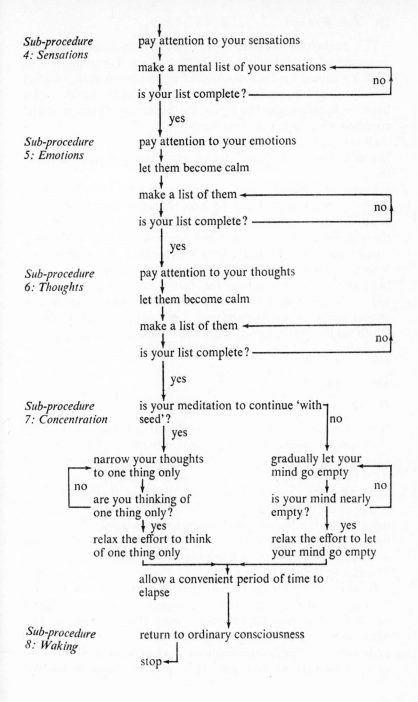

Sub-procedure
4: Sensations

pay attention to your sensations

make a mental list of your sensations

is your list complete? — no

yes

Sub-procedure
5: Emotions

pay attention to your emotions

let them become calm

make a list of them — no

is your list complete? — no

yes

Sub-procedure
6: Thoughts

pay attention to your thoughts

let them become calm

make a list of them — no

is your list complete? — no

yes

Sub-procedure
7: Concentration

is your meditation to continue 'with seed'? — no

yes

narrow your thoughts to one thing only

are you thinking of one thing only? — no

yes

relax the effort to think of one thing only

gradually let your mind go empty — no

is your mind nearly empty? — no

yes

relax the effort to let your mind go empty

allow a convenient period of time to elapse

Sub-procedure
8: Waking

return to ordinary consciousness

stop

This might then account for the fact that such states are also characterized by delusions and hallucinations. For suppose that these are caused by the imposition of agreement on brain-switches already busily engaged in 'representing' aspects of the world. Such a blind imposition might then lead to the distortions of perception and cognition which occur in these states.

(However, I also think that drug-induced states are also, at times low in certainty, or 'Runic'. So my brain theory is inconsistent at this point.)

I suppose I should defend this neologism (my only other one is the term 'mindwork'). I use the term 'Runic' to describe states of unusually *low* certainty which lie, on the Map, along the segment of the circle of certainty between A and Ā, passing through Z (the most Runic place of all). I take the term from the magical inscriptions on Viking swords and such like—my knowledge of Runes is imprecise but I know that the word has the right 'aura'—and I apply it to a wide variety of strange and often poetic states of mind. The 'dreamy mental states' of Crichton-Browne mentioned by William James (1960) fall into this category, and indeed Runic states occupy part of the no-man's-land between neurology and psychiatry.

The mystical path

The seven stages on the path

Now, let us have another look at the mystical path and, in particular, at its various stages. The data we have from the mystics are incomplete and largely unstandardized. That is to say, each mystical author tends to use his own terminology and to select particular experiences to describe, from what must be a much wider set of experiences.

One of the tasks of psychological research, therefore, is to obtain more complete data using a standardized terminology. A start has been made in this direction by Marghanita Laski (1961) and a survey of 'religious experiences' is being planned by Sir Alister Hardy at Manchester College, Oxford.

However, using the data available to us at present, it is possible to compare the different mystics' descriptions of the mystical path and thus to see where their terms coincide, where they overlap and where there are gaps. Since no single mystical author provides a comprehensive descriptive terminology I have been obliged to devise one. I divide the mystical path up into seven stages, as follows:

orientation, concentration, meditation, contemplation, the Void, re-emergence and return.

I can now tabulate these seven stages in table 7.5.

Table 7.5 The stages on the mystical path

Stage number	Name	Symbols
I	Orientation	Ⓐ ↔ A
II	Concentration	A ↔ A, with high concentration
III	Meditation	A ↔ P and A ↔ M
IV	Contemplation	M --›V
V	The Void	V
VI	Re-emergence	V ↔ Z
VII	Return	Z ↔ A′

A few comments are necessary here to explain the symbols. The circle around A in stage I, thus Ⓐ, represents the person's 'attachment' to the conventional world of average life. The circle symbolizes the stability and protection which that attachment offers us. It corresponds roughly to Freud's idea of the ego.

The orientation stage, stage I, is the stage of losing the sense of Ⓐ being the only 'reality'. Hints of a 'greater reality', 'immortal longings' for a different way of life—such as mystics and poets describe— begin to erode the protective wall of everyday reality. This process may take time and be intermittent and so I represent it by a reversible arrow, thus: Ⓐ ↔ A. The next stage, stage II, is the process of concentration as typified in yoga. The degree of certainty remains at A but the person increases his concentration by diminishing the 'things on his mind' while maintaining a high level of attention.

When stages I and II have been diligently pursued for a long time the person may move on to stage III, the stage of meditation, which takes him on temporary 'trips' first to P and later, all the way to M.

The next stage, stage IV, is usually described as being passive. It also appears to be irreversible, unlike the previous stages. Contemplation is therefore shown with an arrow that points only to the Void.

Stage V is meant to convey the idea of a stay in the Void of indefinite duration. When the person re-emerges from the Void, in stage VI, he finds himself in the eerie world of Zen at C_{zero} (Watts, 1962).

I doubt whether a human being can stay at Z for long and mingle with the 'outside world' at the same time. Instead, I suggest, there is a final stage on the mystical path, stage VII, when the person moves from Z, back to A, but re-stabilizes, in the context of everyday life, at a somewhat changed A. This is A' which I call 'A-prime'. Perhaps repeated cycles around the Map move the person to A'', A''' and so on? This idea fits in with the widely held opinion that the mystical path changes people progressively. The nature of the change may be to do with the important process of non-attachment which the person would have already attempted as part of the orientation procedure (Stephen, 1957; Prabhavananda and Isherwood, 1956).

I must agree that the concept of non-attachment is about as ineffable as any, although I suppose it may also be one of the most important concepts in this whole field. I would have to fall back on Louis Armstrong's type of answer to the question 'what is non-attachment?' and, for the moment, I can only refer the questioner to the good books just mentioned.

The mystical spiral

Finally, let me draw your attention to the mystical path once again, by showing how it spirals upward in the three dimensions of the Map of Inner Space (figure 7.9).

The outsider

The opposite path

Parallel to that of the mystic it is, however, possible to posit the path of the outsider (Wilson, 1963). By contrast with the mystic who is an extreme 'insider', feeling more and more identified with the world, the outsider is that lonely character, portrayed by many authors, especially the existentialists (Sartre, 1965; Camus, 1964) who always feels himself to be in the role of a detached observer. He feels 'at home' at Ⓐ a place where the insider, who usually lives at Ⓐ, feels anxious and gloomy. The nature of each place on this subjective Map is thus highly 'relative' to the person's starting place (see figure 7.8).

'The coincidence of contradictories'

The outsider's path has, I think, been combined explicitly with the mystical path in several traditions, particularly that of alchemy and that of Zen. When the alchemist speaks of the 'alchemical marriage' perhaps he is referring to the conjunction of the two paths at V. Perhaps this is also the 'coincidence of contradictories' of Nicholas of Cusa (Happold, 1964).

Cleansing the doors of perception

Zen and psychotherapy

At Z the mystic emerges from the Void into a world where, as we said above, his 'doors of perception' have been 'cleansed' where time has changed character, and where the will is free. This strange world of the newly-illuminated is familiar to the mystics, and is sometimes encountered by persons recovering from mental illness.

This Z-state is best described in the Zen literature, which is nowadays being increasingly studied by psychotherapists.

Speculations on personality

Insiders and outsiders

The rest of this chapter consists of my speculations on personality and everything I say from here till the end should be taken with appropriate reserve! Naturally, this is not to say that I don't believe I am talking quite good sense in general. After all, a 'speculation' is nearly as good as a 'hunch' and far better than a 'hypothesis'. Personality theory may be the Cinderella or even an ugly sister of psychology but I don't suppose the following will turn any pumpkins into golden coaches nor any mice into coachmen.

On the map we can indicate whether a person is an insider—as I think we most of us are—or is a member of that small but fascinating group, the outsiders, mentioned above.

Perhaps mankind has evolved, by genetic and social evolution, in such a way that Ⓐ, that cosy and practical place, is the 'best' place for most of us to be for most of the time. I expect that human society cannot stand too many outsiders at Ⓐ, nor too many enthusiasts at P, nor too many mystics at M, nor too many Zen masters, honest rogues and double-agents round about A'. This last group are the jokers. Society needs them, but not too many of them. (Naturally, jokers never acknowledge one another.)

Intuition

Intuition, so valued by Jung, might perhaps be the ability to see many sides to a question at once or to see a process as a whole, as if events in clock-time were spread out sideways before one, in a celtic pattern. (Is this what Lévi-Strauss means, when he talks of 'Structures'?)

On the Map I conceive of the intuitive person as being at home at Ⓐ and Ⓐ simultaneously. (Or one can imagine the Map folded over along the V–Z line so that Ⓐ and Ⓐ can no longer be distinguished, one from the other.)

Some traditions, particularly the Zen Buddhist tradition, seem to be trying to increase the pupil's intuition. Zen training is first of all, however, meditation. This, as we have discussed above, would seem to lead to states of increased certainty, P, M, and, finally, the limiting state of V. Nevertheless, in addition to meditation, Zen requires the pupil to wrestle with enigmas—the famous *Koans*. These riddles cannot be resolved in their own terms. They have to be transcended, and the meta-language in which that resolution can occur is one in which a particular distinction—a particular yin/yang polarity—is seen not as two separated things but as two-in-one. (The 'sound of one hand clapping' is the 'electric potential at one pole of the dynamo'.)

The three kinds of Zen Master

Maybe the Zen literature is obvious to the intuitive person? To others Zen seems to be a 'closed book'—although in his extreme manifestation the Un-Zen person merges imperceptibly with the Zen master.

Indeed, I think that there are three kinds of Zen master. The first kind talks about Zen; the second kind denies its existence (which is better); but the third and supreme kind has never heard of it.

Little children and most drunks probably belong to this third class. In this connection it is interesting to note that both drunks and babies are held up for emulation as models of Taoist wisdom whereas Christianity, less adventurously, sticks to little children.

Instability

Just as I picture the intuitive person as someone who is at Ⓐ and Ⓐ̄ simultaneously, as a person who does not distinguish between the insider's and the outsider's view of life; so I can also interpret a person who fluctuates between A and Ā on the map, without feeling really at home at either. Such a person would feel insecure and ill-at-ease in our ordinary world. This is the unstable or 'neurotic' person. However, I am not clear how we can distinguish the neurotic from the 'sick soul', as described by William James (1960). The 'sick soul' does not feel at home in the world until he has been 'born again'. Is the mystical path of the 'sick soul' *identical* with the path towards 'integration' of the neurotic?

Psycho-analysis and mysticism

Let us pause at this point to consider the relationship between psycho-analysis and mysticism. Freud disclaims 'mystical practices' as a method of treatment but admits that psycho-analysis has chosen 'a similar line of approach' (Freud, 1964, pp. 72–3).

If psycho-analysts and Zen therapists could agree upon some criterion of success it is tempting to envisage the possibility of setting up a controlled clinical trial to compare them.

(The attempt to compare psycho-analysis with behaviour therapy seems doomed from the start. Some kinds of behaviour therapy are very successful in treating isolated 'sore thumbs', as it were, whereas psycho-analysis regards such symptomatic treatment as misguided. A meta-theory of therapy is needed to resolve these conflicts.)

Where is the super-id?

Freud's concept of the id is very interesting; he says that 'we call it a chaos . . . the logical laws of thought do not apply to the id and this is true above all of the law of contradiction . . . contrary impulses exist side by side, without cancelling each other out . . . there is nothing in the id that corresponds to the idea of time . . . the id of course knows no judgements of value . . .' (Freud, 1964, pp. 79–89).

Consider again the Z-state, where any 'thing' could be 'on the mind' were it not for the exquisite ambiguity which renders nothing certain, everything equiprobable; where the mountain and the non-mountain balance exactly: yin and yang. Here are no concepts, no choices, no will, no judgments and no time.

Timeless, chaotic and amoral, the Z-state bears a strong resemblance to Freud's concept of the id. By 'taking in the id', the ego grows to maturity; by travelling from Ⓐ to Z the person returns, enlightened, to A′.

If, then, I can relate the id to the Z-state, to the 'original face before one is born' of Zen, can I find other parallels between Freud's system and the Map? (After all, if you can't beat them make them join you.)

Well, consider next the little protective circle which I place around the certainty level to indicate where the person is 'at home', where he finds his 'reality': Ⓐ, Ⓐ and so on. This circle could instead be drawn around the point p, to indicate where the person is on the secondary, concentration, dimension as well. Where only the plane of certainty is shown (figure 7.8), from above as it were, then I adopt the convention that the level of mindwork, MW, is at an average level. Then, if the point p is inside the inner circle on the plane of certainty it shows some degree of concentration above 1. This concentration reaches its maximal limit when p reaches the axis, which passes through the origin O. Concentration drops to 1 at Z (figure 7.8).

The little circle around p would indicate where the person is 'at home'. It would correspond, as mentioned above, to Freud's concept of the ego. Within the beleaguered ego p is the centre of a dynamic clash of forces, all seeking to move and change it. From Z comes the pull of, among others, 'Anarchic Aphrodite' (celebrated in W. H. Auden's lament); while from the world of objects at V come the twin forces of immediate circumstances and of all the training that society has imposed on the individual since birth (the super-ego). No wonder Freud's model is still appealing! It may or may not be a model of the mind, but it certainly models the pressures of modern life.

The identification between the super-ego and immediate circumstances and the V-plane needs an explanation. Note that the Map, as it has been drawn so far, is, explicitly a map of the mind. The *phenomenal* aspects (things) of the world are to be found where p is to be found, and that is, usually, at Ⓐ. However, I envisage the *noumenal* world, of objects, to be completely unrepresentable on those parts of the Map where a mind can go. This leaves the plane of C_{100}, of absolute certainty, of the Void, as 'seen' by the mind from the one point on the frontier-zone where p can go, that is to say from the origin (where Michelangelo shows God's finger so nearly touching that of Adam).

The world of objects (our brain, our body, other bodies, and so on) touches our world of things (our mind) at O, and since in terms of the Map of Inner Space—of the mind—the world of objects is the completely unknown (the completely other), it seems appropriate that the world of objects should belong to the V-plane which, in its own way is just as strange as the plane of Zen.

The unknown world of objects ('Roughly speaking: objects are colourless'—L. Wittgenstein) includes our bodies (which include our brains) and, beyond them, other bodies (which include other brains), animals, plants, buildings, earth, sea, sky and all the other contents of the universe. I see this whole world of objects as impinging on the mind at the mysterious origin O, of the Map of Inner Space.

At the origin my mind meets some sort of limit beyond which my body (including my brain) begins. Stored in my brain are my learned patterns of behaviour both self-taught and imposed (corresponding roughly to Freud's ego and super-ego) and also, stored in my brain, are the patterns of perception which result when other parts of the world of objects impinge upon my body. These are the immediate circumstances, which affect my body (including my brain) and also, by way of the mind/body relationship (whose nature, we have already asserted, axiomatically, is quite unknown), which affect my mind.

The unconscious is of course, by definition, 'off the map'. Since the only way 'off' is via the origin we can picture the unconscious, like the super-ego, as stored patterns of objects, (calculi, beads on the neural abacus, nerve impulses or whatever) which can belong to that other world (of objects), exclusively, at any particular moment.

When those patterns leap (with ease from the pre-conscious, or with more difficulty from the unconscious proper) into the mind I envisage a double process, of *calculation in the world of objects* and of *thinking in the world of things*.

The mysterious relationship between them is reflection, consciousness, awareness, or psyche. The things, we name mind; the neural bead-game, we call our brain processes.

My metaphysical axiom can now be re-stated (in the Cartesian manner) as follows: *I think I calculate.* See how psyche, as 'I' in that sentence, does both, and thus embodies the mind/body relationship.

Dreams, by the way, are in the underworld of the Map, near to what Huxley calls the 'Mind's Antipodes' (1971). Dreams are *not* off the Map, not—at any rate—while we are dreaming them.

The jokers

Seeing our 'original face'

The editor of this book, in his own chapter, puts forward the concept of personality as a constraint upon the ability to play roles.

This can be related to the yoga metaphysics which seem to arise fairly naturally from the Map. If our 'true self', or 'Atman', or 'original face' is revealed to us in the Z-state, then perhaps our role-playing person—or persona—(Freud's 'ego'), is the limitation imposed on ourselves by our demand for security, as embodied in the conventional 'reality' of the average world of everyday at Ⓐ.

By contrast with these persons who are still 'attached' to their sense of 'reality', the 'enlightened one' at A' (or A", A''' or A^n), or at anywhere else on the map, plays any role, and in consequence often appears to be somewhat unconventional.

'The joker is wild'

It is this disconcerting unpredictability of the genuine sage that, paradoxically, places him among an odd bunch of characters that I call 'the jokers'. They include the following diverse types: sages (as already mentioned), little children, hysterical personalities, double-agents, actors, comics, psychopaths and some artists, priests and psychiatrists.

What characteristics have they in common? I should say that they are all highly versatile, and have the ability to play many roles. They can all be puzzling, charming, but 'manipulative' (except for the psychiatrists of course—patients *manipulate* psychiatrists whereas psychiatrists only *handle* patients). I suggest that the whole bunch possess these common features by virtue of their non-attachment to the 'reality' of everyday life (Lutyens, 1970).

However, having defined the jokers in this way let me hasten to distinguish them, one from the other. For example, the small child has not yet *learnt* to stick to the rut of convention—to acquire his 'ego'—whereas the psychopath has so far *failed* to do so, in spite of society's efforts to teach him. The hysterical personality, on the other hand, has learnt all the conventions but has, according to Janet, a tendency to 'dissociate' bits of them (Hamilton, 1967) so that one rather brittle mask after another has to be donned until it, in turn, breaks down in the face of stressful circumstances.

Like the hysterical personality, the actor can take up one role after another. But, whereas the hysterical personality plays out his roles in 'real life' where they frequently wreak havoc among the supporting cast (often his family), the actor may, if he so wishes, confine his versatility to the stage (Stanislavski, 1967).

The double-agent is a figure of great fascination. (*Koan:* Did Philby catch himself? Yes, but he didn't let on, so as to see who his contacts were.) Like the actor, the double-agent poses the uneasy question about what is left behind when all Peer Gynt's onion-skins are removed.

A few priests and psychiatrists see themselves as jokers. I know one priest who admits to being a double-agent, preaching the Law which must always hide the Spirit (which is nevertheless there, ready to be decoded by his congregation in their own good time). As for psychiatrists, I recently read that Freud sat out of his patients' line of sight because he used to make faces at what they said.

I have called these jokers a funny bunch of 'characters' but I wonder if a better name for them wouldn't be 'personalities'. They play many roles and surprise us like the actors they are, personalities of stage, screen and the domestic hearth, leaving behind them a wake of healing or devastation or merely entertainment. The term 'character' would be better reserved perhaps for those consistent and hence reliable persons who are, by contrast to the above 'personalities', very poor at playing any but their own settled role—'every man to his humour'.

The healers among my bunch of jokers differ from the others in that they have transcended convention, including conventional morality, but still retain their harmlessness, learnt painfully long ago, as part of their 'preliminary yoga' (figure 7.10). The psychopath can be a close cousin to the sage (especially to real jokers, like Gurdjieff) but he lacks the foundation of moral training which renders the genuine sage harmless, albeit often disturbing and always unpredictable.

Who knocked down the Euston arch?

Joker–politicians make a welcome change from the other sort. Recent examples are H. Macmillan, N. Kruschev and C. de Gaulle. But they may display a childish tendency to destroy beautiful things, or to be rude (He's gone to Kiev to see his dentist), or negativistic.

'Of course it's a Fake; I often paint Fakes'

These words, attributed to Picasso, introduce the joker–artist. Interpreting the word 'artist' widely, other recent examples are V. Nabokov and I. Stravinsky—which reminds me: should we send *Stravinsky* to the Moon? On re-reading this section on the joker I realize how much I owe to reading Alan Watts. So, to sum up, let me quote him: 'the fully liberated man . . . [is] as one completely free to take part in the cosmic and social game . . . He is a joker or "Wild" man who can play any card in the pack' (Watts, 1961, p. 61).

The above passage seems to relate the 'fully liberated man' to the actor or, better still, to the great actor; and consider indeed, how we revere our great actor and, in the person of Prospero, see him as fused with his part. The great actor knows all roles and can play them at will. In this capacity he coincides with the sage. Both, as we have noticed, may also be jokers.

'What are the rules of the bead-game?'

Relativity

If the Map is at all valid, does it hold any message? What strikes me mainly is its relativity. Each place on the Map has a meaning which depends on where a person has come from and where that person places his 'reality'. To the 'enlightened' person—at A', A'', A''' and so on—according as to how many of Don Juan's enemies (Fear, Clarity, Power and Old Age), he has vanquished (Castaneda, 1970) the circle of 'reality' no longer surrounds him at A, nor indeed anywhere. Unless we imagine that the circle of 'reality' now coincides with the circle of certainty (figure 7.3), from Z to V in both directions, that is to say with the entire map, comprising both the known and the unknown world.

For the average man at Ⓐ, to move to Ā is miserable, to move to P̄ is highly unpleasant and to move to M̄ is horrific. Such journeys to 'the wrong side of the map' give rise to anxiety and bodily discomfort. For the manic-depressive carrying his season ticket from P to P̄ and back again, there are two familiar worlds, the universe of horror and the universe of bliss, as described by John Custance (1951). The M-state is valued highly by the apprentice mystic; whereas the yogi believes that it is only one more guise of *Maya*, that is to say, of the play of illusion.

Ringing the changes

And so the dance goes on and all that exists is changeable. In the Book of Changes, the venerable *I Ching*, which shares its circular logic with the equal temperament of Western music (now *there's* a bead-game for you) there are two points of perfection, one at the top and one at the bottom; but neither is a point of rest.

Acknowledgments

I am grateful to the editor of *New Society* for permission to use the flow diagram (figure 7.10) which was first published in *New Society* on 23 July 1970.

The editor of *Pulse* has very kindly permitted me to quote extensively, and to use diagrams, from articles previously published in *Pulse*.

Bibliography

Beer, S. (1970), 'The cybernetic cytoblast: management itself', in *Progress in Cybernetics*, ed. J. Rose, vol. 1, Gordon & Breach.

Brown, G. S. (1969), *Laws of Form*, Allen & Unwin.

Camus, A. (1964) *The Outsider*, Penguin.

Castaneda, C. (1970), *The Teachings of Don Juan*, Penguin.

Clark, J. H. (1970a), 'What are the rules of the bead game?', a paper presented at the Third International Writers' Conference, Harrogate, 1969; *New Worlds*, no. 197, January.

Clark, J. H. (1970b), 'A program for Patanjali', *New Society*, 23 July.

Custance, J. (1951), *Wisdom, Madness and Folly*, Gollancz.

Fremantle, A. (ed.) (1964), *The Protestant Mystics*, Mentor.

Freud, S. (1961 edn), *The Ego and the Id*, Hogarth Press (first published 1923).

Freud, S. (1964 edn), *New Introductory Lectures on Psycho-analysis*, lecture 31, Hogarth Press (first published 1932).

Happold, F. C. (1964), *Mysticism: A Study and an Anthology*, Penguin.

Huxley, A. (1971), *The Doors of Perception* and *Heaven and Hell*, Penguin.

James, W. (1960), *The Varieties of Religious Experience*, Fontana.

Janet, P. (1967), 'The major symptoms of hysteria' in *Abnormal Psychology*, ed. M. Hamilton, Penguin.

Jung, C. G. (1953), *Psychology and Alchemy*, Collected Works, vol. 12, Routledge & Kegan Paul.

Laski, M. (1961), *Ecstasy*, Cresset Press.

Lawrence, D. H. (1959), *Women in Love*, Ace Books.

Lewin, K. (1936), *Principles of Topological Psychology*, New York, McGraw-Hill.

Lovecraft, H. P. & Derlath, A. (1970), *The Lurker at the Threshold*, Panther.

Lutyens, M. (ed.) (1970), *The Penguin Krishnamurti Reader*, Penguin.

Mayer-Gross, W., Slater, E. & Roth, M. (1955), *Clinical Psychiatry*, Cassell.

O'Brien, E. (1964), *The Essential Plotinus*, Mentor.

Sartre, J. P. (1965), *Nausea*, Penguin.

Stace, W. T. (1960), *The teachings of the Mystics*, Mentor.

Stanislavski, C. (1967), *An Actor Prepares*, Penguin.

Stephen, D. R. (1957), *Patanjali for Western Readers*, Theosophical Publishing House.

S. Prabhavananda & Isherwood, C. (translators) (1956), *Bhagavad-Gita*, Phoenix House.

Tart, C. T. (ed.) (1969), *Altered States of Consciousness*, New York, Wiley.

Watts, A. W. (1961), *Psychotherapy, East and West*, Mentor.

Watts, A. W. (1962), *The Way of Zen*, Penguin.

Wilson, C. (1963), *The Outsider*, Pan.

Yeats, W. B. (1937), *A Vision*, Macmillan.

8 Review and commentary

Ralph Ruddock

It might appear that the foregoing chapters lead in different directions. In fact, however, there is some measure of convergence between them and there are no contradictions. It would be possible to set out the corresponding items in tabular form. For brevity, it has been decided to point to some congruences between Ninian Smart's philosophic approach and those of the other contributors, who are all social scientists.

Ninian Smart writes 'the concept of the person is culturally determined', a proposition which is basic to Dan Gowler's essay and partly explicit in others. He argues the reality of individual freedom, a position common to all the approaches. (None argues for the determinist position even as a heuristic device.) Morality is related to imagination, the aesthetic function and sensitivity, which enable us to conceive of other people as persons. His general conclusion that 'personhood is an ethical concept' is echoed in the appeal of Dan Gowler's final paragraphs. This is paralleled by John Morris writing of our responsibility in the creation of each other, and is related to the perspectives discussed in chapter 5. Ninian Smart places man in history, seeing the concept of the person as historically derived, and history as 'always open at its cutting edge'—'we live in an indeterministic historical mode'. This relates to the project and the Marxist account of man as a contingent historical product (see chapter 5). His view of the person as 'a bearer of certain rights and ... imperatives about not infringing certain rights' is parallel to Dan Gowler's definition of the person in terms of social rights and duties. Again, where Gowler exemplifies the possibilities of defining individuals as non-persons or less-than-persons, Ninian Smart writes that for some tribes 'the word for man coincides with the word for a member of the tribe. It is as though all men are people but only some are persons.' He touches on our behaviour towards animals at several points, illustrating the ambiguities of category that are central to Dan Gowler's analysis. By implication he suggests that in defining animals we define an aspect of ourselves. He further argues that 'the appeal of the concept of the person is universalistic'. This is a position that is common to all contributors, but we are reminded here that the employment of the concept represents a moral stance, 'a moral option'. This point would have come naturally to sociologists of an earlier generation, such as Hobhouse and Ginsberg.

Ninian Smart writes of the function of myths, and says they are 'co-ordinated to ritual'. This fits well with John Morris's treatment of ritual. Social scientists generally have treated myths as empirical phenomena, or functional components in a total social process. The possibility that a myth might be 'true' (Ninian Smart uses the term) has not been a point of interest. A phenomenological approach however requires us to recognize that we cannot know about entities outside ourselves, we have no direct access to their state of being. This being so, myths may express in intelligible and summary form certain valid apprehensions or intuitions of reality. R. D. Laing, in an article entitled 'Religious Sensibility' in the *Listener* (23 April 1970), wrote:

> Some of us have a sense of ourselves and of the world as we perceive it, as not derived ultimately from any of the things we can sense. Myths give expression to this sense. Myths are essentially dramatic. And I haven't come across any better way: as far as I know, human spiritual sensibility has not yet found another form to clothe itself.

Ninian Smart writes of the myth of the Eternal, that man is made in the image of the Eternal. This is the language of tradition, and from one position, it could be seen as corresponding to the original (transcendental) self (see chapter 5). The 'infinite range of variation in individual properties' genetically and socially derived, corresponds perhaps to the unique self, the realization of which is the basic drive through life (John Shaw). Ninian Smart's reference to the Buddhist skandas points towards the central mystery, where lies the question of the relation of the original self (the myth of the Eternal) to the self which can be realized under temporal social conditions. All contributors implicitly concur with Ninian Smart in repudiating the concept of a given 'standard essential humanity' constituting personhood.

Ninian Smart's discussion of standardized versus particularized views of the person, with emphasis on the necessity of each, echoes the theoretical discussion in the first chapter. His formulation of Sartrean existentialism 'Genuine life consists in transcending externally derived roles' matches John Morris's view of the individual as most fully a person when involved in a drama.

A reference to psycho-technology (compare the treatment of this by John Shaw) and the corresponding danger of perceiving people as machines, playthings, toys (compare John Morris's metaphors) leads to the position that the concept of the person requires that one person should mean a lot to another.

The above paragraphs have not included references to the essay of John Clark, which is so much concerned with what can happen 'inside the mind' that it does not appear to offer concepts comparable to those deployed by other contributors. There is more relevance than might appear, however. His account of the Freudian ego as 'attachment to the conventional world of everyday life' and the possibility of the erosion of 'the protective wall of everyday reality' shows that he fully comprehends the precarious status of the social personality. Whereas other contributors have emphasized that each person depends upon, and is ultimately created by, others, John Clark is interested in what happens when normal egoic life no longer contains the person's experience. His position is nearest to that of John Shaw; their perspectives are respectively those of a psychiatrist and a psychologist. They share a regard for mysticism, speculate about drug-induced experience, and accept Maslow's account of the super-egoic 'peak experience'. Somewhat divergent however are the centrality of a self-to-be-realized in John Shaw, and the agnostic relativity of John Clark who is content to locate possible positions in relation to each other. Clark is careful to dissociate himself from metaphysical or ontological speculations. When he writes, 'Each place on the Map has a meaning which depends on where a person has come from and where that person places his "reality" ', this is in the direction of Ruddock's concept of identity as selection of a location within the personality; but many of Clark's locations are far out, offering no basis for personal life in society. His positions are not indeed chosen—the person risks experiencing them when he moves, or is moved, out of the A-state.

R. D. Laing, in *The Politics of Experience* (1966), writes of the person experiencing 'schizophrenia' as lost in inner space, in unfamiliar territory and trying to retain his bearings. 'We respect the voyager, the explorer, the climber, the space man. It makes far more sense to me as a valid project for our time to explore the inner space of time and consciousness.' John Clark attempts a co-ordinate geometry of inner space with some indications of the main climatic regions. Such a system might help people to orient themselves when they lose the A-state, or project themselves out of it. The social sciences on the other hand concern themselves with the A-state and with the social determinants of its loss. Clark starts from the margin where the social sciences leave off. John Shaw writes mainly of man as actualizing himself in the social world, but basing much of his thinking on the writings of Jung, sees the life-task of individuation as achieving a unity between one's own inner space, with its universal components, and the social ego.

Common to all of these approaches is a sense of the frailty, contingency and dependency of the social self. Gowler, Morris and Smart register this basic condition of personhood, and require, by implication, that a recognition of it should inform a universal ethic prescribing that individuals should perceive each other as fully endowed persons. Gowler cites many instances, and their consequences, where individuals have been otherwise defined. Smart instances some American soldiers' views of the Vietnamese.

An ethical prescription leaves the ontological problem unresolved, however. Smart fears that scientific control of the human sub-systems may lead to a disenchantment of the person, and argues that it is essential to preserve the myth of personhood; only on this basis can we support each other's personal life. Morris's position is entirely in accord with this, but in addition, he writes as a person writing about persons. He directly explores his state of being, and finds himself most himself when confronted with a dramatic crux— to get his essay finished or not. In this crux, however, he becomes aware of the surface of the table and the light. These experiences may be out of the ego, not properties of the person as eventually re-organized for dramatic action, but undoubtedly properties of the self before such re-organization is accomplished. Shaw, developing Jung's concept of creative fantasy, sets out a relationship between the egoic and non-egoic life. Creativity is seen by Smart as a mani-festation of the freedom which characterizes the person; a concept parallel to Morris's definition of personal drama as being uncertain in outcome.

Although none of the contributors formulate their position in such terms, the following statement may be consistent with all the approaches. Ontologically the individual is a field of experience. He develops as a person in so far as personhood is imputed to him by others, and by himself. If his personhood is not socially developed due to non-recognition or functional incapacity, he continues to exist, while experiencing non-normal, non-egoic states of consciousness. Even in the normal person, non-egoic states constantly interchange with egoic states. In all cases, it is ethically imperative that a recognizably human individual should be accorded the status of a person. The term 'person' thus has two distinguishable meanings. One is the complex of rights and duties imputed to the human individual, embodied in ethical prescriptions and cultural value systems. This meaning is in principle universal. The other is the freely acting participant in a social system, whose capacity for such action has developed on the basis of some attribution of personhood.

Appendix: The identity model

(see chapter 5)

The following paragraphs are added in order to clarify the relationship between components of the model, and its possible application in the study of literature.

Personal identity is established when the original self selects a location from which to organize the personality for role-performance, is able to endorse that performance and lend itself to it, so that self, personality and role become a subjective unity. In that unity, only the role-performance is visible, both externally and internally, It alone appears to constitute identity. This appearance is shattered whenever the self, personality and role are no longer in perfect 'register'—the term is borrowed from colour-printing, where inaccurate super-position of colours blurs all images.

When the three modes of being are no longer in register, the perspectives come into play. Self takes a *view* of personality ('Lack of confidence—my old trouble!'), a view of role ('Perhaps it's not the right job'), and a view of personality-in-role ('I need to learn the required skills'). A printer can re-register on the blue, the red or the yellow. A person may re-register on the role, the personality or the 'real self'.

Self, identity, personality, role, perspective and project are the bases of individual life. They are the elements which the individual brings together into his personal pattern, which shows consistency over time, but is loosely articulated so as to permit some re-arrangement of the elements in response to inner disposition or changing circumstance.

The concern of literature has been to explore and express whatever is central to the human condition. It should be possible therefore to examine situations presented in drama and the novel, in the hope that beneath the richness of observation it will be possible to discern themes which can be expressed in the terms proposed here. Much comedy and narrative might be seen as exploring the area between role and personality. The tragedies of Lear and Othello appear to warn us against the danger of allowing identity to depend upon role. Religious writing informs us that identity-in-the-world is itself transient and contingent, and requires the individual to live in the awareness proper to his 'real self' within a cosmic frame of reference. Twentieth-century literature has been a good deal preoccupied with perspectives, and the extent to which one's ability to function in any way whatever is dependent on the way one is seen.

What, then, of the 'real self'? The case for its reality is argued by John Shaw in chapter 6. A lifetime is the opportunity for its social realization. Daily life is the struggle to secure the conditions which might make that realization possible. Subjectively, it is experienced as a central continuing awareness, separable from personality.

Some of the distinctions proposed in this essay may be identified in passages from George Bernard Shaw's autobiographical preface to his early novels, and written at the age of seventy. (These passages are discussed in somewhat different terms by Erik Erikson, 1968.)

When Nature completed my countenance in 1880 or thereabouts
(I had only the tenderest sprouting of hair on my face until
I was 24), I found myself equipped with the upgrowing
moustaches and eyebrows, and the sarcastic nostrils of the
operatic fiend whose airs (by Gounod) I had sung as a child,
and whose attitudes I had affected in my boyhood. Later on, as
the generations moved past me, I . . . began to perceive that
imaginative fiction is to life what the sketch is to the picture or
the conception to the statue.

If I am to be entirely communicative on this subject, I must
add that the mere rawness which so soon rubs off was
complicated by a deeper strangeness which has made me all my
life a sojourner on this planet rather than a native of it.
Whether it be that I was born mad or a little too sane, my
kingdom was not of this world: I was at home only in the
realm of my imagination, and at my ease only with the mighty
dead. Therefore, I had to become an actor, and create for
myself a fantastic personality fit and apt for dealing with men,

and adaptable to the various parts I had to play as author, journalist, orator, politician, committee man, man of the world, and so forth.

These events might be described as follows. As a boy, Bernard Shaw had experimentally identified with the role of an operatic devil. His appearance (view of himself, perspective) as a young man confirmed for him that this was a role he could play, and it became his project. Later he discovered that this 'imaginative fiction' had become his life. He elaborated it and created 'a fantastic personality . . . adaptable to the various parts I had to play as author, journalist, orator, etc.' This elaboration is the role-tree. All of this role behaviour (which had as much the character of theatre as of drama, to use Professor Morris's terms in chapter 4), was 'complicated by a deeper strangeness' which left him feeling mad, too sane, not of this world, only at ease with the dead. This was the self, the original self which he had not succeeded in realizing. His inner predicament may be seen as an existential universal. It was made acute by the attempt to build personality and establish identity on the basis of role. This is a reversal of the direction needed for integration and self-realization, which requires that roles depend on personality, and identity choice on self-awareness.

Index